WOMEN AND FICTION:

Feminism and the Novel 1880–1920

WOMEN AND FICTION

Feminism and the Novel 1880–1920

PATRICIA STUBBS

METHUEN

First published in Great Britain in 1979 by
The Harvester Press Ltd

First published as a University Paperback in 1981 by
Methuen & Co. Ltd
11 New Fetter Lane, London EC4P 4EE

© 1979 Patricia Stubbs

Printed in Great Britain by
J. W. Arrowsmith Ltd, Bristol

British Library Cataloguing in Publication Data
Stubbs, Patricia
    Women and fiction. – (University paperbacks; 729).
    1. English fiction – 19th century – History and criticism
    2. English fiction – 20th century – History and criticism
    3. Women in literature
    I. Title   II. Series
    823'.8'09352   PR830.W6
    ISBN 0–416–30640–3

Contents

PART FIVE
CONCLUSION

Preface

This book has grown out of the research I did on women and literature as a postgraduate student at Sheffield University between 1971 and 1974. Although it has been enlarged, twice rewritten and generally much altered since then, I should like to thank my supervisor of those years, Christopher Heywood, whose scholarship and close attention I am sure saved me from countless inaccuracies and flamboyantly untenable generalizations. If any errors or distortions have crept in since those days, I only have myself to blame. I should also like to thank Angela Carter, Christine Jackson, Judith Billingham, Jennifer Boshell, Gisela Feurle and Ann Foreman who read all or parts of the book at various stages, and encouraged or helped me in my search for a publisher. Thanks to Harvester Press for being that publisher and to their anonymous literary advisor for his fierce but constructive comments on an earlier draft. Thanks too to the helpful staff of the Sheffield University Library and to my typist, Monica Mosely, but not to the Post Office who lost the top copy of her work. Above all thanks to my parents for their patience, and to Anthony Arblaster for his encouragement and support.

A brief note of explanation is needed on my use of the term 'feminist'. I have deliberately avoided offering a narrow definition for although this would accommodate Olive Schreiner or George Egerton, it would exclude male writers like Meredith, Hardy, Grant Allen or H. G. Wells, who were perceived as feminists by their contemporaries and who must be distinguised from more hostile male writers such as George Gissing or Henry James. It may be unpopular that this usage allows the inclusion of male writers and that many more men than women novelists are discussed in the book. But both these heresies are surely unavoidable if we want an account of an entire period of literary history rather than of women's

novels alone, particularly when the period contains committed anti-feminist women writers such as Mrs Lynn Linton or
Mrs Humphry Ward.

Sheffield 1979   Patricia Stubbs

Introduction

This book is connected with two important changes, one in contemporary politics, the other in literary-academic practice. These are, first, the re-emergence of feminism as a significant political movement, and second, the growing recognition that the relation between the text and its historical and ideological location, between the work and what has for long been dismissed as its 'background', is central to a full and proper understanding of any work of literature. I hope that these two developments come together in this book.

Feminism has already begun to re-examine, and where necessary rewrite, our political and cultural history. Where literature is concerned this is an especially important task, because it is through literature, and particularly through the novel, that the dominant images of women and their experience in our culture have been most easily and, until recently, most widely elaborated.

No matter what part in society individual women in fact play, traditional images focus on their domestic and sexual roles. This has the effect of continually limiting women's notions of themselves and their possibilities; it undermines from within. For images are not an innocent pictorial guide to reality, a neutral mental shorthand which helps us to recall the outside world. We certainly use these simplified ideas of how people and things 'really are' to make sense of our experience of the world; but this is an essentially subjective process. So far from helping us to perceive a supposed 'reality', it in fact creates that reality from within. Our images create the world for us; they shape our consciousness. The women's movement knows this, and so attempts to combat cultural stereotypes of female experience. These are confronted and, hopefully, discredited by the creation of new, alternative images which instead of narrowing women's consciousness of themselves, try to expand it. This process can be incidental – when women act in ways which lie quite outside the roles they are usually expected to play – or deliberate, when women specifically set out to create alternative images or to demolish old ones.

This is where the novel, and nowadays the other popular media, are so important. It is here that the ideological battle is fought out, unconsciously by most writers, consciously by the committed on either side.

It can be argued that film and television are now more important than the novel as sources of insight into today's beliefs and assumptions, not just about women and sexuality, but about most other areas of life as well. But although the novel is clearly no longer the sole art or entertainment form with mass appeal, its status, the diversity of its sub-genres and its huge readership since the development of the paper-back mean that it must remain an important focus for any study of contemporary culture.

More important however is the historical position of the novel as the major literary form of European culture over the last two hundred years. Novelists at work now take as their starting point the culmination of a long tradition. They can choose to reject parts of this tradition; they may even be largely unaware of it; but they cannot hope to escape its legacy altogether. A particularly onerous part of their inheritance is the way the development of the novel has been closely bound up with the social and political position of women. This is especially the case in England. From Samuel Richardson in the eighteenth century up to the present day, beneath the shifts and changes in attitude which have undoubtedly taken place towards women in the novel, there is a fundamental continuity which firmly places them in a private domestic world where emotions and personal relationships are at once the focus of moral value and the core of women's experience. In the novel women are 'prisoners' of feeling and of private life.

There are important historical reasons why the novel has always seen women in this way. It grew up as a literary form at a time when industrialization was beginning both to exclude women from production and to create an artificial split between public and private life.[1] These two developments are closely related, and the connection between them lies in the changing role of women. Increasingly confined to the home, it was they who became the focus of the new value which was placed on private experience once the public 'outer' world of production was stripped of its satisfactions by industrialization and the division of labour.

It was at just this moment, and for much the same reasons, that the novel came of age. For the novel as a form is also characterized by its absorption in private experience, and by the elaboration of the individualistic moral values which emerged as a response to the fragmentation of morality and economics into conflicting areas of activity.[2] The novel, in other words, is inherently bound up with the notion of a private life which has its own autonomous moral standards and values. At its best it explores private relationships and moral behaviour as an expression of external social and economic realities, but its central, its defining preoccupation, remains the elaboration of an intensely personal world of individual experience, the moral structure of which is built up around carefully organized patterns of personal relationships.

But this is peculiarly damaging to women. For within bourgeois society women are confined to this private, largely domestic world, and have become the focus of a powerful ideology which celebrates private experience and relationships as potent sources of human satisfaction. It is of enormous significance that the first novel 'proper', *Pamela*, locked its heroine into the moral centre of this very ideological system. For the essence both of the central action of the novel and of Pamela's own character is her virtue and moral superiority over Squire B. The fact that this virtue is narrowly defined as sexual chastity is broadly irrelevant. For whereas the specific characteristic of sexual chastity has gradually slipped from its primary place in the hierarchy of female virtues, so that Pamela's anxious defence of her 'honour' now seems both ludicrous and prurient, the moral function of women in the novel has continued to resemble that of its first heroine. We shall see that that after about 1880 women no longer needed to be technically chaste in fiction; but they remained the moral centre of the fictional structure.

This becomes ever clearer if we place *Pamela* beside the heroines of Richardson's near contemporary, Defoe. For what is so interesting about the development of the novel in and after the eighteenth century is the way it adopted and elaborated Richardson's conception of womanhood rather than the one we find in *Roxana* or *Moll Flanders*. The reason for this is that Defoe's women, in particular his great creation Moll, were seriously at odds, in a way Richardson's were not, with the way women, at least upper-class women, now lived. It is not just that Moll is sexually promiscuous where Pamela is chaste, but that Moll is essentially amoral in all her dealings with reality. She is a criminal. She is also quite astonishingly independent, even in basic geographical terms, as she wanders freely through the streets of eighteenth-century London. Moll, in short, has none of the disabilities, the emotions or, above all, the morality fostered in women by the new economic order and its ideology. She was quite inappropriate as a prototype novel heroine; she was a subversive, far removed from that focus of moral value which women were becoming, in fiction and in life.

Richardson's *Pamela* then, initiated what has always been a fundamental association in the novel between women and private life. It is from this association that all the familiar images of women in fiction are derived – the virgin heroine, the wife and mother, the prostitute, the spinster, the mistress, the redundant middle-aged woman, the single mother. Though we may deplore this narrow range of 'types' of women represented in fiction, it is important to recognize that they are rooted in the very origins of the form and that they are part of a very strong tradition. This tradition has grown to some extent out of the historical reality of women's experience, but it owes even more to the ideology which developed to disguise that experience.

This is why in the 1880s and 1890s and on into the twentieth century, in spite of an active feminist movement and the expansion of opportunities for women outside the home, the novel showed no signs of evolving a different framework for even some of its women characters. Virginia Woolf expected the novel to make this long delayed transition once women had won a degree of political and economic independence:

The change which has turned the English woman from a nondescript influence, fluctuating and vague, to a voter, a wage-earner, a responsible citizen, has given her both in her life and in her art a turn towards the impersonal. Her relations now are not only emotional; they are intellectual, they are political. The old system which condemned her to squint askance at things through the eyes or through the interests of husband or brother, has given place to the direct and practical interests of one who must act for herself, and not merely influence the acts of others. Hence her attention is being directed away from the personal centre which engaged it exclusively in the past to the impersonal, and her novels naturally become more critical of society, less analytic of individuals . . . The novel will cease to be the dumping ground for the personal emotions[3].

But she was wrong. Specific aspects of women's lives have been scrutinized in the novel – the marriage laws, economic impotence and poor education provision in the nineteenth century, and, in the twentieth, the psychological damage which women suffer in their unequal relationships with men. But few novelists have begun to explore the different ways in which women have lived or have wanted to live since the end of the last century. Almost no heroine in late nineteenth-century fiction works for instance, and though they do tend to have jobs in novels today, this is almost always a relatively marginal part of their experience. And very few writers indeed have discarded the traditional association in fiction between women and private feeling.

A genuinely feminist novel must surely credit women with more forms of experience than their personal or sexual entanglements. Even in 1880 many middle-class women worked; working-class women had always done so. This means that literature which continues to concentrate exclusively on women's private lives is in a sense perpetuating a lie. Women do not live off their relationships. Like other people they work, and even when they do not work outside the home, they still have contact with the material world, with people and things outside their own more intimate feelings.

This is a complicated question; because of the impact of generations of ideological oppression, many women do believe that this other part of their life is unimportant, especially if the work they do is a low-paid factory job, or cleaning, or housework. Yet this is exactly why the image of women which the novel has helped to sustain has been so important. It encourages them to see an enormous area of their lives as irrelevant to their real selves, seducing them with a fantasy world of wholly satisfying relationships, which belittles the problems and inequalities they confront in their everyday lives. In this way it perpetuates what is in fact both a falsification and a limitation of experience. This is admittedly the novel at its worst, but even at its best it has not yet been able to break free of this narrowing interpretation of women's experience.

This criticism clearly applies more to modern writers than to nineteenth-century novelists who were, after all, working at a time when women's experience was more clearly confined to private life. However, even within this overall framework, some mid-century novelists did reject customary oversimplifications of female psychology and experience. Many of the writers whom we now regard as major literary figures recognized the vast discrepancies between the acceptable cultural images of women and what women actually experienced. They built some of their finest work around just this contradiction. But it was only towards the end of the nineteenth century that novelists began to go beyond structuring their work around the dislocation between ideology and reality and started to attack the ideology itself. The steady growth of the women's emancipation movement, and then the political and cultural uncertainties of the end of the century, finally discredited the traditional images. The period between 1880 and the end of the Great War was one of reassessment and redefinition. In the novel the old ideal of women as passive, dependent and, above all, chaste, was gradually but deliberately transformed. Women in fiction became sexual, sensuous beings. A complete about turn had taken place.

This book is about the writers who pioneered that change – they include Hardy, George Moore and H.G. Wells as well as explicitly feminist writers such as Olive Schreiner and George Egerton. These and their critics were all deeply engaged in the debate which the nineteenth century called 'the Woman Question'. For the struggle to acknowledge women as complete human beings with individual and sexual rights was fought out to a very great extent in literature – in books like *Jude the Obscure, Tess of the d'Urbervilles* and *Ann Veronica*. Yet in the widest sense this was an essentially political issue. For recognizing women as individuals with rights as well as duties, with legitimate sexual passions, with an independent, autonomous existence, meant challenging the moral and political orthodoxies of mid-nineteenth-century culture. It meant, in particular, questioning the permanence, even the desirability of marriage, and it raised the question of the role of the family and women's function within it. Not surprisingly then, the relations between these novelists and the literary and moral establishment were far from easy.

The remaking of women's image in fiction was only one aspect of the cultural upheaval which characterized this period, but it was certainly one of the most interesting of the many breaks with Victorian ideology which took place at the end of the century. Part of its interest lies in the fact that this break was not in fact the total rupture which it appeared at the time. With hindsight we can see that what took place was an evolution, not a revolution in the portrayal of women. The new but ultimately disproportionate emphasis it placed on women's sexuality, so far from being a radical departure from tradition, has proved to be a link between the stereotypes of the past and those of the present. The fiction of this crucial period of transition shows us in fact where our current images have come from, how they evolved out of an apparently very dissimilar pattern. For though it may seem at first glance that nothing could be further removed from the feminine ideal of a hundred or so years ago than the sexually active, curious or experimenting women we meet in today's fiction, the virgin heroine of the past and her contemporary fictional sister are not really so very different. Both are defined through their private emotional experience; ultimately neither is allowed any other kind of relation to people or material life.

There is then, an underlying continuity between the dominant images of the past and those of the present. Women in fiction are still 'Pamela's daughters' and are likely to remain so until they are defined through their contacts with the 'outer' as well as their 'inner' world. Whether traditional realism can evolve a pattern which will free women from their association with private feeling, and yet still retain its characteristic concern with individual experience, is an interesting and important question which arises many times in the course of this book and which I take up in my conclusion. It raises in turn a more fundamental question about the relation between literary forms, known experience and desired change. It may be that the novel, and certainly realism as we know it, simply cannot adapt in the way feminists would wish. Monique Wittig's *Les Guerillières*, in which the notions of individual experience and private morality have disappeared altogether and are replaced by a poetic vision of a collective female culture, perhaps indicates the direction in which fiction will move in order to accommodate the notions of reality and experience currently evolving out of contemporary feminism. We are likely to see more experiments of this kind if writers begin to challenge the fictional tradition which identifies women with private experience.

PART ONE

FORERUNNERS

1. Women, Ideology and Censorship in the Nineteenth Century

WOMEN AND IDEOLOGY

Feminist and labour historians are as yet still documenting the radical transformation of women's position in the economy which took place in Britain during the eighteenth and nineteenth centuries. But though some of the detail of this process has yet to be filled out, the outline, the general impact of industrial capitalism on women is now well known. That it threw the working-class woman on to the labour market in the new industrial centres, and at the same time made bourgeois women economically redundant, is an established historical fact.[1] The middle-class woman, with no economic function to perform in the home and debarred by a patriarchal ideology from work outside it, became a dependent in a more direct way than ever before. Economically impotent and with only a social, decorative and childbearing role to perform, there was an ever widening gulf between her life and that of the working-class woman who had become a wage-earner outside the home, albeit an exploited one, and whose life was untouched in any material way by the ideals of Victorian domesticity. So far from leading a stable life of domestic and maternal fulfilment, the mass of wage-earning women worked in the dehumanizing factory system of developing industrialism and lived crowded into the city slums which were so anxiously documented by middle-class reformers. They were left to meet as well as they could the double burden of domestic and factory labour.

There was clearly, even in crude numerical terms, an enormous gap between the domestic ideology of Victorian England and the realities of everyday life. But the disjunction between ideology and reality, though at its clearest between classes, was most acutely experienced within a single class – the middle class where, as both history and literature testify, instead of the fulfilment promised by exalted notions of family life, women all too frequently found the boredom and intense frustrations of a largely meaningless existence. Edward Carpenter, well-known at the end of the century as a socialist who supported feminism and championed sexual liberty, gives in his autobiography an account of his own family life which sums up the oppressive yet trivial existence women were obliged to endure in mid-Victorian society:

There were six or seven servants in the house, and my six sisters had absolutely nothing to do except dabble in paints and music . . . and wander aimlessly from room to room to see if by chance 'anything was going on'. Dusting, cooking, sewing, darning – all light household duties were already forestalled; there was no private garden, and if there had been it would have been 'unladylike' to do anything in it; every girl could not find an absorbing interest in sol-fa or water-colours; athletics were not yet invented; every aspiration and outlet, except in the direction of dress and dancing, was blocked; and marriage, with the growing scarcity of men, was becoming every day less likely, or easy to compass. More than once, girls of whom I least expected it told me that their lives were miserable, 'with nothing on earth to do'.[2]

But women quickly recognized the realities of their new situation, and as the century wore on the problems stemming from economic dependence became the focus of an emergent feminist movement. Pressure for the right to maintenance and custody in the event of divorce or separation began as early as the 1830s. The Governesses' Benevolent Institution was founded in 1843 and was followed by a long campaign to improve women's education opportunities, a campaign which included the foundation of Queen's and Bedford Colleges in 1848, Cheltenham Ladies College in 1853, Girton and Newnham in 1869 and 1871. The first attempt by a woman to register as a medical student was an early as 1856, and the first parliamentary Bill to give married women the right to own their own property was introduced in the same year. The struggle for the franchise began organizationally in the 1860s.[3] We can find traces of most of these activities, certainly of the frustrations and impulses behind them, in mainstream nineteenth-century fiction, in which the conventional characterization of the heroine jostles more critical works on spinsters, governesses, dependency, or the frustration of imagination and abilities. There is a clear pattern linking early feminism with the novel –

both register misgivings, doubts, and discontent with women's position.

The focus of this early feminism was the woman who clearly fell outside the paternalistic family system – the unsupported spinster, the married woman whose marriage, for whatever reason – it could be desertion, divorce or separation – no longer afforded her any protection. Its aims were civic rights and access to employment and education, and, judged by its own objectives, its achievements were substantial. Yet although nineteenth-century feminism drew attention to and remedied at least some of the material problems middle-class women faced in Victorian England, and was in addition well aware of the distance which existed for many women between ideology and everyday reality, it did not regard the ideology itself as either an obstacle or an enemy. Conventional notions of marriage and women's 'natural' sphere were taken for granted as feminists concentrated their efforts on women who, as they saw it, for accidental or numerical reasons were not likely to marry.[4] Spinsterhood was still regarded as a misfortune, marriage as the norm, and feminists and reformers alike supported the factory acts which restricted women's employment in industry not primarily because they objected to factory conditions as such, but because the reality of working women's lives was an affront to the ideal of home and family.

All this meant that important, far reaching and for the novel quite decisive aspects of women's confinement to the home and private life went unquestioned. These included highly tendentious ideas about the relation between private and public life, between the home and work, and about female sexuality.

The separation between domestic life and production, and the consequent identification of men with the external world of work and women with the internal world of feeling, was intensified and exaggerated in the Victorian period through the absolute exclusion of middle-class women from any form of labour. This came about not simply to confine women to the home and so safeguard their chastity, though, as we shall see, this was an important consideration. It came about largely in order to protect the home and family as ideals. The bourgeois notion of the home and women's role within it assumed its extraordinarily elevated position in Victorian ideology because it functioned as a retreat from the external world, where utilitarianism and the mechanisms of competition, capital accumulation and profit, made impulses such as compassion or human sympathy an uneconomical luxury. It provided a refuge for the uneasy conscience troubled by the conditions of the industrial poor, and it became the symbolic centre of the moral values which commercialism could not afford. Ruskin's 'Of Queen's Gardens' (1865) set out to sanctify this new idea of the home, giving it an altogether novel moral and spiritual significance:

The man, in his rough work, in open world, must encounter all peril and trial; – to him therefore must be the failure, the offence, the inevitable error; often he must be wounded, or subdued, often misled; and *always* hardened. But he guards the woman from all this; within his house, as ruled by her, unless she herself has sought it, need enter no danger, no temptation, no cause of error or offence. This is the true nature of home – it is the place of Peace; the shelter, not only from all injury, but from all terror, doubt and division. In so far as it is not this, it is not home; so far as the anxieties of the outer life penetrate into it, and cross the outer threshhold, it ceases to be home; it is then only a part of that outer world which you have roofed over, and lighted fire in. But so far as it is a sacred place, a vestal temple, a temple of the heart watched over by household gods, before whose faces none may come but those whom they can receive with love, – as far as it is this, and roof and fire are types only of a nobler shade and light, – shade of the rock as in a weary land, and light of the Pharos in the stormy sea; – so far it vindicates the name and fulfills the praise of Home.[5]

As far as fiction is concerned, we find the apotheosis of this idea of home as the sacred retreat from unwelcome external realities in Dickens. The split personality of Wemmick in *Great Expectations*, the prototype commuter who has built a drawbridge and moat between his home and the rest of London, whose work and whose private life require of him totally different and incompatible personalities, dramatizes both Dickens's criticism and, disturbingly, his answer to the relation between public and private life.

The burden of sustaining this new idea of the home fell on women; they became custodians of the moral conscience, the repository of all virtue, and as such were obliged to live apart from the sordid everyday cares of material life. Returning home from the pressures of the real world, economic man was supposedly soothed and elevated by the spirituality, virtue and domestic charm of his wife. Ideally, she should be a 'companion who will raise the tone of his mind from low anxieties and vulgar cares'. She must 'lead his thoughts to expatiate or repose on those subjects which convey a feeling of identity with a higher state of existence beyond his present life'.[6] The knowledge that they were providing a refuge from the outside world was supposed to adequately compensate women for their total exclusion from work and public life.

The fear of 'coarsening' women's 'superior moral nature' and so of blurring the distinction between work and home, between public and private, was frequently used as an argument against women's suffrage. ('Where', asked the novelist Mrs Lynn Linton, 'will be the peace of home when women like men plunge into the troubled sea of public life?')[7] And the ideology of home and family was consistently employed to oppose emergent feminism. Women were told that 'to keep the family true, refined, affectionate, faithful, is a grander task than to govern the state',[8] and that the vote would dissipate 'the special moral qualities' of the female sex, qualities of 'sympathy and disinterestedness'.[9]

This rhetoric went some way to disguise the fact that the elevation of the family, posed as an alternative or counter to the amoral world beyond it, meant the imprisonment of its central member, the wife and mother:

The true function of women is to educate not children only, but men, to train to a higher civilization not the rising generation but the actual society. And to do this by diffusing the spirit of affection, of self-restraint, self-sacrifice, fidelity and purity ... as mother, as wife, as sister, as daughter, as friend, as nurse, as teacher, as servant, as counsellor, as purifier, as example, in a word – as woman.[10]

Never, one notes, as herself.

One thing which made it very difficult for women to break through this family ideology was the seductive concept of romantic love, which became a key part of Victorian mythology once it was felt, in the wake of Darwin's *Origin of Species*

(1859), that Christianity could no longer offer a firm moral basis for human actions. In a world rocked by religious uncertainty a superior form of secular love could provide a new spiritual focus, and in a society under continual pressure from an embittered working class, human relationships could become a means of forgetting, of fending off despair.[11] Matthew Arnold's 'Dover Beach' crystalizes, in what is perhaps the most characteristic poem of the Victorian psyche, this mood of bewildered retreat into personal relationships, a mood which adds an important inner, psychological dimension to the split between the public and the private:

> Ah, love, let us be true
> To one another! For the world, which seems
> To lie before us like a land of dreams,
> So various, so beautiful, so new,
> Hath really neither joy, nor love, nor light,.
> Nor certitude, nor peace, nor help for pain;
> And we are here as on a darkling plain,
> Swept with confused alarms of struggle and flight,
> Where ignorant armies clash by night.

Humphry House has offered a perceptive and convincing analysis of the mid-Victorians' dependence on personal relationships:

I see anxiety and worry as a leading clue to understanding them. They were not complacent compromisers. They were trying to hold together imcompatible opposites and they worried because they failed. They clung to an immortality that should not include the possible justice of Eternal Punishment; they wanted a system of administration which should be efficient without expense; in the face of repeated and ferocious strikes and riots they clung to the doctrine that the interests of employers and employed were identical. They knew such things as these were incompatibles; they worried because they could neither reconcile them nor move on to other terms of thought. They worried about immortality, they worried about sex ... they worried about politics and money ... It is not surprising if, to support life at all, they turned to (among other things) an intensification of personal relationships and an unbalanced exaggeration of the domestic virtues.[12]

The only thing House might have added is that these anxieties were evaded or suppressed largely through shifting on to women the burden of maintaining the threatened beliefs, so that while the Victorian householder, disburdened of his unquiet conscience was free to carry on his political and economic life, his wife was shackled by a cramping and inflexible domestic ideology.

The central importance of love and personal relationships in the moral structure of the English novel arises out of this ever-widening division between the private and the public. This split was at its most acute and most conscious in mid-Victorian England when the new industrial system was being consolidated and when men and women had to find new ways of living with a transformed economy. Yet as an underlying ideological principle it has gone largely unrecognized until very recently by authors, critics and feminists alike. One particular manifestation of this general pattern was, however, identified and fought over very bitterly in literature at the turn of the nineteenth century. This was the definition and portrayal of sexuality, particularly of female sexuality.

It is easy enough to link the specific content of nineteenth-century sexual ideology with both earlier and later formations. An association between repressed sexuality and achieved wealth, for instance, is not peculiar to Victorian England.[13] However, it does seem to be the case that Victorian beliefs and assumptions about sexuality were exceptionally oppressive. These have been documented already by Steven Marcus, and by Peter Cominos in his article 'Late Victorian Sexual Respectability and the Social System'[14] All that need be pointed out here is the extent to which the ideal of continence, within marriage as well as outside it, impinged on women rather than on men. Extensive prostitution, pornography and the more or less openly acknowledged mistress or 'second family' are indication enough of the breaches of the official sexual rules. But where men could and did resort to prostitutes or mistresses, middle-class women in particular were obliged to live out the requirements of the official ideology, for the most part actually believing themselves to be without sexuality or desire and morally superior to men because of it. The orthodox view was that 'as a general rule',

a modest woman seldom desires any sexual gratification for herself. She submits to her husband, but only to please him and, but for the desire for maternity, would far rather be relieved from his attentions.[15]

There was of course a central contradiction in this concept of female sexuality. It was based on the assumption that women in different social classes have different psychological and physiological needs. Thus William Acton, the distinguished authority on prostitution felt able to claim that a 'previously incontinent man ... need not fear that his wife will require the excitement, or in any respect imitate the ways of a courtesan'. Prostitutes were obviously 'different'. This confusion, and the unease it generated, set up the contradictions which we find within and between the images of women which emerge from a reading of Victorian literature. On the one hand there is the pure, chaste virgin of respectable fiction who will duly blossom into the model wife and mother, the angel in the house whose charms are strictly domestic; on the other there is the cruel initiate of Swinburne's 'Dolores' or the *femme fatale* whose sexuality corrupts the social order in Tennyson's *Idylls of the King*.[16]

This unease also produced the now infamous double standard of sexual morality, which punished with social ostracism any woman who breached the sexual taboos, but which blandly ignored male offences. This was an effective way of policing women, of penalizing any who demonstrated that they were not the a-sexual beings of popular mythology and so inadvertently reminding the community of the hidden, unacknowledged, and possibly disturbing existence of female desire.

But the double standard with its attendant paraphernalia of ostracism and disgrace did more than keep the lid firmly shut down on Pandora's box. It was an important feature of the monogamy which ensured the legitimacy of offspring and so the safe inheritance of property. A husband could be, and often was, as promiscuous as he liked; this in no way endangered his property, only someone else's. We seldom find any direct admission that it was the anxieties inherent in property ownership which repressed female adultery. However, the debate on the 1857 Divorce Bill produced the following justification for enshrining the principles of the double standard in the new Act. 'A wife', according to the Lord Chancellor,

... might without any loss of cast, and possibly with reference to the interests of her children, or even of her husband, condone an act of adultery on the part of the husband; but a husband could not condone a similar act on the part of a wife. No one would venture to suggest that a husband could possibly do so, and for this among other reasons ... that the adultery of the wife might be the means of palming spurious offspring upon the husband, while the adultery of the husband could have no such effect with regard to the wife.[17]

The exacting patterns of behaviour imposed on women by the dual operation of the double standard and a neurotic sexual ideology, placed enormous pressure on them to deny their sexuality altogether. It is no wonder then that so many Victorian ladies succumbed to the mysterious 'decline'. Edward Carpenter, a homosexual with first-hand knowledge of what it meant for a person to deny their sexuality, believed that the repression and guilt experienced by women forced to regard their sexuality as a perversion, was comparable to the psychological damage society does to homosexuals.[18] Looking back on the personal and social relations of his adolescence in mid-Victorian England, he says that he can hardly bear, even now,

to think of ... the denial and systematic ignoring of the obvious facts of the heart and of sex, and the consequent nerve-ruin of thousands and thousands of women, and even of a considerable number of men ... It is curious – and interesting in its queer way – to think that almost the central figure of the drawing-room in that later Victorian age ... was a young or middle-aged woman lying supine on a couch – while round her, aimiably conveying or consuming tea or coffee, stood a group of quasi-artistic or intellectual young men. The conversation ranged, of course, over artistic and literary topics, and the lady did her best to rise to it; but the effort probably did her no good. For the real trouble lay far away. It was of the nature of hysteria.[19]

The story of Elizabeth Barrett's remarkable recovery from her mysterious illness once Robert Browning appeared at her sofa-side, points again to the sexual/psychological nature of the disorder. But few contemporaries understood the real cause of the 'decline', or if they did suspect it, they preferred to keep it to themselves. It was not until the post-Freudian twentieth century that the decline became the central theme of a novel – May Sinclair's *The Three Sisters* (1914).

If women were to occupy at all convincingly the chaste

niche that nineteenth-century sexual anxieties created for them, it was important that they should be not just technically pure, but innocent in mind and thought as well. In practice this meant a policy of Ignorance for Young Girls. This was achieved by a conspiracy of silence so effective that there could be no danger of a well-bred young English woman obtaining the slightest hint of sexual knowledge. This produced an excessively prudish society whose fear of sex was so acute that over-nice distinctions between what was and was not proper often became downright prurient.

Specifically sexual topics were absolutely taboo because any breach in the wall of silence might lead to women finding out all sorts of dangerous things. Take contraception for instance. One book, R. Ussher's discreetly titled *Neo-Malthusianism* (1898) had this to say on the subject:

It [contraception] would very considerably diminish ante-nuptial chastity on the part of both men and women, especially of the latter. If they came to know that they could indulge all sexual appetite without any fear of becoming mothers, they would undoubtedly surrender their virginity much more readily than if the fear of bearing a child was present.

Worse still,

Women would be enabled to appear outwardly as virgins, yet all the time they might be living in concubinage with their lovers and nobody would be any the wiser.[20]

Ussher reveals some very interesting things here. First, women do not figure in his imagination as the supra-sexual beings of contemporary orthodoxy. On the contrary, their sexuality is so strong that it has to be restrained by artificial checks; they must be prevented from breaking out of their psychological chastity belts and so the 'fear of bearing a child' is used as a deterrent. Second, in keeping with the double standard, the moral effects of contraception are alleged to be more serious for women than for men. Finally, Ussher's dismay at the idea of secret liaisons provides the key to his bundle of anxieties. Contraception would throw into disarray the carefully organized network of taboos which could normally be relied upon to enforce female chastity. He is horrified that property-owning gentlemen would have no way of knowing who was a virgin and who was not ('nobody would be any the wiser').

The spectre of women finding out about and using birth control was also too much for *The Lancet*. On 10 April 1869 it published an article which consisted of medical horror stories about the supposed moral and physical effects of contraception. It told its readers that

A woman on whom her husband practices what is euphemistically called 'preventative copulation' is necessarily brought into the condition of mind of a prostitute ... She has only one chance, depending on an entire absence of orgasm, of escaping uterine disease.[21]

Knowledge of birth control was a key to women's emancipation. It also threatened the ideal of sexual self-restraint. So it is hardly surprising to find that it provoked heavy criticism. But other issues which breached the convention of female ignorance produced exactly the same response. Among these was Josephine Butler's campaign against Contagious Diseases Acts, discreetly known as the C.D. Acts. The Acts allowed, in certain garrison towns, the forcible examination of prostitutes suspected of having venereal disease and the detention of those found to be infected. It was yet another statutory enactment of the double standard and gave wide powers to the police. Mrs Butler's initial problem was to get publicity for the campaign, and indeed even for the fact that such legislation existed. The shroud of secrecy under which the Acts were passed, in 1864, 1866 and 1869, and the reluctance of newspapers to discuss them at all, was because any publicity about them would have meant invading the purity and ignorance of ladies, who were supposed not to know anything about sexual diseases and their transmission, but who yet did glance at *The Times* occasionally. The campaign, led by a woman and supported by women, was a serious affront to the Victorian ideal of womanhood. Henry Austin Bruce, Home Secretary at the time when a modified C.D. Act was introduced into Parliament, after the Government had finally been forced to hold a commission of enquiry in 1871, remarked 'with grief and with sorrow' how much he regretted that the 'reserve and delicacy, for which our women were so distinguished' had been 'broken through'.[22] And a suitably veiled comment in a ladies' newspaper referred to the Acts as a subject 'on which respectable and decent women must of necessity be totally ignorant'.[23]

Sexually transmitted diseases, like contraception, were an explosive topic, but even the mere facts of reproduction were treated, as far as women were concerned, with the same degree of reticence and horror. Ideally, a girl should be totally ignorant about sex when she married. Henry James's Pansy Osmond in *The Portrait of a Lady* (1881) is a piquant literary example of this dangerous state of innocence:

She was such a perfect *jeune fille* ... a *jeune fille* was what Rosier had always dreamed of – a *jeune fille* who should yet not be French, for he had felt that this nationality would complicate the question. He was sure Pansy had never looked at a newspaper and that, in the way of novels, if she had read Sir Walter Scott it was the very most. An American *jeune fille* – what could be better than that? She would be frank and gay, and yet would not have walked alone, nor have received letters from men, nor have been taken to the theatre to see the comedy of manners.[24]

James clearly had his reservations – if not exactly about the desirability of this kind of innocence, then certainly about Rosier's motives in admiring it. But he was writing late on in the century at a time when novelists had begun to question and challenge the conventions which imposed serious, even damaging constraints on literature.

WOMEN AND CENSORSHIP

English literature has always been broadly didactic. But in response to the prudery and caution of the age the conception of morality which it upheld in the nineteenth century was unusually narrow. The majority of English readers and critics, and writers for that matter, believed that:

The object ... which the writer of fiction should always hold in view is to exercise the phantasy in pleasant lawful subjects, to fill it with novel and happy images, and by this indirect, as well as by direct appeal to the heart, so to temper and control the passions as may be most suitable to the formation of virtue and the extirpation of vice. For this reason, his representations should be chaste, his sentiments pure, and his leading characters noble-minded and virtuous.[25]

No matter what the overall ethical position of a novel might be, if it so much as contained a morally dubious character it was suspect as,

the moral nature is exposed to contamination by prolonged imaginative companionship with the very evil against which the moral warning is directed.[26]

Nor can we 'by an effort of the will, so to speak, close our nostrils to moral putrescence'.[27] As long as this simple-minded moralism dominated literary responses, the critic's task was reduced to allotting a work to an ethical category somewhere on a wide spectrum between 'good' and 'evil'; and writers, to avoid censure, were driven either to adopting crude devices of poetic justice and black and white characters, or to writing in long didactic passages which spelled out the unexceptionable morals of their work. This was a kind of moralism which could, and did, easily degenerate into a purely nominal observance of respectability which in fact allowed prurient sensationalism or titillation.

All this was bad enough, but even more serious is the way those who demand morally edifying fiction automatically equate morality with the moral imperatives of their own class, so that the assumptions and behaviour of a small group then take on the appearance and authority of Moral Truth. This is certainly what happened in the middle of the nineteenth century. To illustrate, James Ashcroft Noble in an article on 'The Fiction of Sexuality', written towards the close of the century when the argument about morality in literature was intensifying, argued that 'civilization' dictates what is and is not acceptable in literature, and compared reticence in writing about sex with putting lavatories in 'comparatively obscure and unobserved corners of our dwellings'.[28] Another example (which, incidentally, also compares sex with lavatories) comes from a review of the notorious Dr Bowdler's second edition of *The Family Shakespeare*. It justified expurgation because,

as what cannot be pronounced in decent company cannot well afford much pleasure in the closet, we think it is better in every way, that what cannot be spoken, and ought not to have been written, should cease to be printed.[29]

It was class assumptions like these that made the critics react so angrily to Hardy's Arabella – the coarse, blowsy wife of *Jude the Obscure*. To most critics she was simply revolting. Among other things she was 'a woman so completely animal that it is at once too much and too little to call her vicious', a 'human pig',[30] 'loathsome and repulsive in the highest degree'.[31] These responses to Arabella's sexuality illustrate what could happen when an author deviated from his class's ideology, in particular its sexual ideology. Henry Vizetelly, English publisher of Zola, was a victim of the same prejudices. An old man in his eighties, he was tried and imprisoned for producing, among other novels, *La Terre*, even though his was an expurgated translation. An account of the trial written by Vizetelly's son shows why the book was banned:

> The jury expressed their views clearly enough by interrupting a passage describing how the girl Francoise Louch brings the cow, La Coliche, to the bull at the farm of La Broderie. The mere idea that such a thing could happen evidently amazed and disgusted them.[32]

A publisher's life was not necessarily an easy one in nineteenth-century England. Sex could be discussed in fiction only if author and publishers were prepared to accept certain conventions. These usually ended in evasion and dishonesty.

'Society's' judgment in these matters was based on the vulnerability of its weakest member, the person most likely to be contaminated by contact with suspect fiction – in other words the innocent virgin who had to be protected from sexual knowledge. The obsession with protecting women from 'improper' literature grew up in the late eighteenth century, during the early phase of women's confinement to the home, so we can find a good many pre-Victorian homilies on the subject. Take John Bennett's *Letters to A Young Lady* (1789) for instance. He believed that,

> delicacy is a very general and comprehensive quality ... It extends to everything where woman is concerned. Conversation, books, pictures, attitudes, gesture, pronunciation should all come under its statutory restraints ... A girl

should *hear*, she should *see*, nothing that can call forth a blush, or even stain the purity of her mind.[33]

But in spite of these early manifestations of Podsnappery, women were still reading writers like Fielding and Aphra Behn at the turn of the century. It was in the following decades that the moral clean-up took place, the definition of the improper steadily widening so that by the time Aphra Behn's novels were re-issued in 1872 her work was damned as 'literary garbage' and compared to 'rotting corpses'.[34] Trollope, whose views as a remarkably successful mid-century writer carry some weight, was particularly worried that girls might be corrupted by novels. He points in his autobiography to the predominantely female readership of fiction and warns aspiring novelists against 'the peril of doing harm' in characterizing 'spuriously passionate' or 'heartless, unfeminine and ambitious' women.[35] Alternatively, with the right blend of sentimentality and exhortation, Trollope believed a novel could instil correct notions of conduct into its impressionable female readers. It could assert the values of home-and-family and wifely devotion. Of Thackeray's Laura Bell in *Pendennis* he said that her love

... was so beautiful and the wife's love when she became his wife so womanlike, and at the same time so sweet, so unselfish, so wifely, so worshipful, – in the sense in which wives are told to worship their husbands, – that I cannot believe any girl can be injured, or even not benefited, by reading of Laura's love.[36]

Even though 'Pendennis was not in truth a worthy man, nor did he make a very good husband'. Trollope had a very firm grasp indeed of the ideological function of literature.

If we again turn to Hardy, this time to *Tess of the d'Urbervilles*, we can see quite clearly how assumptions like these could colour standards of critical judgment. The novel raises the problem of the double standard and probes conventional ideas of sexual morality. But the majority of critics chose to overlook these issues and concentrated instead on an angry and literal-minded discussion of the book's subtitle, 'A Pure Woman'. They were anxious, above all, to prove that Tess is not pure. Mrs Oliphant, writing for *Blackwood's Magazine*, typifies this approach to the novel. A pure woman, she says,

is not betrayed into fine living and fine clothes as the mistress of her seducer by any stress of poverty or misery ... we do not believe for one moment that Tess would have done it ... we do not believe him ... Whoever that person was who went straight from the endearments of Alec d'Urberville to those of Angel Clare ... Mr. Hardy must excuse us for saying pointedly and firmly that she was not Tess, neither was she a pure woman.[37]

What Mrs Oliphant really means is that she does not want to believe it. In Hardy's own characteristically ponderous words, she shows the usual 'inability to associate the idea of the sub-title adjective with any but the artificial derivative meaning which has resulted to it from the ordinance of civilization'.[38]

The widespread custom of family readings made things even more difficult for the novelist. For Dr Bowdler this was the principal justification for cleaning up Shakespeare. His first expurgations were apparently impromptu and took place when he was reading the plays to his family circle. He was so good at it that they were unaware that they were not hearing the full text.[39] In his preface to the 1818 edition of the suitably named *Family Shakespeare* he explains his reasons for preferring a mangled text to a complete one:

It is certainly my wish, and it has been my study, to exclude from this publication whatever is unfit to be read aloud by a gentleman to a company of ladies. I can hardly imagine a more pleasing occupation for a winter's evening in the country than for a father to read one of Shakespeare's plays to his family circle. My object is to enable him to do so without incurring the danger of falling unawares among words and expressions which are of such a nature as to raise a blush on the cheek of modesty, or render it necessary for the reader to pause before he proceeds further in the entertainment of the evening.[40]

Texts were not the only thing to be expurgated. Appropriately enough, the vocabulary of censorship was itself censored. Until 1800 'castrate', 'geld' and 'mutilate' were the customary words for expurgation, words which indicated clearly enough why censorship was taking place. After approximately 1800 the euphemisms 'purge', 'prune' and 'chasten' began to appear. 'Bowdlerize' was first used in 1836, a sexually neutral term which effectively concealed the motives of the bowdler-izer.[41]

If a novel violated social and sexual conventions it was not just frowned upon or ignored. Society operated an extensive apparatus for banning as well as bowdlerizing and it did not hesitate to use it. This meant that if they wanted to be published at all, writers had to accept severe restrictions on the scope and treatment of their material. Most stayed well within the moral conventions, but if a novelist did step out of line he or she was likely to be silenced by publishers, editors or librarians. There was also the possibility of prosecution under the Obscene Publications Act (1857), but as a general rule unofficial, private censorship worked efficiently enough to enforce 'public morality'.

The system worked well because the price of books was kept artificially high throughout the greater part of the century. Novels were published in three expensive, elaborately bound volumes, and at one and a half guineas a time were far beyond the pocket of even quite well-off readers. So the public had to rely for its fiction on the private lending libraries and the periodicals, which serialized novels before publication. This meant that between them the libraries and the magazines monopolized the fiction market. The libraries did particularly well out of the high retail price as they bought in bulk from the publishers at five or six shillings a volume instead of the usual half guinea. The publishers were happy too, as they could rely in turn on large orders from the libraries. Needless to say, with the novel-reading public expanding all the time, libraries were very big business indeed. This is how the firm of W.H. Smith began.[42]

The 'three-decker', as the three-volume novel was called, forced writers into unnecessarily complicated plots, lengthy descriptions and commentaries. These were all packed in to make up the required length. But its predominance also gave the magazines and libraries considerable political power. They made good use of their monopoly, censoring and banning anything they disapproved of. Magazine editors for instance often bowdlerized the manuscripts they accepted for serialization. They would alter or suppress what they regarded as risky passages. The author usually accepted the suggested changes and then restored the full text when the novel was later published in three volumes – though, as we shall see, he then ran the risk of being banned by the libraries. Occasionally, however, a manuscript was bowdlerized without the author's consent. This happened to Wilkie Collins, who forced the editors of *The Graphic* to print a revealing apology, which ran as follows:

In last week's installment of *The Law and the Lady* the following paragraph, which occurs on page 83, column 2, was printed thus:-
'He caught my hand in his and covered it with kisses. In the indignation of the moment, I cried out for help'.
The author's proof of the passage stood as follows:
'He caught my hand in his, and devoured it with kisses. His lips burnt me like fire. He twisted himself suddenly in the chair, and wound his arm round my waist. In the terror and indignation of the moment, vainly struggling with him, I cried out for help.'
The editor of the journal suppressed a portion of the paragraph on the ground that the description originally given was objectionable. Mr. Wilkie Collins having since informed us through his legal advisors that, according to the terms of his agreement with the proprietors of *The Graphic*, his proofs are to be published verbatim from his M.S., the passage in question is here given in its original form.[43]

But *The Graphic* still continued with its policy of bowdlerizing sexually suspect passages. We can see this from its treatment of Hardy's *Tess* which it serialized from 4 July to 27 December 1891. M.E. Chase in her very useful study *Thomas Hardy from Serial to Novel*, has traced the numerous alterations Hardy had to make before the novel was inoffensive enough for the editor. Two important episodes were cut out altogether – Tess's seduction and the death and baptism of her baby.[44] He also made extensive alterations in Tess's relationship with Alec. These are a useful guide to what the editor considered dangerous. In the magazine version it is made laboriously clear that Tess thought she was actually married to her seducer. This emerges from changes Hardy made in the conversation Tess has with her mother after her return from Trantridge. In the book version Tess has no illusions about her situation:

Get Alec d'Urberville to marry her! He marry *her*! On matrimony he had never said one word.[45]

But in *The Graphic* version Hardy writes in a false marriage:

'He made love to me, as you said he would do, and he asked me to marry him, also just as you declared he should ... He said it must be private even from you ... I drove with him to Melchester, and there in a private room I went through the form of marriage with him as before a registrar.'[46]

Another example from M.E. Chase's study shows just how ridiculous the bowdlerizations could be. The very sensuous episode where Angel Clare carries the milkmaids over a large pool of water is laughably altered. In *The Graphic* version Clare prudishly goes to fetch a wheelbarrow, and so the girls are trundled across without any physical contact.

A fascinating exchange of letters between Hardy and Leslie Stephen, editor of *The Cornhill* at the time it serialized *Far From the Madding Crowd* in 1874, gives us a glimpse into another magazine's policy on women, sex and fiction. Stephen wrote to Hardy saying that he had:

ventured to leave out a line or two in the last batch of proofs from an excessive prudery of wh(ich) I am ashamed; but one is forced to be absurdly particular. May I suggest that Troy's seduction of the young woman will require to be treated in a gingerly fashion, when, as I suppose must be the case, he comes to be exposed to his wife? I mean that the thing must be stated but that the words must be careful—excuse this wretched shred of concession to popular stupidity; but I am a slave.[47]

This was from one of the leading intellectuals of the century. But as the novel progressed he became even more anxious about what Hardy was letting the magazine in for:

I think that the reference to the cause of Fanny's death is unnecessarily emphasized. I should, I think, omit all reference to it except just enough to indicate the true state of the case ... I have some doubt whether the baby is necessary at all and whether it would not be sufficient for Bathsheba to open the coffin in order to identify the dead woman with the person she met on the road ... it certainly rather injures the story, and perhaps if the omission were made it might be restored on publication. But I am rather necessarily anxious to be on the safe side; and should somehow be glad to omit the baby.[48]

Where the magazines bowdlerized, the libraries suppressed

altogether. They simply refused to stock books they considered 'improper'. Meredith, George Moore and even the
fiercely moral George Eliot all ran into difficulty with the
libraries at least once. Mudie's was the largest and most successful of the circulating libraries. He virtually ran a fiction
empire, which meant that he was one of the most powerful
men in England when it came to dictating standards of literary
morality. His library was called Mudie's Select Circulating
Library, and select is just what he did. He believed that 'the
public are evidently willing to have a barrier of some kind
between themselves and the lower floods of literature'.[49] But
as his narrow-minded moralism was considerably more pronounced than his literary judgment, he managed to include
among the lower floods *Adam Bede, Esther Waters* and *The
Ordeal of Richard Feverel*, to name only three of the more
important books he excluded from his branches at one time or
another. Innocuous, mediocre fiction on the other hand was
assured of a speedy passage from the publishing houses to his
shelves.

In the 'eighties George Moore waged what began as an
almost one-man campaign against the circulating libraries. He
singled out Mudie as the chief enemy, declaring him to be 'the
greatest purveyor of the worthless, the false and the commonplace' and an impediment to 'the free development of our
literature'.[50] He had no illusions about *why* the libraries kept
such tight control over their fiction:

It may be a sad fact, but it is nevertheless a fact, that literature and young girls
are irreconcilable elements, and the sooner we leave off trying to reconcile
them the better. At this vain endeavour the circulating library has been at
work for the last twenty years.[51]

Hardy shared Moore's view of the libraries' impact on literature, describing most circulating library fiction as 'a literature
of quackery' and demanding that the 'regulation finish that
"they married and were happy ever after"' be abandoned in
favour of 'catastrophes based on sexual relations as it is'. To
this, he added, 'English society opposes a well-nigh insuper-
able bar'.[52]

The three-volume novel was finally phased out in the mid-
nineties when novels began to appear even in the first edition

in cheap, single volumes.[53] The libraries then lost their mono-poly. This partially eroded their moral influence, but it was only with the spread of public libraries after the Public Libraries Act of 1919 and, finally, well into the twentieth century, with the appearance of the paper-back, that the private lending system became really marginal. We can see from the Circulating Libraries Association's response to H.G. Wells's *Ann Veronica* (1909) that even at this comparatively late date they could still hope to interfere with the market. One librarian wrote to *The Spectator* complaining about the novel and 'all this literary filth passing into the hands and minds of the public and thereby polluting the moral atmosphere of our home life'. Another letter, from the Circulating Libraries Association itself, called on publishers to give the libraries time to carry out pre-release censorship. They wanted, they said, to be quite sure that none of their stock 'by reason of the personally scandalous, libellous, immoral or otherwise disagreeable nature of its contents is, in our opinion, likely to prove offensive to any considerable section of our subscribers'.[54]

Unofficial, private censorship was not the only way of protecting women from 'harmful' literature. As a last resort there was always the law. The 1857 Obscene Publications Act, was, in principle, designed to control only pornographic literature, books written

for the *single purpose* of corrupting the morals of youth, and of a nature *calculated* to shock common feelings of decency in any well regulated mind.[55] (my italics)

But this is not the way it was used. The act was interpreted in the light of the so-called 'Cockburn definition' of 1868. According to Judge Cockburn's ruling the 'test of obscenity' became whether or not

the *tendency* of the matter charged as obscene is to deprave and corrupt those whose minds are open to such immoral influence and into whose hands a publication *may* fall.[56] (my italics)

Under this ruling, the author's intentions became irrelevant. All that mattered was the impressionability of the weak-minded, so that it became very easy for busybody organizations to bring private prosecutions against publishers whose books had, in their opinion, a 'tendency' to corrupt. Groups like the National Vigilance Association (NVA) were able in this way to drag the statutory power of the state into upholding their own extremely tendentious definitions of morality and obscenity. The most famous action brought by the NVA was the Vizetelly/Zola prosecution in 1888 (see page 16). The case was particularly important because the Government, agreeing under pressure from the NVA to take over the prosecution, gave official sanction to the witch-hunt against Zola's publisher. Another important case was the Bradlaugh–Besant trial in 1877. Their offence was to publish a book on contraception. Another less sensational trial re-enforced the damage already done by the Bradlaugh–Besant affair. This was the prosecution over Havelock Ellis's *Sexual Inversion* in 1898. This was the first volume of Ellis's pioneering work *Studies in the Psychology of Sex*. But as a result of the successful prosecution, it was never sold in England during Ellis's lifetime. Edward Carpenter had a similar publishing experience. It shows how the Obscene Publications Act could intimidate publishers who, for fear of prosecution, would shy away from certain topics. In Carpenter's case T. Fisher Unwin, who had already agreed to publish *Love's Coming of Age*, panicked when he heard about *Homogenic Love* – a book about homosexuality which had been brought out by the Labour Press in Manchester. Without even seeing *Homogenic Love*, Unwin refused to go on with *Love's Coming of Age* and even withdrew a further book by Carpenter – *Towards Democracy*, a lengthy political poem in the style of Whitman which has nothing at all to do with sex. The Wilde trial in 1895 had made publishers more wary than usual where homosexuality was concerned, and both Ellis and Carpenter were caught up in the shock waves that followed it. But intimidation is always the effect, and often the aim of this type of legislation. In the words of the confirmed liberal E.M. Forster:

The public ... determines to be on the safe side, and to do less, say less, and think less than usual. That, rather than the actual exercise of the law, is the real evil. A psychological censorship is set up ...[57]

The spate of obscene publications trials in the 'eighties and 'nineties was part of an attempt to re-impose orthodoxy on writers and intellectuals who, by the end of the century, were no longer prepared to accept moralistic interference with the development of literature or science. But it was no easy matter to break the moral hold of the establishment. Finding new ways of writing about sexuality and new images of women was a political as well as an aesthetic struggle. It meant attacking a whole ideology and the network of state and social controls which had evolved to re-enforce it. The inoffensive heroine who could shock no-one was a highly political creature, and only the most determined of writers were prepared to modify, let alone transform her.

2. The Well-Regulated Heroine

Now that we have seen something of the constraints and conventions under which novelists worked in the nineteenth century, it is easier to understand why the typical Victorian heroine is so insipid. Chastity was the foundation of her personality, and its superstructure was made up out of a judicious arrangement of emotionalism, passivity and dependence. Wilkie Collins for one thought she was wholly delightful:

I love her blushing cheek, her gracefully rounded form, her chiselled nose, her slender waist, her luxuriant tresses which always escape from the fillet that binds them. Any man or woman who attempts, from a diseased craving after novelty, to cheat me out of one of her moonlight walks, one of her floods of tears, one of her rapturous sinkings on her lover's bosom, is a novelist whom I distrust and dislike. (*Household Words*, Dec. 1865)[1]

Not only was she gentle and submissive, but her story, the novelist's fiction, was expected to articulate and demonstrate the belief that a woman can reach happiness through her relationships, is fulfilled in her domestic role. She was to reassure. So it was disturbing if a novelist rose above the stereotype, probing these assumptions about the automatic felicity of marriage and the satisfactions of the female lot. Burne-Jones, for example, was disconcerted by *Anna Karenina*. He could not 'bear', he said,

A tale that has in it a woman who is knocked about and made miserable and mad, and thrown away on a wretch, and is altogether heart-breaking. I like such a one, after due troublesomeness and quite bearable anxiety, to marry the hero and be happy ever after.[2]

Burne-Jones may have been being facetious, but he was still expressing the expectations of the average reader, and indeed the average writer, of fiction.

One of the things which sets the major Victorian novelists apart from the orthodoxy of the minor writers is their refusal to accept this dishonest and misleading representation of women. They were aware of (though they could never resolve) the contradictions between the ideology of womanhood and the all too frequent reality of unhappy marriage or the indignities of spinsterhood and dependence on the charity of often grudging relations. The recognition of the distance between the Victorian ideal of how a woman should live her life and the way many women actually lived is a continual theme of nineteenth-century fiction, even reaching down, in Mrs Gaskell, to a well-intentioned, if distorted account of the lives of working-women in Manchester. The Brontë sisters, Mrs Gaskell, Thackeray in some moods, George Eliot, even Dickens (in parts) are often claimed as feminists, or at least as writers with some degree of feminist consciousness. Up to a point this is true, and it is certainly helpful to identify the critical insights of these mid-century novelists, forming as they do an important tradition of dissent. It is in this context that we should see the Huntingdon marriage in Anne Brontë's *Tenant of Wildfell Hall*, the isolation, yet independence and strength of Charlotte Brontë's single women, Mrs Gaskell's attempts to write about prostitutes and 'fallen' women in *Mary Barton* and *Ruth*, the interesting ambiguities of Thackeray's portrayal of the 'good' Amelia and the 'wicked' Becky in *Vanity Fair* and Dickens's horror at the encroachment of wealth and power into what was for him the sacrosanct realm of marriage and the affections. George Eliot's identification with the aspirations and thwarted potential of women like Maggie Tulliver and Dorothea Brooke are clearly part of this pattern.

The insight and critical power of these novelists should not be underestimated – their work clearly forms the basis on which the more thorough-going literary feminism of the 'eighties and 'nineties was built. Yet this group of mid-century writers did not repudiate or, at a fundamental level, even question the system of personal and sexual relations which gave rise to the unhappiness and frustrations, and to all the contradictions between ideal and reality which their fiction so deftly pinpoints. In short, their imagination operates, as far as women are concerned, within fairly sharply defined limits, so that though they often focus powerfully on what they see as abuses of the marital or domestic system, the system itself generally escapes criticism.

Charlotte Brontë is perhaps the most interesting of the group in this respect. Her own and her sisters' experience as teachers, governesses, above all as spinsters, together with the inner conflict she experienced between what she saw as her domestic duty and her desire to do something else, to write, uniquely qualified her to understand and articulate the frustrations of her contemporaries. She was able to create a range of women characters whose experience and consciousness in many ways typify the dilemmas of her age: strong independent-minded women like Shirley; self-supporting but intensely lonely women like Jane Eyre and Lucy Snowe; dependent, protected, yet intelligent and frustrated women like Caroline Helstone, who has nothing but the prospect of spinsterhood to contemplate day after day at the parsonage. Yet Charlotte Brontë, for all her acute diagnosis of women's emotional and economic problems, always engineers a fictional resolution which ensures the ultimate happiness and fulfillment of her lonely, hard-pressed heroines. This resolution takes the form of marriage. The curious ambiguity of the ending of *Villette*, the doubt about Paul Emanuel's ultimate return and marriage to Lucy, indicates an uncharacteristic degree of unease on Charlotte Brontë's part, an unease which I think we should relate to the unlikeliness of the entire relationship; but there is no such unease in the marriages to Robert and Louis Moore in *Shirley*, to Rochester, or to Crimsworth in *The Professor*.

This recurrent pattern, the resolution of the heroines' problems in marriage, reflects more than the fictional convention of the happy ending. It is rather the inevitable culmination of Charlotte Brontë's commitment to the legitimacy, the desirability of passionate love. The emphasis on passion sets up similar tensions in all the Brontës' work, but these are most acute in Charlotte. On the one hand the insistence of the rightness of love, especially for women, is liberating and radical in the context of the late 1840s and 50s, the period when bourgeois domestic and sexual ideology was being consolidated. Raymond Williams has argued this point in *The English Novel From Dickens to Hardy*. What he did not argue here is another, essentially non-radical role of passion in the Brontës' work, which only becomes apparent in relation to their portrayal of women. Thus in Charlotte's novels the overwhelming emphasis on the need to love and be loved finally submerges all the other essentially feminist issues – the problems of women's employment, their economic dependence, their restriction to a purely domestic range of activities and ambitions, the isolation of the self-supporting woman. All these problems are resolved, or rather simply disappear, on the marriage of the heroine. So that passion, and it is always Passion in the grandly romantic manner of the Angria cycle – the hero ultra-masculine and slightly demonic, the heroine suddenly passive and adoring – this passion, which begins as an additional source of unhappiness, even torment, once safely contained within marriage, emerges as a solution to what the rest of the novels demonstrate as insoluble problems. This collapse of her heroines' independence into welcome submission within the conventional marriage relationship (always preceded by the tell-tale master-pupil relationship) creates a serious rupture in the texture of the novels. This is particularly the case in *Jane Eyre*, with its melodramatic maiming of Rochester and convenient incineration of his wife, and in *Villette*, with its faltering ending. But the insistent emphasis on love, on the notion that only through a passionate relationship with a man can a woman find happiness, is also a serious limitation in Charlotte Brontë's understanding of what women's lives could be. Steeped as she was in the Byronic romanticism of her childhood fantasies, the emphasis of her work cannot be surprising, but we should recognize the essential conformism of a fiction which characterizes women largely through the frustrations or joys of their love relationships.[3]

It is generally recognized that of all the major nineteenth-century novelists, Dickens's work was the most scarred by the prevailing sexual ideology, and offered the least resistance to it. His fictional women simultaneously borrow from and contribute to the readily available range of feminine stereotypes. More important, the moral structure of his novels often rests on, or is amplified by, carefully contrasted female types: the quietly competent, domesticated wife versus the incompetent, negligent or nagging one; the gently affectionate woman versus the cold and distant; the pure innocent virgin versus the guilty adulteress or prostitute.

Dickens always identifies the ideal woman with the ideal home, that Ruskinean sanctuary of affection and right-feeling which the outside forces of materialism, exploitation, money-getting and violence must not be allowed to invade. It is at this point, the point of intersection between the home and the world beyond it, the degree to which the world is seen to invade the protected area of feeling and affection, that Dickens's portrayal of women is at its most interesting. Like the role of passion in Charlotte Brontë, it points Janus-like in two opposing directions. Idealized women like Biddy in *Great Expectations*, Esther Summerson in *Bleak House*, Florence in *Dombey and Son*, Lizzie Hexam in *Our Mutual Friend* or Little Dorrit embody the values and human affection Dickens poses against the inhuman world of industrialism and *laissez-faire* liberal economics. Conversely, the distortion of nature in Edith Dombey, Lady Dedlock, Estella, Louisa Bounderby and, temporarily, Bella Wilfer, is an important part of Dickens's version of a world which places money and power above affection and community, and uses marriage to buy or sell status. His versions of womanhood are thus an important part of his increasingly hostile interpretation of the new society brought into being by industrial capitalism. Yet *as* versions of womanhood, his abstracted ideals and caricatures are without substance or inner complexity; indeed they are without any kind of reality at all, so that they can never become more than symbolic functions of the fictive pattern.

Perhaps the most arresting aspects of Dickens's women is their now famed desexualization. Dickens was certainly not alone in desexualizing both women and love in nineteenth-century fiction, but in him the process of deodorization goes well beyond what most major novelists achieved. We have already noted the emphasis on feeling in the Brontë sisters, can recall Becky Sharp's open manipulation of her sexual attraction in *Vanity Fair* and even George Eliot's admittedly covert allusions to impotence and sterility in *Middlemarch*. Dickens's good women have affections and warm hearts, but never sexual desires; his tainted women, the adulteresses, are or may have been involved in liaisons, but they are essentially cold, emotionally aloof and icy.[4] None of his women display anything faintly resembling sexual passion, so that love in Dickens is either a very tame, essentially domestic affair, or a horror of disgrace and guilt.

An important part of this domestication of what one might expect to be sexual relationships is the continual confusion in Victorian fiction between different kinds of love, often combined with curiously frequent age discrepancies between the partners. Thus in Dickens what are essentially father-daughter relationships between Little Dorrit and Arthur Clennam, and between Esther and Jarndyce, shade off into love relationships; the ideally affectionate household in *Martin Chuzzlewit* is built around a brother and sister; and the Dora-David marriage in *David Copperfield* is more like a boy-girl relationship than a sexual partnership. This merging of different kinds of love, so prominent in Dickens, is not peculiar to him. We find it for instance in Charlotte Brontë, where Jane Eyre and Lucy Snowe both love and finally marry men much older and more experienced than themselves, men who can be seen as surrogate fathers. And the same emotional configuration is repeated and amplified through the master-pupil relationships which encorporate Shirley and Louis Moore, Frances Henri and Crimsworth as well as Lucy and Paul Emanuel, Jane and Rochester. We find a similar pattern in Thackeray and can possibly trace it as far back as Jane Austen – in Fanny Price's tutelage and subsequent marriage to Edmund Bertram, and in Emma's relations with the significantly older Knightley.

We can relate this pattern, so common in Victorian literature, to the sexual ideology of the middle classes, more specifically to the demand for sexual restraint and the consequent desexualization of relationships generally. The cult of the innocent young girl, affectionate, but not passionate, was of enormous importance in curbing any open display or acknowledgement of sexuality. To us now there is something disturbing, perhaps even perverse, in the ideal of the innocent virgin or the sexually neutral marriage. But its appearance in so much Victorian fiction was no more than a legitimate reflection of everyday realities. Take for example E.W. Benson's record of his engagement and marriage. His future wife was eleven at the time he made the following diary entry; he was twenty-three:

I, who from the circumstances of my family am not likely to marry for many years ... and who am fond indeed (if not too fond) of little endearments, and who also know my weakness for falling suddenly in love, in the common sense of the word, and have already gone too far more than once in these things and have therefore reason to fear that I might on some sudden occasion be led (here the manuscript takes refuge in cipher) ... Is it not strange that I should have thought first of the possibility that some day dear little Minnie might become my wife?[5]

Benson became Archbishop of Canterbury and a highly respected member of the English establishment. What is so interesting about his account of his early relationship with Minnie is that it demonstrates how his interest in her when she was so young was essentially a defence against what he regarded as his dangerously physical temperament. Minnie's innocence and youth guaranteed his continence.

In their treatment of sexuality then, the mid-Victorian novelists reflect fairly uncritically the dominant assumptions of their age. They certainly worked within the limits of frankness laid down by Mrs Grundy and the circulating libraries and made no serious attempt to challenge or break these down. This was left to the late nineteenth-century writers with their more rigorous notion of realism. But we can make two interesting and valid comparisons here. One is with the treatment of sexuality in historically comparable European novels, the other is with English poetry. Balzac, Flaubert, and Tolstoy, working within a different cultural and social *milieu*, enjoyed an artistic freedom denied to their English contemporaries. Their fiction consequently contains, and in Flaubert and Tolstoy is often built around, the sexual as well as social conflicts experienced by women living through the repressive social mores of nineteenth-century Europe. Balzac in particular wrote with a degree of sexual explicitness quite alien to the English tradition. This was something he was aware of and remarked on in the preface to the *Human Comedy* (1842) where he discusses his indebtedness to Scott:

Walter Scott was obliged to conform to the ideas of an essentially hypocritical country, and consequently, in terms of humanity, he was false in his
portrayal of women, because his models were protestant ones. The Protestant woman ... can be chaste, pure, virtuous; but her love cannot grow. It
will always be calm and well-behaved like a duty performed.[6]

As an account of women in Victorian fiction this is extremely
accurate. But we cannot apply it quite so systematically to
Victorian poetry. Where fiction, with its ever growing and
largely female readership remained discreet and well within
the bounds of literary propriety, some of the poets, Swinburne
in particular, were considerably freer to touch on sexual
themes. We can detect a consciousness of sexual fears and
anxieties in their work which would never have been permitted in the more explicit fictional form. Then there is also the
huge underworld of Victorian pornography, where we find
the underside of the public protestations of chastity and morality. These books are in their way as revealing as the omis-
sions or evasions of the official, licensed product, marketed
with the seal of approval of the circulating libraries.

European fiction, some nineteenth-century poetry, pornography, the realities of everyday experience – all these are a
measure of the sexual timidity, even hypocrisy, of most mainstream Victorian fiction. But by the time of George Eliot the
strain of silence is beginning to show, so that the integrity and
texture of the novels themselves are affected by it. This is
particularly the case with the Gwendolen-Grandcourt part of
Daniel Deronda which, although it incorporates the sinister
and, for George Eliot, unusually awkward, even melodramatic figure of Grandcourt's discarded mistress, Lydia Glashier,
is weakened by the silence over Gwendolen and Grandcourt's
sexual relationship. The novel sets out to explore this marriage
and its destructive effect on Gwendolen, yet omits what the
reader must always sense as perhaps its most crucial aspect.
The nearest George Eliot comes to discussing this aspect of
Gwendolen is in establishing from the earliest stages of the
novel that she shies away from what she calls 'love making',
from physical contact – one of the things she dislikes about her
cousin Rex is his attempt to handle her, one of Grandcourt's
saving graces as a suitor is his physical discretion. Gwendolen's sexual nature is clearly hinted at in this way, but Eliot

does not return to it after the marriage takes place. We are left wondering.

George Eliot had to confront a similar problem in her account of the Dorothea–Casaubon marriage in *Middlemarch*, and we sense her struggling to find an acceptable way of indicating the sexual as well as spiritual failure of the relationship. She manages to do it, through her imagery, but she is less successful in her handling of the attraction between Dorothea and Ladislaw. Here, at the moment when the couple finally declare their love, she falls back on the stale device of using a thunderstorm to dramatize the strength and intensity of their passion.

It is of course the degree of honesty, rather than the explicitness with which writers handle sexual conflicts or relationships which is important. But there is some degree of overlap between the two if we are considering the portrayal of women in the nineteenth century, when most novelists preferred to deny their women any sexual feelings at all, so that even adultery or prostitution become entirely moral, rather than sexual states.

George Eliot's realism avoids the extremes of moral piety we associate with Dickens or Mrs Gaskell, so that characters like Gwendolen or Hetty Sorrel do have a limited degree of sexual authenticity (Hetty so much so that *Adam Bede* was, as we have seen, banned for a time by Mudie's). Yet in other more important ways Eliot operates well within the bounds of patriarchal orthodoxy. She clearly has a degree of feminist consciousness – we can see this in her handling of Dorothea, Gwendolen, Maggie Tulliver and Mrs Transome, the latter a prototype of the now familiar figure of the redundant, middle-aged woman. But George Eliot's moral philosophy, more especially her ultimate belief in the complete moral autonomy of the individual and her commitment to the notion of duty, conflicts with her more radical understanding of the frustrations society imposes on its female members. It leads, among other things, to a serious inability to extend her sympathy to women who are not able to meet the heavy demands of her moral imperatives – Rosamond Vincy in *Middlemarch* and Hetty in *Adam Bede*. Rosamond and Hetty are really quite logical extensions of popular notions of womanhood, as

George Eliot fleetingly recognizes in her references to Rosamond's education at Miss Lemon's Academy. Yet, though the connection between these women and the bourgeois ideal of decorative domesticity are plain enough, George Eliot is simply not interested in this aspect of the problem. For her, these girls are a moral not a social deviation, and she is involved in exploring the destructive impact of their feminine egoism or narcissism on other people – on Adam and the Poysers, and on Lydgate. Lydgate is not blameless, he has his 'spots of commonness' – which include conventionally stupid ideas about women and marriage – but, like Dorothea, he is capable of the moral growth which takes the form of compassion for his weaker spouse. Rosamond is patently not capable of this; she is the marital millstone, at once a test of Lydgate's humanity and the cause of his failure. We are made to feel enormous sympathy for Lydgate, despite his arrogance and folly, whereas for Rosamond we are allowed to feel none. She fares badly even in comparison with Casaubon, the male counterpart to her domestic and personal selfishness, for where we are carefully taught to see inside and to understand Casaubon's meanness of soul, Rosamond is systematically characterized from the outside, through her chilling gestures and cold mannerisms.

Perhaps George Eliot was aware of the narrowness of her moral sympathies, of the limits to her compassionate tolerance. Her return to and reworking of the spoiled egoistical woman in *Daniel Deronda* is certainly interesting in this respect. Here Gwendolen Harleth, a grander and more sensitive version of Rosamond is the centre of interest, and George Eliot tries hard to see and understand the world from Gwendolen's point of view. But we are never left in any doubt that Gwendolen has acted wrongly, and that though she struggles earnestly towards a true sense of morality and duty, she is in every way weaker than Daniel or the saintly Mirah.

The use of Mirah as a contrast to the sinning and struggling humanity of Gwendolen brings us to another significant point about George Eliot's portrayal of women. She continues their traditional association with moral principles. They are not quite so wholly good or wholly bad as in earlier or less complex novelists, but it remains true that the women characters in George Eliot's novels tend to separate out into the ones for whom the author feels compassion and sympathy and those for whom she does not, and that this division corresponds to the moral distance between those who try to act and live rightly and those who cannot or will not. She never oversimplifies her women, her notions of morality are infinitely more subtle than most of her contemporaries, and she invariably places an ironic distance between herself and the positive, ardent women characters. But the underlying moral patterning is still there, placing and pigeonholing the good and the bad. This moral framework, George Eliot's confident and ultimately rigorous standards of judgment, is quite different from the moral relativism we find in the late nineteenth-century realists, for whom abstract principles have ceased to have anything but a negative, and, in Hardy, oppressive significance.

Very different too is the drift in George Eliot's novels towards a workable compromise between her characters and their world, a compromise which is always at the expense of the individual, not the society or group. And where this compromise is not possible, in *The Mill on the Floss* or *Daniel Deronda*, it is because of the moral weakness of the character. The resolution of *Middlemarch*, with Dorothea's marriage to Ladislaw, is certainly realistic in the sense that historically the most likely outcome of a non-fictional Dorothea's struggles would have been a lowering of her sights, an acceptance of the possible rather than a continuing and possibly tragic search for the ideal. But is this the best or most satisfactory resolution for the fictional Dorothea, and if it is not, why does George Eliot end the novel, and some would say Dorothea, in this way? These questions have been asked before, but it is not enough to say in reply that George Eliot is aware that in marrying Ladislaw Dorothea is possibly still wasting herself, is burying herself in marriage for a second time, or again that she cannily entitles the closing section 'Finale' and deftly makes 'many who knew her' voice their misgivings about Dorothea's future. This is the voice, after all, of demonstrably unreliable Middlemarch; using it leaves Eliot's own position ambiguous, non-commital. This evasiveness, even if it indicates a degree of unease about Dorothea's 'ending', falls well short of the uncompromising tragedies of Emily Brontë or Hardy.

It is instructive to compare the closing chapters of *Middlemarch*, or for that matter almost any mid-century English novel with a degree of feminist awareness, with the very different ending of Turgenev's *On The Eve* (1860). In the Russian novel the marriage of the strong and idealistic heroine, Elena, has a very different function. In *Middlemarch*, in Charlotte Brontë, in Mrs Gaskell, marriage magically resolves conflicts and contradictions. In Turgenev it is only one step on Elena's journey towards freedom. The novel does not end with the marriage, but with the husband's death and the crystalization of Elena's political commitment. But even more significant is the open-ended, essentially non-realist closing pages where the reader is deliberately left in doubt about what Elena's future will be. This deliberate inconclusiveness reflects a recognition on Turgenev's part that the future of a woman like Elena, who abandons her home and country for personal freedom and political action, has to be uncharted by the novelist. As far as women were concerned, Elena's is a step into the unknown, into the future. But the realist novel can only describe the real and the known, and so Turgenev leaves her at the point the nineteenth-century novelist had to leave such a woman, unless, like George Eliot, he reconfines the woman to the known available world of marriage and domesticity.

It is a strength in George Eliot that she returned to re-explore more fully in *Daniel Deronda* the meaning and implications for a woman of a marriage which is seriously wrong, and where there is no possibility of escape or even temporary comfort in the support of friends or any wider community. Yet even here, after Grandcourt's death and Daniel's marriage to Mirah, she finally abandons Gwendolen; she is brushed away into the background, an unhappy widow, whose reassurances to Deronda that she is strong enough to bear separation from him and to live bravely are made at a distance, through a carefully worded letter. This letter allows George Eliot to keep Gwendolen at arm's length, not just from Deronda, but from us, so that what we know must be a life and a future without real meaning is presented, almost by a sleight of hand, as an implausibly resigned calm.

The tendency to stop short, the failure of vision, takes

different forms in the various mid-century writers, but what they all share is the ultimate compromise, the fictional reconciliation between the dilemmas of their female characters and the demands, or possibilities held out by existing social structures. Only one mid-century novel pushes the contradictions in the woman's position to its logical tragic conclusion, and that is Emily Brontë's *Wuthering Heights*, the one novel before Hardy's to reject compromise, and to depict instead the total, inevitable clash between the desire to live freely and the crushing weight of social convention and prejudice. The only possible resolution of conflict in *Wuthering Heights* is in the unrepentant, the defiant death of its anti-heroine and anti-hero, because they and their aspirations cannot be contained within the world as it is structured. When Catherine Earnshaw adopts the feminine and domestic conventions of bourgeois gentility she precipitates her own and Heathcliff's destruction. This destruction is a measure of the compromises, the hesitations and implausible resolutions of so many of the major novelists of the century.

But if the major novelists of the mid-Victorian period contain their critique of women's role within an overall concurrence in moral and social imperatives, what can we expect of the countless minor writers? Here, though the moral framework is considerably less flexible, the portrayal of the heroine is perhaps more directly responsive to public interest in specific women's problems.[7] Long before the consciously feminist novels of the 'nineties, the minor novel had registered a growing awareness of the special difficulties women faced in Victorian society. Once recognized as some kind of social problem, factory girls, governesses, spinsters, even prostitutes, were taken up in the novel and became, if not always heroines, at least an important focus for discussion. 'Fallen' women for example, figured more frequently and were treated with greater understanding in fiction once the campaign against the Contagious Diseases Acts had publicly raised the question of prostitution. And the beginnings of an organized feminist movement in the 'seventies, marking a degree of relaxation in the conventions defining 'ladylike' behaviour, is also registered in the lesser novels, though not always favourably. The novelist Mrs Lynn Linton for example complained that the 'girl of the period' was:

> a hybrid creature perverted out of the natural way altogether, affecting the licence but ignorant of the strength of a man, alike as girl or woman valueless for her highest natural duties, and talking largely of liberty while showing at every turn how much she fails in the coessential of liberty, knowledge.[8]

She was never reconciled to the idea of any extension of women's activities outside the home – even the vote was anathema to her – nor did she tire of criticizing what she called 'modern youngladyism', returning to the attack in the 'nineties with a series of articles on what she now termed 'the wild women'.[9] But changes in manners and conduct led in the work of her contemporaries to a lively and in many ways likeable heroine who was efficient and resourceful and more likely to think for herself than her earlier counterparts. But occupational fashions and changes in manners did not mean a change in the ideological framework of fiction, so that the superficially emancipated heroines of novelists like Miss Braddon, Rhoda Broughton and Mrs Oliphant, to name the best known of this group, remain well within the limits of moral and social convention. Their independent-minded young ladies have shed the fragility and insipidity so admired by Wilkie Collins, but they are in no way a serious challenge to patriarchal stereotypes of feminine character or behaviour. These are left intact. Even the notorious Ouida (Louise Ramée), who delighted in shocking Mrs Grundy and was repeatedly banned from the circulating libraries, had an essentially safe, 'establishment' view of women. In short, even the most sensational of these women writers demonstrates the truth of J.S. Mill's perceptive remark that although 'literary women are becoming more free-spoken and more willing to express their real sentiments', the 'greater part of what women write about women is mere sycophancy to men'.[10]

To get a clear idea both of what the latter nineteenth-century writers achieved and of what they had to contend with, we need to understand exactly what this 'sycophancy' led to in the portrayal of women. The remainder of this chapter aims to make this clear through a brief analysis of three popular Victorian novels – Mrs Oliphant's *Miss Marjoribanks*, Miss Braddon's *Aurora Floyd* and Ouida's *Moths*. The first two are from the 1860s, the third appeared in 1880. The three together present a coherent and not unfair picture of the mid-Victorian heroine inherited by the more iconoclastic writers of the 'eighties and 'nineties.

Mrs Oliphant was a professional who wrote to support her own and her improvident brother's family. She was no amateur dabbler, and as the breadwinner for five children she might be expected to have had advanced views on the 'woman question'. But this was not the case, and like Eliza Lynn Linton she maintained a consistently conservative attitude towards the emancipation movement. We have already seen something of this in her review of Hardy's *Tess*, but her comments on *Jude* are equally revealing. For her

... nothing so coarsely indecent as the whole history of Jude in his relations with his wife Arabella has ever been put into English print.[11]

This gives us some idea of how Mrs Oliphant saw the novelist's responsibility when it came to depicting women and their sexual relationships. Her own practice as a novelist is well illustrated by *Miss Marjoribanks* (1866).

Miss Marjoribanks is a story about the social success of its heroine, Lucilla, whom we see establish herself as the social centre of a small provincial town. She has a natural flair for social diplomacy and is an independent-minded young lady of the 'managing' sort. We see her successfully manage her widowed father, who quickly abdicates the government of the household in her favour, her cook, whom she must win over if her dinner parties are to be the success she wants, her upholsterer, and a succession of young or not so young admirers, whose periodic proposals of marriage punctuate the narrative and provide a diversion from the theme of Lucilla's domestic and social triumphs. After ten years of uninterrupted reign as 'the queen of Carlingford', the novel ends with her graceful abdication and marriage to her cousin, Tom.

As this outline of the plot suggests, the range of interest and activity in *Miss Marjoribanks* is confined to Lucilla's drawing-room. The social and class limitations of the subject are obvious, but if we compare the novel with what Jane Austen does in *Emma*, where the skeletal idea of the book is very similar

(Emma too tries to manipulate people through her sex and social position), we see that a severely restricted social range need not exclude important concerns. *Miss Marjoribanks* is trivial in a way that *Emma* is not, and it is so because of the author's attitude, endorsing as she does Lucilla's exploitation of her traditional female role.

Lucilla understands the possibilities and immunities her sex offers her when it comes to manipulating the people she is interested in socially, and in achieving her (admittedly harmless) aim of establishing social harmony in Carlingford, she ruthlessly exploits these advantages. Although it is true that Mrs Oliphant describes Lucilla's manoeuvering among her acquaintance with a degree of amused irony, she still approves of both Lucilla and her activities. Unlike Emma, Lucilla is allowed to sail through life without a setback or a come-uppance of any major sort, and both Mrs Oliphant and Lucilla's admiring entourage of kindly matrons find her pursuit of success as a hostess a worthwhile, even commendable occupation. And when Mrs Oliphant generously arranges for Lucilla a future of social challenges and philanthropic activity among the gentry we are made to feel that virtue has yet again been rewarded. 'It was', we are told, 'but the natural culmination of her career that transferred her from the town to the country.'[12]

Mrs Oliphant's admiration is slightly qualified by her habitual attitude of detached amusement. For instance she shrewdly indicates the degree of egocentricity in Lucilla's apparently disinterested ambition to improve the run-down village which is attached to the estate to which she and Tom graduate at the end of the book, and which prefigures, incidentally, Dorothea's disappointment over the healthy condition of the cottagers at Lowick in *Middlemarch*:

> If it had been a model village, with prize flower-gardens and clean as Arcadia, the thought of it would not have given Miss Marjoribanks so much pleasure. The recollection of all the wretched hovels and miserable cottages exhilerated her heart. (p. 595).

But the purpose of the irony here, and throughout the book, is not to critically 'place' Lucilla and her ambitions; instead these sly criticisms of Lucilla's motives make us like her even more, endearing her to us as someone who, for all her apparent perfections, does, after all, have human failings. The irony is not used to modify the general approval of her lifestyle, so that ultimately the novel still implies that the proper place for a talented young woman is in queening it over the dinner or tea table and in gracefully dispensing charity to the agricultural poor. There is no suggestion that Lucilla is in any way wasted, or that she could become bored or frustrated with the social whirl. Indeed, when her father inconveniently loses all his money and dies, and Lucilla has to look about her for something else to do, the plot immediately provides her with a husband and the second readily available female role, that of wife and mother.

The novel is also a celebration of romantic love. To begin with it looks as if Lucilla is determined to free herself from the claims of love and family, so great is her desire to concentrate on those of home and hostess – she even refuses or discourages four tempting 'offers' rather than desert her father's drawing-room. But we see how superficial this level of emancipation is when she finally accepts Cousin Tom. She has already rejected him once, in the opening chapters, dismissing him to a period of colonial administration in India. But Tom returns to Carlingford in time to oust all rivals and carry Lucilla off in triumph. At this point Mrs Oliphant's sophisticated tone falters; she becomes sentimental and falls into plot clichés as Tom re-enters only just in time to forestall another 'offer'. He actually bursts into the hall with his bag and baggage just as the other suitor is about to propose in the drawing-room upstairs. Destiny and the conventions of romantic love have more to do with the marriage than the internal logic of the novel:

Fate and honest love had been waiting all the time till their moment came; and now it was not even necessary to say anything about it. The fact was so clear that it did not require stating. It was to be Tom after all. (p. 580)

Even though they have not seen one another for a decade. The reason why Lucilla rejected all her other suitors in favour of the absent Tom is, we are told, because she loved her cousin all the time – unconsciously:

'I did not know it at the time,' said Miss Marjoribanks, with sweet confidence and simplicity, 'but I see it all now. Why it never came to anything before, you know, was that I never could in my heart have accepted anyone but Tom.' (p. 600)

And someone else comments,

'She bore up a great deal too well against all her little disappointments ... When a girl does that one may always be sure there is somebody behind – and you know I always said, when she was not just talking or busy, that there was a preoccupation in Lucilla's eye.' (p. 603)

And so Lucilla's reluctance about marriage, the great enviable state of being, is explained away as an unshakeable prior attachment to the one-and-only lover.

We see little of Tom, but when we do meet him his manliness is carefully emphasized. He returns from his ten years' oblivion equipped with a beard and forceful manner which allows him to bully Lucilla into accepting him. Bold and decisive, he is at once a simplification and an idealization of masculinity. Tailor-made to fit the literary stereotype, he is the polar opposite of, for example, Hardy's men, whom Mrs Oliphant found almost as objectionable as his women, though for the opposite reasons. They are,

... passive, suffering ... victims of [the women] and of fate. Not only do they never dominate, but they are quite incapable of holding their own against these remorseless ministers of destiny.[13]

Mrs Oliphant could never have created, and never wished to create characters like Angel Clare or Jude. In her novels the relationship between hero and heroine adheres strictly to the conventions which impose dominance on the man and submission on the woman. So Lucilla, for all her former independence, accepts the likeable but overbearing Tom and the dependence which follows from their marriage.

But Mrs Oliphant does not leave things even at that. She goes out of her way in the novel to build up a careful contrast between Lucilla and another woman, Barbara Lake. The comparison is very much in Lucilla's favour. She has what the author calls a 'well-regulated mind – another aspect of her partial emancipation – whereas Barbara's is a jealous, ill-governed temper. But the contrast between this and Lucilla's self-restraint, poise and initiative, establishes Lucilla not so much a forerunner of emancipation, but as a new kind of womanly ideal. She is set up as a pattern of female conduct while poor Barbara, who cannot and will not try to conceal her emotions, is made ridiculous. She is an 'under-bred' young woman who knows no better than to show her feelings.

All this brings out Mrs Oliphant's traditional views about women clearly enough, but on a number of occasions in the novel she cannot resist making them quite explicit – with damning references to the emancipation agitation which had begun in earnest in the 'sixties. For instance, she describes Lucilla at twenty-nine as having reached 'that condition of mind when the ripe female intelligence, not having the natural resource of a nursery and a husband to manage, turns inwards, and begins to 'make protest' against the existing order of society, and to call the world to account for giving it no due occupation – and to consume itself'. (p. 477) With this brisk assigning of discontent to the frustration of women's natural destiny, Mrs Oliphant avoids any real discussion about women's unsatisfactory social condition. Needless to say, Lucilla's well-regulated mind prevents her from plunging into revolutionary activity on the part of her sex.

One last aspect of the novel deserves some attention. This is Lucilla's politics – or rather the character of her political influence. She feels no frustration at being excluded from direct participation when there is an election in Carlingford; instead she is happy to be the proverbial woman-behind-the-scenes who influences, guides or inspires the male candidates. Her influence is based, moreover, entirely on her sexual and personal attractions. (One of the candidates has proposed to her and the other is about to do so.) Her preferences are sexual and personal, not political. One 'knowing' female character in the novel is right when she says that she 'knows what it means when young ladies take such an interest in elections'. (p. 567)

In giving Lucilla this kind of political influence, Mrs Oliphant was adopting one of the stock arguments against women's suffrage – that through manipulating their men women had all the political power they needed. For example, as late as 1910, speaking on the second reading of the 'Conciliation' Bill which would have given the vote to women house-holders, Arnold Ward commented that,

Innumerable unseen women will guard the entrance to those Division Lobbies tonight, and will be voting through us. It is now proposed, in addition, that they should have votes for themselves, thus practically having two votes, while we have none at all.[14]

The idea of the woman as the political inspiration or power behind the successful man is certainly not peculiar to Mrs Oliphant. Mrs Humphry Ward's Marcella Boyce in *Sir George Tressady* (1896) provides the moral force and the social vision which motivate her husband, an influential Tory minister. And Marie Corelli's *Temporal Power* (1902) illustrates the same assumption – that women are the 'power behind the throne' and that they are satisfied with this invisible, shadowy role, with the illusion of power instead of the substance. Admittedly *Temporal Power* takes this belief to ludicrous and laughable extremes, but even so, we cannot dismiss the ideas in the novel as so much nonsense, if only because Marie Corelli was a popular and extremely successful writer. Her crude simplifications of contemporary ideology very largely account for this success, and a reading of her work, though it requires stamina, does reveal dominant social and political assumptions in a particularly clear way. What we find in *Temporal Power* is that the two leading male characters, a king and a revolutionary of unspecified persuasion, are both motivated by love of the mysterious woman-of-the-people, Lotys. The revolutionary, for one, has this to say about his activities,

'All for Lotys!' he murmured. 'working for Lotys, plotting, planning, scheming for Lotys. The government intimidated – the ministry cast out – the throne in peril – the people in arms – the city in a blaze – Revolution and anarchy doing their wild work broadcast together – all for Lotys! Always a woman in it!'

When Lotys dies both king and revolutionary commit suicide over her corpse. The plot is absurd, but indicates clearly enough in its exaggerated way, the lengths to which the idea of woman as inspiration could be stretched. It remains doubtful, however, whether the woman-behind-the-man theory has ever been based on reality for any but a very few exceptionally strong women. Yet it was a seductive notion, and even feminists writers adopted it; Sarah Grand for instance in *The Heavenly Twins* (1893). Here one of the author's rebellious women, Angelica, is finally content to marry a political husband and write his parliamentary speeches for him. We are expected to accept this as a satisfactory solution to the problems Angelica has been facing in fighting the restrictions imposed on her as a woman. But it cannot work for Angelica, and it does not work for the novel, which ends lamely. Grand was chasing a chimera which could never be a substitute for freedom.

My next novel, really very different from *Miss Marjoribanks*, is perhaps closer to Marie Corelli's fantasies. Mrs Oliphant's book is essentially a light-hearted comedy of manners, but *Aurora Floyd* (1862), disingenuously described by its author, Miss Braddon, as 'a simple drama of domestic life'[16] is in fact a full-blooded sensation novel. It uses all the favourite themes of bigamy, blackmail and murder, woven into a suitably far-fetched and extravagant plot. The sensation novel, descendant of the gothic romance, created a fantasy world of villains and heroes, poetic justice and beautiful but misunderstood heroines, and as such is clearly far removed from more sophisticated novels like Mrs Oliphant's.[17] But what differences there are between the two types of novel – the sensational and the popular domestic – are essentially differences of style and imagination. At a more fundamental level a flamboyant work like *Aurora Floyd* treats women and sexuality in much the same way as more obviously genteel works.

Aurora is another 'spirited' heroine; she is wilful and has a quick temper, flashing black eyes and a passion for physical exercise. But she is utterly traditional in her desire for husband and home. The value of these is deliberately thrown into relief by the plot, which almost prevents Aurora from obtaining either. We learn at the beginning of the novel that while very young she ran away with her groom and married him. Although she has left him when the book opens and the marriage has been hushed-up, she seems doomed to a life of pretence and celibacy because she cannot marry the man with whom she is now in love. However, she is unexpectedly reprieved when she learns of the sudden death of her groom-husband. The second marriage still does not take place, for the severe and upright fiancé insists on knowing all about Aurora's 'past', declining to marry her when she refuses to enlighten him. She eventually marries another, less priggish young man. It looks at this point as though she is about to live happily ever after when more complications develop: the former husband reappears. He was not dead after all. It is here that the blackmail and murder aspects of the plot take over. It is unnecessary to go into these, except to say that they cause great misunderstanding and unhappiness between Aurora and her second husband John, and almost break up their relationship. Eventually the plot unravels itself, and with the groom properly dead this time, Aurora remarries John. But the main point to notice about the suspense and dangers Aurora is put through before the obligatory happy ending is that they make her future domestic happiness seem that much more valuable.

The novel works through suspense rather than insight; various unpleasantnesses arbitrarily arise to block Aurora's path to happiness, building up what Miss Braddon calls a 'dark wall' of misunderstanding and mistrust between herself and John. Marital problems could be, and did become, important themes in the novel later on in the century, but here they are simply components of clever plotting rather than class or psycho-sexual obstacles to compatibility. It is interesting, however, that Miss Braddon thought she was doing something very different in her decision to deal with a marriage as well as a courtship:

Now my two heroines being married, the reader versed in the physiology of novel writing may conclude that my story is done, that the green curtain is ready to fall upon the last act of the play ... Yet, after all, does the business of the real life-frame always end upon the altar steps? Must the play needs to be over when the hero and heroine have signed their names in the register? Does man cease to be, to do, and to suffer when he gets married? And is it necessary that the novelist, after devoting three volumes to the description of a courtship of six weeks' duration, should reserve for himself only half a page in which to tell us the events of two thirds of a life-time? Aurora is married, and settled, and happy; sheltered, as one would imagine from all dangers, safe under the wing of her stalwart adorer; but it does not therefore follow that the story of her life is done. She has escaped shipwreck for a while, and has safely landed on a pleasant shore, but the storm clouds may lower darkly upon the horizon, while the hoarse thunder grumbles threateningly in the distance. (p. 151)

But these melodramatic forebodings tell us clearly enough that the marital problems the book goes on to deal with are closer to the complications of an extended courtship than a serious exploration of real difficulties. The novel follows the pattern of the troubled engagement, where the writer places obstacles in the way of the couple which they then have to overcome before the happy outcome of marriage is possible. Aurora's bigamy, in spite of what Miss Braddon says about it, is merely an extra obstacle which happens to crop up after the marriage instead of before it. Miss Braddon was not doing anything revolutionary.

Though the plot of *Aurora Floyd* centres around bigamy, this does not mean either that the book takes an 'advanced' attitude towards sexual problems. It is certainly unusual to find a 'nice' heroine who is bigamously married (Jane Eyre recoiled from the idea in horror), and Miss Braddon's sympathetic treatment of Aurora does suggest a degree of tolerance within a tradition which classes the bigamous wife with the adulteress. In this respect Aurora is an advance on Lady Audley, her bigamous predecessor in Miss Braddon's fiction. But because Aurora ia an unintentional bigamist, Miss Braddon never has to confront the marriage laws which might tempt a woman into either bigamy or adultery. Instead the whole problem is sensationalized; it becomes a useful peg to hand a plot on and no more. Because they could always neutralize sexual problems in this way, the sensation novelists managed to write about taboo subjects and get away with it. A novelist could safely include adultery, bigamy or seduction provided he or she did not question basic moral categories. On the other hand writers who later challenged the assumptions of sexual ideology were instantly labelled 'immoral', in a way the sensation novelists were not, even though at a more fundamental level they were profoundly serious moralists. *Aurora Floyd* is characteristic of its kind in the way it exploits, rather than confronts contemporary ideologies.

Ouida's *Moths* (1880), though in some ways quite daring, is really just as timid in its treatment of women and sexuality.

The book has many strong points: Ouida is critical of the double standard, the marriage-market, the education and wasted lives of upper-class girls, the legal position of the unhappily married woman. But at the same time the function of these social evils is to emphasize the moral beauty of her heroine, Vere. In her purity and incorruptibility Vere is as irreproachable a heroine as any conventional author could wish for. There is 'immorality' in the book, even dark hints of unmentionable vices:

... he knew that his sins against his wife were heavier and grosser than even his mistress knew or guessed.[18]

There is even an almost-bedroom scene when Vere finds her husband in his mistress's room (p. 429), but there is no hint of physical love between hero and heroine. They never exchange so much as a kiss throughout the whole novel. They remain exaggeratedly pure and unreal figures, while the other depraved characters provide the titillating thrill Ouida's readers doubtless enjoyed. In this way she technically stays within the 'correct' moral framework – keeping her heroine chaste, but exploring the possibilities of vice for her 'evil' characters. She both has her moral cake and eats it.

But perhaps the most conventional aspect of Ouida is her fairy-tale idea of love. In *Moths* we find an absurdly romanticized relationship between Vere and the hero, Correze. This would-be lover is a brilliant operatic tenor, young, brave and persistent in his adoration of the unattainable Vere. He is content to worship her from a distance rather than encourage her to act unworthily and leave her husband. He even serenades her under her window and languidly haunts the neighbourhood so he can be near her:

He had the lover in him of southern lands, of older days. He would watch in long hours of cold midnight merely to see her image go by him; he would go down to the cliff on the northern coast only to gather a spray of sweetbriar on the spot where he had seen her first; he would row in rough seas at dark under her villa wall in the South for the sake of watching the light in her casement; his love for her was a religion with him, simple, intense, and noble; it was an unending suffering, but it was a suffering he loved better than all his previous joys. (p. 805)

It is this romanticized notion of love which, more than anything else, unites the novelists examined in this chapter, major and minor writers alike. Few take it to such extremes of masochism and unrewarded devotion as Ouida, but it is there all the same, underlying and conditioning their whole outlook. The love interest is central to these novels and women are at the heart of the love interest, experiencing life almost exclusively through their emotions. Mrs Humphry Ward is a novelist who will figure more prominently in a later section, but her views on the connection between the novel and the emotions neatly summarize a central tendency in the writers looked at so far. For her,

The tenderness, faith, treason, loneliness, parting, yearning, the fusion of heart with heart and soul with soul, the ineffable illumination that love can give to common things and humble lives – these after all are the perennially interesting things in life ...

and are the things novelists should be writing about.[19] One measure of the success of the less complacent, more critical novelists of the following decades must be how far they managed to redefine love and its attendant features of marriage, sexuality, domesticity and motherhood.

PART TWO

REALISTS AND FEMINISTS

3. Introductory

The eighteen eighties and 'nineties saw the beginnings of a
major revision in thinking about women and about sex, a
process in which literature played an important part. Novelists
in particular were moving towards new and radical images of
women. It is tempting to believe that these changes came
directly out of the feminist movement, which by 1880 had a
firm organizational basis in suffrage committees in all the
major cities, and was rapidly becoming a large, if not broad-
based movement with some important achievements to its
credit. The first Married Women's Property Act had been
passed in 1870, and another, more far-reaching one became
law in 1882. These had given many women their first taste of
economic independence. Custody and maintenance rights had
been steadily extended by women taking cases to court in the
middle decades of the century. Women with the necessary
property qualifications won the local franchise in 1882, and
after this began taking up posts in provincial administration,
sitting on school boards or even working as factory inspectors.
Women clerks were employed by the Post Office from 1870,
and by 1877 women had won the right to enter medical
schools.[1] Just as important as all these 'firsts' in various fields
was the political experience and confidence many women
developed during the prolonged campaign against the C.D.
Acts. The campaign had begun to break down some of the
absurd pretences and conventions about women's purity and
sexual ignorance. And it undermined the rigid separation of
women into categories of good and bad, prostitutes and ladies,
which had been such an effective method of dividing and
ruling.

    With agitation on so many issues going on, awareness of
women as constituting a special 'problem' had become acute
by the end of the century. The 'woman question' had arrived

in earnest and the vague but popular phrase 'the new woman' was coined in the 'nineties in an effort to describe women who had either won or were fighting for, a degree of equality and personal freedom. It can hardly be surprising then to find that even established male writers like Hardy, George Moore, Meredith or Henry James show an interest in or an awareness of contemporary women's issues. But this must immediately raise the whole question of the connection between literature and social change. Can we, for instance, reasonably interpret novels like *Jude*, *Esther Waters* or *The Bostonians* as simple reflections of, or responses to, highly specific social pressures or feminist demands? It is a question that is easier to answer if we ask it of explicitly feminist women writers such as Olive Schreiner or George Egerton, whose work is largely conditioned by their conscious experience as women. But when it comes to men like Hardy, Meredith or Moore it becomes misleading to look for any direct link between their novels and feminism, except possibly, in James and in Gissing, a negative one. Their primary commitment was, reasonably enough, not to any explicit political ideology, but to literature, and to their own vision. This does not, of course, make them ideologically unconditioned, but it does point to a more complex relation between their work and feminism than can be accommodated by any reductionist notion of reflection, especially if we recognize that a novelist like Hardy was working towards a potentially more disturbing version of women than anything envisaged by contemporary political feminists. Their work shows that these novelists were undoubtedly sympathetic to at least some of the women's dilemmas and demands, but this sympathy is embedded in and often limited by their own private constructions of reality or by formal difficulties in the novel itself. Their battles were those of realists attempting to redefine existing social and sexual realities, not feminists seeking to change them. Their portrayal of women was incidental to their conception of realism, of what it should do and how it should do it.

By the close of the century a significant number of writers had become severely alienated from the values of British political and social orthodoxy. For them the complacent ideology of mid-Victorian optimism had become an irrelevance and was untenable. Indeed it was soon to be swept away in the wake of the unemployment and resurgence of working-class militancy which greeted the recession of the 1870s. The unease about *laissez-faire* industrialism, urban poverty and exploitation which was so marked a feature of the early Victorian novel re-emerged at this point. We can see it clearly enough in Gissing and in the rediscovery of the working class as subject; it is there too in Moore's *Esther Waters* and especially in Hardy, where it is not simply the class of characters like Tess or Jude that is important, but Hardy's entire outlook, the so-called pessimsim which repudiated the glib meliorism of conventional assumptions.

But more central, and more specific to late nineteenth-century realism in England was its rejection of the individualistic moral imperatives which had accompanied the consolidation of the bourgeoisie in the middle years of the century. As part of this moral re-orientation, important disputes took place, at first over certain continental works, increasingly over indigenous products.[2] French fiction in particular had long been viewed with suspicion by the English, largely because it was free of sexual reticence. French realism and English realism had come to mean two very different things. Briefly, if somewhat crudely, Balzac, Flaubert and Zola wrote about reality as they believed it to be. English novelists tended, as we have seen in Part One, to write about it as they believed it ought to be. This produced two conflicting notions of morality, succinctly characterized by Zola:

The question of morality in the novel boils down to these two opinions: the idealists claim that it is necessary to lie in order to be moral, the naturalists[3] affirm that it is impossible to be moral outside the realm of the true ... We teach the bitter science of life, the uncompromising lesson of the real ...[4]

Zola and Ibsen were the focus of this conflict in England in the 'eighties and 'nineties. *Ghosts*, in which venereal disease is both the key mechanism of the plot and a symbol of social and moral decay, shocked London when it was first produced in England in 1891. One paper called it 'garbage and offal'; to another it was 'as foul and filthy a concoction as has ever been allowed to disgrace the boards of an English theatre'; a third found it 'unutterably offensive', while *The Daily Telegraph*, spoke of 'Ibsen's positively abominable play ... this disgusting representation ... an open drain; a loathsome sore unbandaged; a dirty act done publicly'[5] *A Doll's House*, first performed publicly in England in June 1889, had also produced a critical storm, this time because of Ibsen's insistence that women have every right to determine the shape of their own lives. The play exploded many myths, particularly those which assumed women would always find fulfillment in marriage and motherhood. Here and in *Hedda Gabler* Ibsen openly disputed the whole ideology of womanhood which English literature had barely begun to question. Just as disturbing as Ibsen's subversive dramas was Zola's attempt to write frankly about sexual relations – we have already noted the obscene publications prosecution which greeted the first English translations of his work.

By the end of the century morality had become for many writers a relative, not an absolute matter. The realist no longer believed in absolute free will or, beyond a point, in individual moral responsibility, certainly not in individual moral autonomy. For him or her the dilemma of the individual character grew out of social structures which the character could confront but never control, so that the whole burden of failure or injustice could no longer be pushed, as it was in most mid-century fiction, onto the erring, weak individual. This approach to reality, and to fictional formulations of it, implied, for English writers, the rejection of the greater part of nineteenth-century moral and sexual ideology. It meant in particular major revisions in the portrayal of women. Although English writers did not adopt Zola's 'scientific' theory of fiction and human relations, or his commitment to average experience, to literal truth and verifiable fact, Moore, Hardy and Gissing all shared Zola's and Ibsen's belief that it was time to redefine morality. Meredith and James, though moving in a very different direction aesthetically, also challenged sexual ideology if and when it interfered with their notion of truth, so that even the sexually reticent James could write about the 'feebleness' of most contemporary English fiction, saying that 'our English literature is a good thing for virgins and boys, and a bad thing for the novel itself'.[6]

These developments coincided with comparable advances in the new science of psychology which, though still in its infancy, was making serious attempts at just this time to understand and interpret the nature and function of sexuality in the human personality. Freud was at work in Vienna and in England, Havelock Ellis published his first work on sexual psychology in 1894. Volume III of his *Studies in the Psychology of Sex*, devoted as it was to female sexuality, was particularly important. He saw frigidity in women as a historical phenomenon, not a biological one as Acton and other authorities had claimed. As far as Ellis was concerned it was 'pathological'.[7] And Carpenter, in a series of pamphlets on sex and society, was arguing at much the same time for the recognition of sexuality as a natural and enjoyable part of human relations and behaviour.

Yet there is no direct, causal link between developments in the novel and the emergence of either feminism or sexual psychology in the late nineteenth century. In the case of feminism there was, on the contrary, a definite breach between the novelists and parts of the movement, many women fearing anything which might associate their cause with 'loose morals'. Yet although there was no specific connection between the three developments, they were clearly related. They were all part of the disintegration of what had been a highly homogeneous culture, but which was now rapidly changing under new political and economic pressures. As far as literature was concerned this process both included feminism and went beyond it into a general repudiation of moral imperatives which were being rapidly outgrown by new experiences and new expectations.[8] As far as the novelists discussed in the following pages are concerned, their attempts to write about women and sex with a degree of honesty laid them open to the same kind of attacks as Zola and Ibsen had experienced before them. No matter how reticent or tame they may seem to us now, we should remember that, at the time, they were challenging almost the entire literary and moral establishment. The opposition to them and their books was sustained and bitter, just as it is today over the other quasi-moral, really political issues.

4. Thomas Hardy, A Study in Contradiction

The generation of novelists who begin with Hardy and end with the Great War were moral iconoclasts, social critics who rejected Victoriansim and its ideology of self-help and self-restraint. As far as the development of fiction in England was concerned, their innovations, criticisms and revisions of female stereotypes formed a new tradition which led directly to D.H. Lawrence and his quasi-mystical celebration of sexuality and personal relationships. Whatever we may think of Lawrence, there can be little doubt that his apparently startlingly new emphasis on sexuality was an extension of the earlier efforts of Hardy, Moore, Carpenter, Wells, Forster and others, to break down sexual taboos in literature and escape from the grossly oversimplified images of women and mid-nineteenth-century culture. In a very real sense these writers were pioneers. They almost had to re-invent women in the novel, introducing the inner conflicts and the sexual feelings which had been denied to women in English fiction for nearly a century.

But these writers still lived in and were formed by late nineteenth-century England. It must also be added that they were mostly men and that they shared in a culture which, though changing under pressure from an increasingly articulate women's movement, was still essentially patriarchal, so that its available images and forms were likely to be able to accommodate only an attenuated version of what women themselves were feeling and thinking. Up to a point writers always step aside from contemporary reality in order to interpret it and to communicate their interpretation through their work. This relatively detached, often alienated position provides the vantage point from which the writer assimilates and evaluates. Yet in spite of this, no writer can see his or her own time with complete objectivity. Writers, like everyone else, live in history, and like everyone else the structure of their thought is shaped by the character of the age in which they live. Their vision is also conditioned, and often sharply limited by available forms. These can be modified or reshaped, but are transformed only in a period of such revolutionary change in politics and culture that new structures become essential and inevitable. English politics and culture were going through a period of upheaval and redefinition during the period we are looking at, and literary forms did change. But the novel was not transformed beyond all recognition between Hardy and Joyce or Virginia Woolf; nor was English society. Particularly interesting from our point of view is the persistence of underlying cultural and fictional stereotypes of women and female experience. These received images and patterns are certainly remodelled, largely to accommodate female sexuality, but are not transformed, even by feminist novelists.

Here Hardy is particularly interesting. His fiction is very much a product of a contradiction between his uncompromising vision of life in society and the available form of the realist novel. This begins to break down under the pressure of his analysis. Multiple coincidences, impossible child suicides, sexual consummation in the shadow of Stonehenge – these are not within the tradition of nineteenth-century realism as it is usually understood. Like Dickens and Balzac earlier in the century, Hardy breaks through naturalistic verisimilitude and uses symbolism, exaggeration and melodrama of a type which even contemporary readers find disturbing, and disruptive of the texture of the novels. This tension between idea and received form is especially prominent in Hardy's portrayal of women. Here there is an uneasy co-existence between an intensely modern, even feminist consciousness and what are essentially archetypal patterns of feeling and relationship. This contradiction produces some of the strengths as well as some of the weaknesses both of his fiction and of his feminism.

But first the strengths. I want to look here at Hardy's achievements, at how far he was able to redefine women in the novel, before going on to isolate the contradictions which ultimately limit this redefinition.

Any discussion of Hardy's fiction must at some point touch on his handling of marriage. It was, after all, his cynicism about the formalized marriage relationship in *Jude* which won him the notoriety and unpopularity which contributed to his decision to give up fiction altogether. He was well-known as a public critic of the legal situation which was the legacy of the 1857 Divorce Act. This had made divorce virtually unobtainable for a woman, and a real possibility only for wealthy men. In 1912 when a Royal Commission was at last set up to examine the 1857 Act and caused a flurry of public discussion, Hardy wrote in an article called 'How Shall we Solve the Marriage Problem?'[1] that marriages should be 'primarily' for the happiness of 'the parties themselves' rather than for any abstract notion of the good of the community. As for the existing laws governing marriage, he called them 'the gratuitous cause of at least half the misery of the community', and could only account for them as the product of 'a barbaric age' of 'gross superstition'.

There is probably an autobiographical basis for Hardy's vehemence. The details of his first marriage, to Emma Gifford, are still largely unknown, and due to Hardy's secretiveness will probably remain so, but all the biographies agree that it was not a happy relationship, which may be why in the novels Hardy returns time and again to the 'unnaturalness' of a contract which permanently bound together people whose temperaments were, or had become, incompatible. This won him the reputation of an immoral writer bent on destroying marriage altogether, the sinister organizer of Mrs Oliphant's 'anti-marriage league'. But though Hardy had reservations about marriage as an institution, at least in its contemporary form, he was not opposed to monogamy. His main objection was to the irrevocability of the marriage contract. The unhappy marriages in *Jude* do, at least temporarily, result in divorce, but Hardy still uses the ceremony to emphasize the folly of a permanent union between such an ill-assorted couple as Jude and Arabella:

The two swore that at every other time of their lives till death took them, they would assuredly believe, feel and desire precisely as they had believed, felt and desired during the few preceding weeks. What was as remarkable as the undertaking itself was the fact that nobody seemed at all surprised at what whey swore.[2]

Jude quickly realizes his mistake, although it is then too late for him to withdraw. He sees that

> ... their lives were ... ruined by the fundamental error of their matrimonial union; that of having based a permanent contract on a temporary feeling which had no necessary connection with affinities that alone render a life-long comradeship tolerable. (p. 76)

Sue Bridehead makes a similar mistake in marrying the middle-aged and (to her) physically repulsive schoolmaster Phillotson. At least Jude's marriage to Arabella had a temporary basis in mutual desire; Sue's to Phillotson is a sexual disaster. She can't bear him even to touch her and endures real mental anguish before deciding to leave him. She has to tolerate even greater distress when, driven by guilt, she later goes back to Phillotson and forces herself into his bed. Sue experiences and makes herself overcome a similar repugnance to Jude, and we must see her terror of sex in a critical light. But it is a part of her and she has the right to refuse sex if she wants to. Indeed Hardy goes out of his way to criticize the brutal belief that if a woman showed any hesitancy about sex once married, then she should be 'broken-in'. Arabella, who clearly never needed any 'breaking-in' herself, suggests to Phillotson that this is how he should have dealt with Sue, rather than following the humane and tolerant course of letting her go:

> 'That's the only way with these fanciful women that chaw high – innocent or guilty. She'd have come round in time. We all do! Custom does it! It's all the same in the end ... You were too quick about her. *I* shouldn't have let her go! I should have kept her chained on – her spirit for kicking would have been broke soon enough! There's nothing like bondage and a stone-deaf taskmaster for taming us women'. (p. 329)

Hardy clearly disagreed. He believed that sexual compatability was a vital part of marriage, and that no woman should go against her sexual nature.

Marriage, more particularly unhappy marriage, is a key theme in *Jude*, embracing not just the central characters but other, marginal figures as well. Jude's family, for instance, has a long history of bad marriages; other figures are brought in purely to amplify the theme – such as the two nameless couples whom Jude and Sue briefly encounter at the registry office:

> The soldier was sullen and reluctant; the bride sad and timid; she was soon, obviously to become a mother, and she had a black eye ... Their little business was soon done, and the twain and their friends straggled out, one of the witnesses saying casually to Jude and Sue in passing, as if he had known the before: 'See the couple just come in? Ha! Ha! that fellow is just out of gaol this morning. She met him at the gaol gates, and brought him straight here. She's paying for everything.'
>   She turned her head and saw an ill-favoured man, closely cropped, with a broad faced, pock-marked woman on his arm, ruddy with liquor and the satisfaction of being on the brink of satisfied desire. (p. 293)

On other occasions Hardy attaches cynical comments about marriage to quite unimportant characters. Jude's landlord, for example, observing a show of affection between Jude and Arabella is about to give them notice on suspicion of their not being a married couple,

> ... till by chance overhearing her one night haranguing Jude in rattling terms, and ultimtely flinging a shoe at his head, he recognized the note of genuine wedlock, and concluding that they must be respectable, said no more. (p. 399)

All this creates an almost obsessively closed system in which no marriage in the novel can be happy. It is a depressing view, but one which shows just how far removed Hardy was from the fictional convention of marriage as the resolution of previous difficulties.

Marriage is attacked in *Jude* because it is seen as the cause of so much suffering. But at least those characters in the novel who want a divorce are able to get one. This is true of both the men and the women. Yet, as we have seen, the divorce law as it then stood discriminated against women. This is an issue which is not taken up in the novel. But Hardy did explore it elsewhere, in *The Woodlanders* (1887) where Grace Melbury is misled by her father into believing that she will, under the provisions of 'the new law', be able to divorce her unfaithful husband Fitzpiers. She then discovers to her cost that this is not in fact possible. Fitzpiers has only committed adultery. Hardy does not go into the details, but the problem is that the husband has not committed the additional sodomy, rape, incest, bestiality or cruelty which the law required before a woman could divorce her spouse. His conduct, Grace finds, 'has not been sufficiently cruel ... to enable her to snap the bond'.[3] This causes a great deal of misery. Building her hopes on her father's false information, Grace has allowed herself to look forward to marriage with her old lover, Giles Winterbourne. The two even come to an understanding about their future life together before Grace learns that she has no hope of being free to marry him. There is, of course, no question that they might establish the alternative domestic arrangement of living together. They are both scrupulously moral people who, unlike Sue and Jude, accept contemporary patterns of behaviour. Hardy also makes it quite clear, when Giles is dead and Fitzpiers has come back to her, that Grace will finally be left with no alternative to living with a man who, no matter how temporarily repentant, will soon revert to his philandering. As one of the local sages put it:

'... at present Mrs. Fitzpiers can lead the Doctor as your miss'ess could lead you ... She's got him quite tame. But how long 'twill last I can't say'. (p. 378)

As his wife, Grace has no rights; all she can hope for is to keep Fitzpiers content at home.

Jude and *The Woodlanders* are unusual in that they begin to explore quite explicitly the marital unhappiness and sexual incompatibility which law and social custom refused to acknowledge. But an even more significant innovation in *Jude* is the way Hardy questions the value of marriage and motherhood, even sexuality itself, for a woman such as Sue Bridehead. (The name is significant.) The question is complicated by Sue's sexual neurosis (though even this can be reasonably construed as a response to the narrow and limiting options available to her), but there is little ambiguity in the glimpse Hardy gives us of Sue two years after she finally accepts sexual relations with Jude. She is selling her gingerbread cakes at a stall as a way of raising money while Jude is too ill to work. She has one child with her, two more at home and is pregnant with a fourth. As Arabella complacently points out, all her proud independence has gone, her vitality drained by her new circumstances so that we can hardly recognize in her the 'bright intellect' of her 'bachelor' days. (p. 322)

One aspect of Hardy's characterization of Sue which is particularly interesting, even remarkable for its time, is his almost prescient understanding of the psychological contradictions which independent thought and action could set up in a woman who has come to consciousness from within repressive assumptions. Sue is devastatingly critical of moral and religious orthodoxy, yet at the same time she is still emotionally bound by it. It is this co-existence of intellectual emancipation with emotional dependence which makes Sue such a perverse and contradictory, yet prophetic figure. It ultimately destroys her when, overwhelmed by her children's death, she superstitiously re-embraces the moral dogma she has apparently already repudiated but which now seems to provide an 'explanation' for her suffering. The Christian concepts which she ridiculed in Jude finally drive her back to her living death with Phillotson. Hardy understands how this kind of mental, and in Sue's case, sexual masochism can grow up in a woman who cannot break free emotionally from an ideology which her mind tells her is damaging. When Sue's children die, as she sees it because of her 'immoral' life, the intellectual framework of emancipation in her breaks down. As Jude says, 'bitter affliction came ... her intellect broke, and she veered round to darkness'. (p. 414)

This unconscious dependence is evident in Sue right from the beginning, for example very early on in the book when she buys the two plaster statuettes of Venus and Apollo – gods of love and beauty ousted by sin-soaked Christianity. Apparently trivial, this incident is in fact very significant as it is the first time we see Sue at all closely. The statuettes symbolize Sue's emancipation from conventional religion – Hardy carefully contrasting them with the images of Catholic saints Sue sells every day in the religious knick-knack shop where she works: 'anything is better than those everlasting church fallals!' she says. But although much excited by her purchases, Sue also feels guilty and embarrassed by them:

They seemed so very large now that they were in her possession, and so very naked. Being of a nervous temperament she trembled at her enterprise ...

After carrying them a little way openly an idea came to her, and, pulling some huge burdock leaves, parsley and other rank growths from the hedge, she wrapped up her burden as well as she could in these, so that what she carried appeared to be an enormous armful of green stuff gathered by a zealous lover of nature ... But she was still in a trembling state and seemed almost to wish she had not bought the figures. (p. 101)

The incident must be seen as characteristic of Sue's emotional instability over issues where she wishes to assert her intellectual independence; it provides the pattern for her later self-contradictions and inconsistencies.

Sue's psychological oppression and her failure to combat it effectively add up to a convincing account of a plight many women found, and still find themselves in. Rationally able to demolish damaging beliefs about themselves and their role, women can recognize and understand their emotional involvement in a system of exploitation. But that does not necessarily mean that they can also liberate themselves from emotional complicity in their own oppression. Hardy's grasp of this problem is one of the most far-sighted things in the novel.

One thing I have not yet mentioned in relation to Hardy is the way he presents female sexuality. I shall discuss this more fully below (see p. 80), but meanwhile we can note that he is almost unique in the English nineteenth-century novel in that he creates women who are sexually exciting. Critics continually comment on the relative weaknesses of Hardy's male characters, and are right to do so. It is the women who dominate, and they do so through their sexuality. In *Jude* Hardy acknowledges the power and energy of female sexuality (Arabella), but also shows us, in Sue, the psychological damage done by repression and fear.

We have already seen that Arabella shocked a good many critics. Given the facile moral expectations of large numbers of contemporary readers, this is not difficult to understand – especially in view of our introduction to her. She is supposed to be the 'complete and substantial female animal – no more, no less' (p. 44), and we first meet her when she attracts Jude's attention by throwing a pig's genitals at him over a hedge – hardly a conventional literary introduction. Her subsequent actions are all of piece with this initial gesture. She seduces

Jude, where the male villain would normally seduce the inno-cent virgin (for example Alec d'Urberville and Tess); she dupes him into marriage with her by pretending she is preg-nant when she she is not – the woman, really pregnant, would normally be abandoned at this stage of a more conventional novel (for example Hardy's own Fanny Robin and George Eliot's Hetty Sorrel); she commits bigamy without thinking twice about it (at least Lady Audley was hard put to it to cover up her crime) and she finally re-seduces Jude and persuades him to re-marry her when according to convention she should, by this point in the novel, have been an abandoned whore dying in the streets. She even has another prospective husband lined-up for when Jude dies.

Arabella triumphs because she knows how to use her sexual-ity; she exploits people where they are most vulnerable. Yet her unashamedly amoral attitudes are an eloquent criticism of the supposed morality of the usual sexual arrangements. For she, of all people, always manages to appear respectable. On the other hand, Sue and Jude who try to establish a truly caring relationship, but outside marriage, are crushed. The moral conventions could accommodate Arabella, who is well set to end her life as a rich censorious widow, but they had no place for the sexual and moral honesty of Sue and Jude.

Arabella's real counterpart in Hardy's fiction is not really Sue, who has no sexuality at all, but Tess. Tess is not simply very beautiful. Hardy makes it quite clear that, like Arabella, she is also sexually very attractive. This makes her a target for the amorous advances of the young libertine, Alec d'Urber-ville, who half rapes, half seduces her. So Tess is the victim of her own physical charms. But she is also, more interestingly, the victim of her own high moral standards. Unlike Arabella she is incapable of using her sexuality to her own advantage, so that when her newly-married husband, Angel Clare, tells her he must leave her because of her 'past' with Alec, Tess meekly accepts his decision. Had she been more like Arabella, she would simply have seduced Clare there and then, making it impossible for him to abandon her. Hardy suggests as much when he mentions Clare's 'fear' of her 'exceptional physical nature', which she might have used 'promisingly' had she wished to do so.[4] As it is, her trusting decision to tell her husband about Alec is a complete reversal of the Arabella 'morality', represented in this novel by Tess's mother, Joan Durbeyfield. When Tess tells Joan about Clare's defection, she immediately bursts out with 'O you little fool – you little fool! ... My God! That I should ever live to say it, but I say it again, you little fool!' (p. 290) And there is certainly some common sense if little morality in what she says. In effect Tess's scrupulous conscience deprives her of the instinct to survive which is shared by Joan and Arabella. Once again it is the genuinely moral woman who suffers.

The obvious and quite possibly deliberate similarities and contrasts in *Tess of the d'Urbervilles* with Richardson's *Pamela* re-enforce this criticism of orthodox morality. The plot of *Tess* is a realistic account of what would have happened nine times out of ten to the innocent country girl pursued by the wicked aristocrat or 'gentleman'. Not only does it reverse the vulgar success story of *Pamela* but Tess's open, vulnerable character acts as a complete contrast to Pamela's moral opportunism. Because she is not a virgin, Tess is 'impure' according to society's definition of the term. Yet it is the technically chaste Pamela who is morally deformed by her society – she has learned the cash value of virginity and knows how to exploit it to the full, skilfully fending off Squire B. until he offers to marry her. Tess is too spontaneous to put a financial premium on her chastity, and so comes to grief, but Pamela, who is only too well aware of how best to play the virginity 'card', is rewarded by promotion to the gentry. Richardson's comedy shows us the only way a woman could survive in the new bourgeois world. Hardy's tragedy demonstrates how easily that world could destroy a woman who did not understand or accept its values.

Tess shows us just how unnatural the bourgois notion of sexuality really was, especially female sexuality. Hardy carefully points out that in blaming herself for her seduction by Alec, Tess is substituting a false idea of sexuality for a natural one. Her own poor opinion of herself and her conduct, he tells us,

based on shreds of convention, peopled by phantoms and voices antipathetic to her, was a sorry and mistaken creation of Tess's fancy – a cloud of moral hobgoblins by which she was terrified without reason. It was they that were out of harmony with the actual world, not she. Walking among the sleeping birds in the hedges, watching the skipping rabbits on a moonlit warren, or standing under a pheasant-laden bough, she looked upon herself as a figure of Guilt, intruding into the haunts of Innocence. But all the while she was making a distinction where there was no difference. Feeling herself in antagonism she was quite in accord. She had been made to break an accepted social law, but no law to the environment in which she fancied herself such an anomaly. (p. 105)

Hardy comes back to this contrast between spontaneous morality and the artificial distinctions of a code based on social and economic convenience, when he once more identifies Tess with animals – this time with the wounded and dying game-birds who have been shot at by the sporting country gentry. In their different ways, both Tess and the birds are helpless victims of a society which distorts Nature – Tess of a repressive moral code, the birds of a calculated cruelty which 'protects' them so they can be later shot at for fun. Seeing the dying birds Tess exclaims:

'Poor darlings – to suppose myself the most miserable being on earth in the sight of so much misery as yours ... And not a twinge of bodily pain about me! I be not mangled, and I be not bleeding, and I have two hands to feed and clothe me!' She was ashamed of herself for her gloom of the night, based on nothing more tangible than a sense of condemnation under an arbitrary law of society which had no foundation in Nature. (p. 315)

Tess thinks her suffering is slight in comparison with the birds', but her mental anguish is really no less in kind than the pain felt by the pheasants. Her consoling remarks that 'I be not mangled, and I be not bleeding' are poor compensation for her destitution and desertion; they strike a note of unconscious pathos rather than one of thankful deliverance from a worse fate.

Tess is, above all, a study of true and false ideas of sexual morality. This is worked out through the injustice and suffering thrust on a spontaneously moral woman by a distorted value-system. But more interestingly, the reason why Tess cannot survive her misfortunes is because she herself has absorbed the false code and so is prepared to accept Clare's judgment of her, even though her instincts tell her he is unjust and hypocritical. Her relationship with Alec, her seduction, the birth and then the death of her illegitimate baby, all take place in the context of the traditional agricultural community. In this setting Alec d'Urberville plays the recognizable and so 'accepted' role of the aristocratic seducer, even if his family is actually an upstart one. Only Tess is at all embarrassed by her pregnancy. Everyone else accepts it and no-one blames her for what has happened. We see this from the episode where Tess, who is helping in the fields at harvest time, suckles her baby during a meal break:

As soon as her lunch was spread she called up the big girl, her sister, and took the baby off her ... Tess, with a curiously stealthy yet courageous movement, and with a still rising colour, unfastened her frock and began suckling the child.

The men who sat nearest considerately turned their faces towards the other end of the field, some of them beginning to smoke; one, with absent-minded fondness, regretfully stroking the jar that would no longer yield a stream. All the women but Tess fell into animated talk, adjusted the disarranged knots of their hair ... (p. 109)

This studiously kind indifference is in strong contrast to the outraged moralism of Clare when he discovers that Tess is not the virgin he thought her. It is her experience of rejection by Clare, the self-confessed agnostic, which crushes Tess, not her seduction by the 'wicked' Alec. She is undoubtedly much changed by her experiences with Alec, but as long as she stays within her class and its expectations, her seduction is bearable. It is only when she becomes involved with the tortuous morals of the bourgeosie that she is broken, trapped by the double standard which allows Clare to excuse his own past as 'wild oats' while he condemns his wife. On this level the book becomes a sustained attack on bourgeois morality which, with its inflexible demand for purity in women, but only in women, reduces Tess to terrible poverty and so finally drives her back to Alec and eventually to murder and hanging.

Clare's feebleness and inconsistency play an important part in this pattern. They illustrate the unconscious hypocrisy of the whole moral system. But his *volte face* from liberal agnostic to severe puritan moralist also shows just how deep sexual prejudice can be, even among supposedly progressive people.

This, I think, goes some way towards explaining what has often been criticized as a failure in Hardy's characterization. Clare, it is said, is too contradictory to be true. But there is really no reason at all why male sexual vanity, the desire to secure an 'unsullied' bride, should not co-exist with a degree of resistance to other traditional beliefs – in Clare's case Christianity. This is especially likely to be true when, again as in Clare's case, the rejection of a bourgeois life-style has taken the form of opting instead for an ideal of bucolic innocence. This is what Clare expected to find in Tess, as a sort of compensation prize for giving up a promising career in the Church:

'My position is this,' he said abruptly. 'I thought – any man would have thought – that by giving up all ambition to win a wife with social standing, with fortune, with knowledge of the world, I should secure rustic innocence as surely as I should secure pink cheeks'. (p. 270)

A position with which Hardy has scant sympathy.

But even more important perhaps is Hardy's criticism of the tendency to idealize Tess which underlies Clare's complaint, and is now shattered by her revelations. Both Tess and Clare are alike guilty of idealizing the person they love. This carries as much responsibility for the collapse of their relationship as the double standard. It is only because Clare has been seeing not Tess, but his image of Tess, that he cannot endure the knowledge of her liaison with Alec. His immediate reaction to her story is to say that 'you were one person; now you are another', and that 'the woman I have been loving is not you'. (p. 259) Tess realizes that this is absurd:

'I thought, Angel, that you loved me – me, my very self! If it is I you do love, O how can it be that you look and speak so? It frightens me! Having begun to love you, I love you for ever – in all changes, in all disgraces, because you are yourself, I ask no more. Then how can you, O my own husband, stop loving me?' (p. 260)

But even though Tess, unlike Clare, goes on loving, she makes the same mistake of idealizing the person she is in love with. It is because she almost literally worships Clare, looking to him for guidance and wisdom in everything, that she cannot see how his moral judgment of her is simply wrong, and so accepts without demur his decision that they cannot live together:

'I shan't do anything, unless you order me to; and if you go away from me I shall not follow 'ee; and if you never speak to me any more I shall not ask why, unless you tell me I may.' (p. 261)

She submits because she has always seen Clare as infallible, godlike:

There was hardly a touch of earth in her love for Clare. To her sublime trustfulness he was all that goodness could be – knew all that a guide, philosopher and friend should know. She thought every line in the contour of his person the perfection of masculine beauty, his soul the soul of a saint, his intellect that of a seer. The wisdom of her love for him, as love, sustained her dignity; she seemed to be wearing a crown. The compassion of his love for her, as she saw it, made her lift up her heart to him in devotion. He would sometimes catch her large, worshipful eyes, that had no bottom to them, looking at him from their depths, as if she saw something immortal before her. (p. 220)

All very flattering. This fatal idealization of Clare is more understandable and excusable than is Clare's of her; after all he has both education and experience on his side. But it is not a question of apportioning blame to either party, rather one of realizing, as Hardy does, the dangers of a relationship based not on real knowledge, but on a false, self-induced vision of the other person, a vision fulfilling an ideal of womanhood or of manhood but bearing little relation to the facts of individual personality.

Hardy's most important criticism of romantic love is not, however, *Tess*. It is *The Return of the Native* (1878). In this novel Eustacia Vye (her name indicates her glamorous, romantic personality) attempts to escape the boredom and lack of fulfilment imposed on her by her lonely life on Egdon Heath by immersing herself in passionate love affairs. She first takes up with the somewhat satanic Damon Wildeve (again the name hints at his role in the romantic pattern), and then with the idealistic young Clym Yeobright. She effectively destroys both these men and herself.

But we must place Hardy's criticisms of Eustacia as a

romantic escapist in the right context, and the context is his essential sympathy for the way Eustacia feels about her cramped, empty life. It is this, after all, that leads her to turn, like Emma Bovary, to the idea of passionate love as a way of gratifying her need for excitement and, more important, as a way of fulfilling herself as a person.[5] Eustacia's relation to Egdon Heath is very important here. It defines her not only as a destructive 'outsider' (in the same way that Fitzpiers and Felice Charmond are outsiders in *The Woodlanders*), but also, if we see Egdon as a microcosm of society as a whole, as an alienated woman, barred from useful activity. 'The heath', she says, 'is a gaol to me.'[6] Admittedly Eustacia herself does not see things in quite this light – all she is interested in is having a good time, represented in her mind by going to Paris, or failing that, Budmouth. But if Clym's experience is considered here, it is clear that Hardy sees this desire for material goods as a necessary step on the road to true self-fulfillment. Clym has already passed through the phase Eustacia is only entering at the beginning of the novel, a phase, Hardy believes, that cannot be cut out of the natural stages of development – as Clym learns to his cost when he tries, futilely, to educate the Egdon men into spiritual awareness. Hardy makes this point very clear when he comments on Clym's teaching ambitions:

Yeobright loved his kind. He had a conviction that the want of most men was knowledge of a sort which brings wisdom rather than affluence.

But, Hardy adds:

... in passing from the bucolic to the intellectual life the intermediate stages are usually two at least, frequently more; and one of these stages is almost sure to be worldly advance. We can hardly imagine bucolic placidity quickening to intellectual aims without imagining social aims as the transitional phase. (p. 179)

The same thing applies to Eustacia who cannot, any more than the local rustics, pass from a stage of comparative ignorance to spiritual wisdom without going through intermediate phases. So she wants to go to Paris. Clym overlooks this to his cost. He idealizes Eustacia in the same way that he idealizes the Egdon labourers, and so fails to see that she has never given up her worldly ambitions, believing instead that she would make a good teacher. 'Take me to Paris, and go on with your old occupation,' she asks him some time after their marriage:

'I don't mind how humbly we live at first, if it can only be Paris and not Egdon Heath.'
   'But I have quite given up that idea ... Surely I never led you to expect such a thing?'
   'I own it. Yet there are thoughts which cannot be kept out of mind, and that was one of mine ...' (p. 253)

Hardy admits that Eustacia is fanciful, impractical and finally destructive. Mrs Yeobright, the essence of the practical housewife, is a mouthpiece for Hardy here, and her criticisms of Eustacia as 'lazy and dissatisfied' (p. 200) are in a sense quite true. But Hardy still sympathizes with Eustacia's spirit of revolt, even though it is misdirected towards materialistic aims. Otherwise there could be no sense of tragedy when her ambitions fail and she is reduced, first to living in a furzecutter's cottage with a blind man who does not understand her, and then to running away with a lover for whom she has no respect and whom she recognizes is unworthy of her. (p. 360) This compassion for Eustacia in her dilemma, for her thwarted, frustrated energy, co-exists with Hardy's recognition of her triviality and selfishness. The tension which exists between these two aspects of Eustacia produces both Hardy's ambivalent attitude towards her rebellion, and the complex feelings of loss and waste, coupled with disapproval, which the reader experiences at her death. This sense of loss and our lingering impression of Eustacia as a heroic figure, trapped by her environment, grow out of Hardy's sensitivity to the problems of frustrated potential clearly present in his heroine. She is a woman of undoubted ability and intelligence, but her abilities turn inwards and become self-destructive in a society which has no use for them simply because she *is* a woman.[7]

A pejorative comparison can be made between Eustacia (destructive, neurotic and unable to adjust to Egdon society) and Tamsin Yeobright (practical, stable, the 'little woman' in harmony with her world). But it is most unlikely that Hardy meant this as a conclusive criticism of Eustacia. An alternative interpretation of the contrasts between the two women, which does justice to Hardy's interest in Eustacia, is to see Tamsin as a woman who never questions, is content with her female role, and is under no inner psychological pressure to accept something distasteful or repugnant to her. Eustacia, on the other hand, is a rebel who wants something more. Eustacia rejects society's definition of female 'normality'. Tamsin is never likely to challenge it.

It is in relation to her sense of frustration and boredom then, that we must see Eustacia and interpret her self-dramatization, gloominess and feverish search for excitement, not, as Mrs Yeobright would have it, as some sort of innate character defect. Eustacia herself puts down her gloomy depression to the effects of the Heath, saying she was 'happy enough at Budmouth'. (p. 71) When Clym detects her masquerading as the Turkish Knight in the Christmas mummers' play and asks her why she has dressed up as a man, she replies, 'to get excitement and shake off depression', (p. 152) a depression caused by her lonely existence with her old grandfather in a remote corner of the Heath.

Eustacia's principal strategy to counter depression is to fancy she is passionately in love with attractive men:

To be loved to madness – such was her great desire. Love was to her the one cordial which could drive away the eating loneliness of her days. And she seemed to long for the abstraction called passionate love more than for any particular lover. (p. 77)

Hardy never lets us forget that it is the abstract idea of love, rather than love for an individual, that animates Eustacia. For instance, she is well aware of Wildeve's shortcomings, but prefers to put them from her – at least until another, more interesting man appears, complete with the seductive charm of Paris in his travelling bag. She fills up time by 'idealizing Wildeve for want of a better object'. (p. 79) her need to love eclipsing even her realization that she is not loved in return:

Eustacia sighed: it was no fragile maiden sigh, but a sigh which shook her like a shiver. Whenever a flash of reason darted like an electric light upon her lover – as it sometimes would – and showed his imperfections, she shivered thus. But it was over in a second and she loved on. She knew he trifled with her; but she loved on. (p. 73)

Eustacia's love for Clym is equally ungrounded in any real understanding of his personality. She is attracted to him by rumours about his glamorous life abroad and loves him because she has decided to do so, even before she has seen him. (p. 116) Her obsession with him is self-induced; it is based on fantasies and daydreams which follow the conventional pattern of (lonely) maidens being saved by knights in armour (shining white). She dreams, for instance, a dream 'as wonderful as a dream could be' in which:

She was dancing to wondrous music, and her partner was the man in silver armour who had accompanied her through the previous changes, the visor of his helmet being closed. The mazes of the dance were ecstatic. Soft whispering came into her ear from under the radiant helmet, and she felt like a woman in Paradise. Suddenly these two wheeled out from the mass of dancers, dived into one of the pools of the heath, and came out somewhere beneath into an irridescent hollow, arched with rainbows. (p. 152)

Sustained by fantasies like these, Eustacia drags out her monotonous life on Egdon. But once she is married to Clym, even she is forced to recognize the discrepancies between her romantic image of the Clym who was her lover, whom she thinks of as 'like a man coming from heaven', (p. 116) and the priggish Clym who is her husband. Her vision of Clym disintegrates; but she is not strong enough to overcome her emotional dependence on the old idea of their future together in a sophisticated metropolitan society. Then, at the one moment when it seems as if she might be able to reconcile herself to what marriage to Clym means in reality, Hardy's usual chain of unfortunate coincidences intervenes and pushes her, against her will this time, into the fatal decision to re-open relations with Wildeve. In the event, although she finally sees its folly, Eustacia's blind romancing about the man she is in love with brings disillusion and unhappiness. It is the initial mistake which leads eventually to her death.

Another aspect of Hardy's criticism of romantic love in *The Return of The Native* is the complicated web of relationships he builds up between the five principal characters. Eustacia and Wildeve, the two people more or less incapable of sustained affection, blow hot or cold, are attracted to each other or repulsed, according to how unobtainable they are at different moments in the novel. The 'true lovers', Diggory, Tamsin and Clym are victims in Eustacia and Wildeve's game of hard-to-get. So the book presents romantic passion as a perverse and undisciplined desire which tramples on other people; it destroys Eustacia, Clym and Wildeve and, in Hardy's first draft of the novel, it ruins Tamsin's and Diggory's lives as well. The gloomy mistrust of romantic love emerges in this way as one of the main thrusts of the book.

What Hardy does in *The Native* is to take the nineteenth-century elevation of romantic passion at face value and pursue it to its logical conclusion. He shows how cultivating the emotions, to the exclusion of every rational occupation, could overbalance into a dangerous pursuit of feeling for its own sake. In nineteenth-century society women were forced into just this position by the ideology which confined them to purely personal and emotional sources of satisfaction. They were told that the only way they could 'fulfil' themselves was through their affections, their personal and family relationships. The satisfaction they allegedly found in this way of life was supposed to be more than adequate compensation for any of its irksome restrictions. With Eustacia Vye, Hardy provided a timely reminder of just how unsatisfying and how dangerous this total dependence on emotional satisfaction could become.

Hardy's other emotional vampire is Felice Charmond in *The Woodlanders*. She is a later and in some ways more daring version of Eustacia, for Hardy is much more explicit about Felice's sexual desires than he ever was about Eustacia's ten years earlier. In *The Return of the Native* Eustacia's sexuality is played down in favour of a more general sense of frustration, and Hardy is very evasive indeed about whether or not she has been Wildeve's mistress. But Felice's desires in *The Woodlanders* are explicitly sexual. She is a youngish, not quite respectable widow who is used to an exciting city life. Naturally enough she is bored living in the heart of rural Wessex, and looks about her for diversion, which appears in the shape of Grace Melbury's husband, Fitzpiers. She seduces him and so embarks on an affair which has serious implications for at least four other people.

Even more than Eustacia, Felice depends on emotional excitement. She herself believes that women 'are always carried about like corks on the waves of masculine desire',[8] but makes no effort to break away from this emotional parasitism in her own life. With nothing else to do or think about, she cultivates her sexual and emotional responses until she becomes their slave. Hardy gives the chapters where we see her brooding on her own at home a claustraphobic, heavily sensual atmosphere; curtains are drawn against the sun and candles blaze at midday, (p. 204) the artificiality of the scene suggesting the hot-house artificiality of her emotions. As for when Fitzpiers, a doctor, visits Felice for the first time, it ressembles a visit to a courtesan rather than to a patient:

He was shown into a room at the top of the staircase, cosily and femininely draped, where by the light of the shaded lamp, he saw a woman of elegant figure reclining upon a couch in such a position as not to disturb a pile of magnificent hair on the crown of her head. [Although Fitzpiers does not know the hair is false, we do.] A deep purple dressing-gown formed an admirable foil to the peculiarly rich brown of her hair-plaits; her left arm, which was naked nearly up to the shoulder, was thrown upwards, and between the fingers of her right hand she held a cigarette, while she idly breathed from her delicately curled lips a thin stream of smoke towards the ceiling. (p. 194)

She is made into a melodramatic temptress, and Hardy, at this point, clearly does not approve of her.

Yet Felice's conscious sensuality and self-indulgence over Fitzpiers do not carry quite the condemnation one might expect from these lurid beginnings. Hardy certainly wants us to see her as a destructive force; she disrupts the easy flow of community life both through her sexuality and through her role as landlord, evicting tenants and pulling down houses when leases expire. But at the same time Hardy also understands how Felice is tormented by her sexual desires, and he finally shows her, not as a depraved monster of sexuality, but as the victim of these desires. She wants to break off the relationship with Fitzpiers, but cannot do so; she is swept along by an irrational fixation. For instance when Grace's father foolishly visits Felice to beg her to leave his son-in-law alone out of kindness for Grace, Hardy has her react like this:

As soon as he was out of the room she went to a corner and there burst into tears ... She had never so clearly perceived till now that her soul was being slowly invaded by a delirium which had brought about all this; that she was losing judgment and dignity under it, becoming an animated impulse only, a passion incarnate. A fascination led her on; it was as if she had been seized by a hand of velvet; and this was where she found herself – overshadowed with sudden night, as if a tornado has passed. (p. 241)

Although Felice was the one who began the affair, Fitzpiers develops a hold over her which she cannot break. We then see that it is not Felice who is exploiting Fitzpiers, but Fitzpiers who is using her. She is the one who suffers most, especially after she becomes his mistress. Hardy is unusually explicit on this point. (When he has Grace exclaim, 'He's had you!' (p. 250) there can be no doubt in anyone's mind what the relationship between Felice and Fitzpiers actually is.) This revelation comes in a conversation between the two women. But in spite of the shock it initially gives Grace, they can still establish an alliance based on their knowledge that they are both victims of male selfishness. Their mutual sympathy is more important than Felice's confession of sexual relations with Grace's husband, and the two part, 'kissing each other almost unconsciously'. (p. 252) In this way Fitzpiers' affair with Felice and the adultery it involves is presented as a double male offence against two women, and the reluctant alliance between Grace and Felice becomes a challenge to the social gulf between 'good' and 'bad' women, 'innocent' and 'guilty' which had divided women from each other for so long.

Where Felice is an emotional casualty of sexual ideology, Grace is a victim of legal and social injustice. Her whole life is ruined because she is persuaded to marry for class and status and cannot unmarry them again when she wants to. By raising her price on the marriage market, the fancy education which her father provides for Grace cuts her off from her former plain way of life and from her old love, Giles. Her education is regarded by her father as an investment which will pay a handsome dividend in the shape of a gentleman for a son-in-law. Although meaning no deliberate harm, Mr. Melbury thinks of his daughter as 'a chattel', (p. 94) a piece of human coinage which he can use to buy higher social status. Hardy presses this point home when he gives us a scene in which

Melbury shows Grace his cash and share certificates, hoping in this way to 'sow in her heart cravings for social position'. (p. 93) He encourages Fitzpiers' attentions to Grace and deprecates Giles to her, and is quite overcome with materialistic glee when the 'gentleman' finally proposes:

'This takes me unawares', he said, his voice well-nigh breaking down. 'I don't mean that there is anything unexpected in a gentleman being attracted by her; but it did not occur to me that it would be you. I always said,' continued he with a lump in his throat, 'that my Grace would make a mark at her own level some day. That was why I educated her. I said to myself, "I'll do it cost what it may"; though her stepmother was pretty frightened at my paying out so much money year after year. I knew it would tell in the end. "Where you've not got good material to work on, such doings would be waste and vanity," I said. "But where you have that material, it is sure to be worthwhile."' (p. 160)

The overriding economic considerations in this passage indicate clearly enough the purely material view Melbury takes of his daughter. 'Good material', 'cost', 'paying out so much money', 'waste' and being 'worthwhile' are the characteristic terms of his interest. The irony is that 'waste' is exactly what comes about; not material waste, but human waste, a commodity which Melbury leaves out of his calculations.

Fitzpiers on his side, too, is attracted almost entirely by Mr. Melbury's guineas:

... apart from his lover-like anxiety to possess her, the few golden hundreds of the timber dealer, ready to hand, formed a warm background to Grace's lovely face, and went some way to remove his uneasiness at the prospect of endangering his professional and social chances by an alliance with the family of a simple countryman. (p. 177)

Grace realizes she is being manipulated by her father and suspects that Fitzpiers, far from being the ideal gentleman, has 'had' Suke Damson. She is also still drawn to Giles, who has doggedly gone on loving her. But she is too weak to withstand what is for her the overwhelming pressure of her father and fiancé, so she marries Fitzpiers in spite of her misgivings. Her life is ruined because she is treated by the people closest to her, not as a person, but as a commodity to be used in purchasing social status.

Taken as a whole *The Woodlanders, Tess, Jude* and *The Return of the Native* seem to me to be an expressive, irrefutable criticism of society's debilitating version of womanhood. These are four of the major novels, but Hardy's position is much the same in the earlier works and in the short stories, which are so often an exploration on a smaller scale of the themes taken up in the major works. He was consistently interested in women and became more compassionate towards them, less judgmental, as his work matured, so that the vanities of a Bathsheba Everdene and the fickleness of a Fancy Day grow into the complex, *self*-tormenting contradictions of Eustacia Vye or Sue Bridehead. With characters like these, Hardy showed how women's lives were distorted simply because they were women, trapped in a moral order rooted in sexual discrimination, and in a social structure which refused to acknowledge them as complete human beings. Women are almost always at the centre of Hardy's tragic, uncompromising vision, not merely of the universe, as is so often claimed, but of men and women in society. What his work shows is not so much the indifference of the gods (in whom he did not believe), but the sufferings of human beings in a society which frustrated individual abilities and crushed natural, loving human impulses.

But though the overall tendency and meaning of his work is critical, even subversive in the depth of its alienation from orthodox values, Hardy's radicalism is often attenuated by the weight of received assumptions and literary forms. This is particularly the case in his portrayal of women, where his powerful moral iconoclasm is often in conflict with the use of essentially traditional character types which either cannot comfortably accommodate his ideas or, alternatively, place a sharp limitation on his thinking.

This becomes clear when we look at the overall pattern of sexual relationships in the novels. In a very real way Mrs Oliphant was quite right about this: with the important exception of Tess (to whom I shall return below) Hardy's women are almost always destructive and dominant and his men are invariably passive, worked on by the whims, designs or perversities of various *femmes fatales*. Boldwood, Oak, Clym, Jude, Phillotson, Giles Winterbourne – the overall picture of men suffering from the actions of selfish, vascillating, unpredictable women is inescapable and barely modified by the occasional woman victim – Fanny Robin, Tamsin, Tess and Grace Melbury. And of these only Tess and Grace are central characters. The usual pattern casts the central female figure as a destroyer. She is often either a charismatic beauty of irresistible charm (Eustacia, Bathsheba), or a seductress (Felice, Arabella). Because of this tendency to approach women as the 'fatal sex', Hardy often underplays them as individuals, and their personal psychology is lost in his habit of seeing them first as sexual agents of a destructive destiny, and only second as people. They are all too often sexualized Eve, the eternal temptress or betrayer.

This anxiety about women's sexuality is at its clearest in *Jude*. Here the gentle but pliable hero is destroyed by two stereotypes of female sexuality – the scheming seductress and the fascinating, tantalizing prude. And the two women, Arabella and Sue, are defined almost entirely by their sexual responses (rapacious sensuality and obsessive virginity), a split image of female sexuality which is neatly re-enforced by class 'characteristics' – sexy Arabella is a labourer's daughter, inhibited Sue is an intellectual.

The quotation from the Bible which ominously introduces the first section of the novel refers specifically to Arabella, but it also suggests the important message which underlies the book as a whole:

'Yea, many there have been that have run out of their wits for women, and become servants for their sakes. Many also have perished, have erred, and sinned for women ... Oh ye men, how thus can it be but women should be strong, seeing they do thus?'

This warning about the awful power of women is reiterated by the crude symbolism of a picture of Samson and Delilah which hangs on the wall at a tavern Arabella and Jude visit together, (p. 52) a reference which reappears later in the novel when Jude goes on a drinking bout in a temporary effort to escape his unhappy marriage. (p. 78) The 'moral' of the Arabella relationship is clear enough – sexuality is a trap. Yet so in the novel is its opposite, for Sue's inhibition and frigidity cause Jude as much misery as his original temptress.

Other things contribute to Jude's downfall – the frustration of all his ambitions, ill health, weakness, despair – but the seeds of all his failures lie in his sexual entanglements. The same is true of Clym and Wildeve in *The Return of the Native* and of Giles in *The Woodlanders*. Frank Chapman in an interesting essay, 'Hardy the Novelist', brings out this connection which Hardy invariably makes between sex and failure or death, suggesting that it stems from a deep-rooted fear of sex in Hardy himself.[9] But whatever its psychological basis, the destructive nature of sexuality is a prominent aspect of all Hardy's novels. Sexual passion destroys Tess, Clare and Alec, kills Boldwood, Fanny and Troy in *Far From the Madding Crowd* and leaves a permanent scar on Bathsheba and Oak. So even though Hardy rightly highlighted the importance of sexuality and was prepared to look squarely at some of the problems and conflicts it throws up, he remained apprehensive and sombre. There is no joy in sex in Hardy – only conflict, suffering and, very often, death.

Tess is of course an almost perfect antithesis of the more usual Hardy heroine who brings calamity through sex, for although there is the usual suffering and waste in the novel, this time the woman is the chief victim, not the culprit. But although Tess is clearly an exception to the general rule, she embodies as damaging a stereotype of womanhood as the sexual harpies. Where Eustacia, Bathsheba and Arabella are essentially active agents, passionate women able to dominate and impose their will on the people around them, Tess is docile in the face of her sexual and personal misfortunes. As we have already seen, it is her characteristic passivity and humility which is the fundamental cause of her troubles, rather than her seduction itself. Tess's conditioning as a woman has been all too effective; she has embraced the ideology of purity and passivity and is left defenceless because of it. Yet even though Hardy recognizes that this is what happens to Tess, he still asks us to admire her patience and meekness.

This is a contradiction which lies at the heart of the novel and of women's predicament in Hardy's society, for the very qualities which in contemporary belief made women morally superior, once internalized, as they are in Tess, also left them defenceless and vulnerable to sexual exploitation. Tess's whole history suggests that Hardy understands the crippling effect of such 'qualities' of character, but he never really rejects them. He still believes in Tess's virtues of self-effacement and humility. It is these, after all, which make her 'superior', set her apart from her mundane friends Marian, Izz and Retty, make her worthy of the love of a gentleman and place her in a moral class way above her mother and her companions. Her fatal decision to 'confess' to Clare is determined by her very finely tuned moral conscience which tells her she is cheating her friends (who also love Clare) by remaining silent about her past:

> They were simple and innocent girls on whom the unhappiness and unrequited love had fallen; they had deserved better at the hands of Fate. She had deserved worse – yet she was the chosen one. It was wicked of her to take all without paying. She would pay to the uttermost farthing; she would tell ...
> (p. 254)

This inner moral compulsion ruins her; it borders on masochism. But paradoxically, Hardy still sees her self-effacing character structure as good and admirable, so that he implicitly endorses a moral pattern of womanhood which the whole novel demonstrates is damaging and repressive.

If we look at Olive Schreiner's heroine, Lyndall, in *The Story of an African Farm*,[10] we can see more clearly the shortcomings of this idea of women's moral nature. Lyndall, like Tess, suffers sexually. But she is angry, volatile and rebellious. Her girlhood teaches her very early on that life could be unjust and hard, especially for women. She has none of Tess's innocence and pliability. Seeing how marriage can crush a woman's independence, she refuses to marry, choosing instead a head-on collision with society and the double standard when she goes away with her lover. She is cynical and mistrustful of men's love:

> 'Your man's love is a child's love for butterflies. You follow till you have the thing, and break it. If you have broken one wing, and the thing flies still, then you love it more than ever, and follow till you break both; then you are satisfied when it lies still on the ground.'[11]

This is something Tess learns only through bitter experience.

Lyndall is educated and intellectually incisive. She is able to recognize and denounce the moral hypocrisies which made women into sexual victims, even if she cannot avoid becoming a victim herself. Because she has this firm intellectual grasp of women's oppression, it is meaningless, in a way, to compare her to Tess, the half-educated peasant girl. But in spirit and disposition she is an enlightening contrast. She represents a defiant challenge, not only to existing social and sexual arrangements, but more important, to all the usual assumptions about woman's moral nature. She has no patience with passivity and could never live like her traditionally homely, acquiescent cousin Em. Lyndall dies because she dares to challenge the norms of sexual behaviour, just as Tess dies. But in Lyndall we see the possibility of rebellion. Through her we learn that a new, free sexual morality can only be won if women are defiant and 'immoral', not passive, pure and docile.

Hardy's *femmes fatales* and betrayed, long-suffering heroines are part of his general tendency to see characters as types. The use of symbolic names (Wildeve, Yeobright, Oak, Charmond, Angel, Bridehead, Jude[12] and so on) is a symptom of this habit of mind. So too is the way he groups his characters into formal patterns. These are determined by the structure of relationships in the novels. Thus, Alec is a conventional seducer and Tess is an archetypal betrayed maiden; Fitzpiers, Clym and Troy are exciting newcomers; Gabriel, Giles and Boldwood are worthy but rejected suitors; Marty South and Diggory Venn are faithful lovers. This careful patterning of character types has a clear sexual basis, so that a casual glance at Hardy's fiction can leave the reader with an impression of forsaken lovers, patient wooers, unscrupulous seducers, betrayed maidens and stolid worthies of ballad-like simplicity. This essentially archetypal view of sexual relationships tends to inhibit Hardy's exploration of individual psychology; more important, it can also be at variance with his usual ability to see his characters in relation to social structures.

It is when he shows men and women shaped or bound in their relationships by external events, by class or environment that Hardy is at his most compelling. He is then showing us what it means to live in a particular time in a particular kind of society. We have already seen, for instance, how the compassion he makes us feel for Eustacia Vye grows out of his ability to make us sympathize with the intense frustration she experiences because of the futility of her existence on Egdon. But for the purposes of the plot and in her relationships with the other characters, Eustacia is a stereotype – a Bewitching Beauty, who is always mysterious and always irresistible. And she is an idealized stereotype at that. A 'goddess', the 'raw material of a divinity' who for all her selfishness and extravagance, is still cast in a romantic, dignified role. She is queenly in her lonely isolation on the Heath, a female variant of the misunderstood Byronic hero in her desperate flight and death.

Hardy resists or at least maintains a critical distance from Eustacia's romantic image, until he comes to her death. Here he gives way to a final celebration of her 'queenly' qualities, so that we forget the petty details of much of her life and are left remembering only the romance. The sordid death of Flaubert's Emma Bovary, whose impulses stem from the same boredom and frustration as Eustacia's, points to this contradiction in Hardy's conception of his heroine. (The very fact that we can call Eustacia a heroine, whereas one hesitates to call Emma a heroine at all, is a measure of the distance between these two writers even when their subjects are so close.) Emma dies a horribly painful, protracted death from self-poisoning. Her death is a final degradation. But Eustacia's is an escape from degradation and further compromise. It gives her the tragic stature which she has always yearned for:

They stood silently looking upon Eustacia, who, as she lay there still in death, eclipsed all her living phases ... The expression of her finely carved mouth was pleasant, as if a sense of dignity had just compelled her to leave off speaking. Eternal rigidity had seized upon it in a momentary transition between fervour and resignation. Her black hair was looser now than either of them had ever seen it before, and surrounded her brow like a forest. The stateliness of look which had been almost too marked for a dweller in a country domicile had at last found an artistically happy background. (*Native* p. 383)

Eustacia's calm repose in death obliterates her former weaknesses.

Tess is a more successful synthesis of the sexual stereotype with an individualized yet socially representative character. She is both seduced, discarded innocence and typical of the declining English peasantry whose labour and life-style was being eroded by the mechanization of agriculture. But in *The Woodlanders* the result is not so happy. Here Giles, Marty and Grace Melbury are once again social types as well as archetypal lovers. Through them we see the disastrous impact of an alien, essentially urban value-system on a traditional rural culture. In the opening chapters they are entirely successful in their social roles, Hardy tracing in their relationships with each other and with the 'outsiders' Felice and Fitzpiers, the moral and emotional complications arising out of the clash between radically different patterns of feeling. Giles, for instance, is very effective as a pre-Lawrencian character-type. Associated with the natural goodness and fertility of the woods, he is in tune with his environment of woods, trees and apples, with the natural cycle of growth and decay. Marty South also 'works' as a representative of a particular life-style; her natural, spontaneous way of living, working and feeling for people is cleverly contrasted with Felice when she is persuaded to cut off her beautiful long hair so Felice, who is artificial in appearance and feeling, can wear it as a wig. (It is this 'pile of magnificent hair' that so impresses Fitzpiers when he first meets Felice.) Grace too is successful as the inexperienced country girl confused by her fashionable education and taken in by the apparent charms of the supposed gentleman, Fitzpiers.

Yet once Fitzpiers has run off, the story loses its careful balance between the social and love themes. The plot collapses into sentimentality as the love roles take over completely, stripping the characters of their social and psychological complexity. They become unhappy lovers, no more and no less. The absurd circumstances of Giles's death are a symptom of this collapse. Hardy wrings the last possible drop of pathos out of the Giles/Grace situation when Giles, by this time a ludicrously high-principled lover, condemns himself to an early death by refusing to come in out of the rain when to do so would mean compromising Grace. Marty too, in her determined faithfulness to Giles's memory, becomes a purely symbolic figure – the eternally faithful maiden who stands always by the tomb of the dead knight. She is not a real woman any longer, only a stereotype, an ideal of perpetual faithfulness.

This kind of unevenness of tone arises out of the conflict between the overall tendency of the novels and the employment of conventional character types. It is one of the characteristics of Hardy's writing which readers find the most difficult to accept, yet it is, I believe, the outcome of a struggle in the fiction between available literary and sexual images and Hardy's efforts to portray real women, characters who are individualized and yet demonstrate convincingly women's predicament in society as a whole. This was a problem he never completely solved; though in Sue Bridehead he perhaps came as near to doing so as possibly any writer could have done at the historical moment at which he wrote.

5. George Moore and George Meredith

The internal contradictions which we have identified in Hardy's novels, the uneasy jostling of feminist ideas with conservative character types and assumptions, is present in some form or other in all the fiction of this period. In Hardy the reliance on sexual and social archetypes is at the heart of the problem, perhaps because, with the notable exception of *Jude*, his novels always rest on the traditional patterns of feeling he associated with rural life. In Moore and Meredith the problem is one of how to resolve within the fiction the aspirations permitted to the women characters, a difficulty which does not arise in Hardy because his is an essentially tragic vision in which the woman is defeated. This has always been a very pressing difficulty for realist fiction and is one which has yet to be solved. Indeed, it may be impossible to solve it within a literary form which diagnoses and interprets existing realities which themselves exclude any resolution of women's problems. As we shall see, it was certainly something from which even the more deliberately feminist late nineteenth-century writers still could not escape.

GEORGE MOORE

George Moore's work, like Hardy's shows that he was well aware of women's social and economic subordination; it also shows a deliberate attempt to break away from the sexual stereotypes of mid-Victorian culture. We have already seen, for instance, how his determination to write relatively openly about sexual relations brought him into public conflict with the circulating libraries. The position he took up here over sexuality in fiction is reflected in his early novel, *A Mummer's Wife* (1885) in which the central character, Kate Ede, slides into alcoholism and prostitution. Interestingly, her original weakness is neither alcohol nor men, but an addiction to romantic fiction of the kind stocked by Mudie's. She reads it because, like Emma Bovary and Eustacia Vye, she is bored. It provides her with a fantasy world into which she can escape. Fantasy ultimately becomes reality as she allows herself to be seduced by an actor (the 'mummer' of the title), leaves her husband and elopes into the world of a travelling light-opera company.

Moore's treatment of the seduction is an important new departure. Kate is far from the passive, pliable victim of literary convention. She is willing and active:

'Let us prove our love one to the other,' he murmured, and frightened, but at the same time delighted by the words, she allowed him to draw her into his room.

'My husband will miss me', she said as the door closed, but she could think no more of him; he was forgotten in a sudden delirium of the senses; and for what seemed to him like half an hour Ralph waited ...[1]

Although all this now seems ludicrously melodramatic in its phrasing ('let us prove our love', the 'sudden delirium of the senses'), in 1885 it was remarkably frank. Even Hardy, some years later, hedges over describing what actually happens when Tess is seduced, and resorts to invoking spirits – 'where was Tess's guardian angel? Where was the providence of her simple faith?' (*Tess*, p. 90) Moore on the other hand, firmly places the 'blame' for Kate's seduction not on the oversight of the ministers of fate, but on Kate herself. He also forces our attention onto what is going on in the bedroom; we are deliberately encouraged to wonder what is happening in that 'half an hour' while the husband, Ralph, waits downstairs. Hardy, it will be recalled, deflects our attention away from the scene and moves instead into the realms of the eternal and infinite: 'darkness and silence ruled everywhere around. Above them rose the primeval yews and oaks of the Chase ...' (*Tess*, p. 90)[2]

This concentration on the moment, on physical detail rather than on abstract generalizations, gives Moore's style a peculiarly sensuous texture. This was an important innovation in English writing, and came out of Moore's interest in the French realists. (It seems to me no accident that the sudden glimpses he gives us, of the way someone is sitting for example, or of a group of people gathered in a room, very often suggests the Impressionist painters, who were working in France at the same time as Moore's mentor, Zola. They were trying to create a new visual reality in much the same way as the realist writers were creating a new moral and material world in fiction.) This sensuousness is particularly evident in the way Moore writes about women, so that in his work they seem to repossess their bodies in fiction for the first time in nearly a century. A typical example of the way his style casually captures and makes us feel the presence of real living bodies, comes from *A Mummer's Wife*:

Hender lolled with her legs stretched out; Kate rested her head upon her hand. Wearily, Mrs. Ede sat straight, apparently unheeding the sunlight which fell across the plaid shawl that she wore winter and summer. (p. 43)

Or, again from *A Mummer*, we have a similar description of the actors gathered for a convivial evening in a lodging house:

Three gas-burners were blazing, wine-glasses were on the table, and Mr. Lennon stood twisting a corkscrew into a bottle which he held between his fat thighs. On the little green sofa Miss Lucy Leslie lay back playing with her bonnet strings. Her legs were crossed, and a lifted skirt showed a bit of striped stocking. (p. 48)

This way of describing people often goes beyond physical detail. Moore uses it to establish or reinforce important themes in his novels. This is clearly the case in *A Drama In Muslin* (1884) where casual physical descriptions help create the tawdry atmosphere Moore associates with a society where sexuality is debased into just another item for sale. In the novel he uses the consciousness of an 'outsider', Alice Barton, as a vehicle to comment on the degradation brought on women by their having to sell their sexuality. Everyone regards Alice as a born spinster, so she stays on the fringes of the marriage market, watching her parents display her sister, who is up for sale to anyone who can bid high enough. In the following passage we see her observing her family with an elderly admirer. Here a particular moment is framed in Alice's memory, and ours, and a series of movements and physical details creates a world of comment and meaning:

It was a long time before she forgot Olive's blond, cameo-like profile seen leaning over the old beau's fat shoulder. Mrs. Barton laughed and laughed again, declaring the while that it was *la grace et la beauté reunies*. Mr. Barton shouted and twanged in measure, the excitement gaining on him until he rushed at his wife, and, seizing her round the waist, whirled her and whirled her, holding his guitar above her head. At last they bumped against Milord, and shot the old man and his fair burden on to the nearest sofa.[3]

Mr Barton is an amateur painter who dabbles in his studio at canvases of doubtful propriety, giving the nudes in his pictures the faces of his wife and daughter. Alice catches him at work, and once more the brief glimpse is made to capture the seedy debasement of sexuality:

Arthur was rushing backwards and forwards, streaking crimson along the thighs of his lady, but, when he saw his daughter, he hurriedly turned the picture to the wall. (p. 37)

Sex and suggestiveness, guilty and furtive in Mr Barton, are overt in another of Olive's admirers, Captain Hibbert, but Moore's technique remains the same:

Captain Hibbert twisted his brown-gold moustache, and with the critical gaze of the connoisseur, examined the undulating lines of the arms, the delicate waist, and the sloping hips; her skirts seemed to fall before his looks. (p. 41)

Although this passage has salacious overtones, it is still quite remarkable to find a novelist writing and writing critically, about a man mentally undressing a woman in 1885.

Moore's handling of his subjects was an innovation; but his actual choice of themes could be an even more startling departure from tradition. In *A Mummer's Wife*, for instance, once Kate has become an alcoholic, Moore insists on the details of her drinking bouts, her violent quarrels with her lover and her sordid death in a cheap lodging house. All of this Zolaesque naturalism flatly contradicted the squeamishness of more conventional tastes. The fact that the squalor and drunkenness were part of a *woman's* life was even more shocking.

Moore also shows the same kind of interest in Kate's psychology as Hardy was later to show in Sue Bridehead, and although the theme is less well developed than it is in *Jude*, it is an important part of the novel. Kate is subjected to the stress of being uprooted from her strict Methodist background and then being transplanted into the radically different environment of Dick, the Mummer's, opera company – secular in morals, bohemian in life-style, having no permanent home, only a series of lodging houses dotted over the country. In the closing scene of the novel Kate's delirium reveals the tremendous mental pressure this has built up in her. As she lies dying she recalls, but jumbles together her two very different lives:

The most diverse scenes were heaped together in the complex confusion of Kate's nightmare; the most opposed ideas were intermingled. At one time she told the little girls, Annie and Lizzie, of the immorality of the conversations of the dressing-rooms in theatres; at another she stopped the rehearsal of an opera bouffe to preach to the mummers – in phrases that were remembrances of the extemporaneous prayers in the Wesleyan Church – of the advantages of an earnest, working, religious life. It was like a costume ball, where chastity grinned from behind a mask that vice was looking for, while vice hid his nakedness in some of the robes that chastity had let fall. Thus up and down, like dice thrown by demon players, were rattled the two lives, the double life that this weak woman had lived, and a point was reached where the two became one, when she began to sing her famous song ... alternatively with the Wesleyan hymns. (p. 399)

Esther Waters (1894) has none of the calculated squalor of *A Mummer's Wife*, but it shows the same refusal to idealize women's lives. The life-story of Esther, the seduced servant-girl, her struggle for survival and her determination to bring up her illegitimate child in spite of almost insurmountable social and economic barriers, is told without any sensationalism and with only a slight tendency towards sentimentality. Romantic love is never any more for Esther than the original cause of her seduction and the hardships which follow it; it has no room in her hard daily battle. Nor is marriage seen as the only possible solution for her. The achievement of Esther's life is in her own efforts to support her son – her marriage to William, when it finally takes place, is only a brief episode of comparative happiness and security in the lifetime of work and care which is resumed after his death. As the life-story of a seduced and penniless girl thrown back on her own resources of character, the novel is more successful than Hardy's *Tess*.

Tess's story is sensationalized by murder and hanging; Esther's life is one of unrelieved, uneventful toil. And as a rewrite of *Pamela*, Moore's sober concentration on the day-to-day difficulties of Esther's situation is a more impressive refutation of Richardson's glamorous falsities.

Moore was not breaking new ground in choosing a working-class heroine for his novel.[4] But earlier 'working-girl' novels had either been written by moralists intent on instilling bourgeois values into working-class readers or, if designed for an upper-class readership, had romanticized or in some other way distorted the lives of their women characters. (Mrs Gaskell's patiently Christian heroines are a good example of this tendency.) Moore was among the first writers in English to attempt a completely honest picture of a working-class woman's life – of what she might have to endure and how she could cope with it.

His unsensational approach to Esther's life apart, perhaps the most important aspect of Moore's attempt at a truthful account is his treatment of Esther as a servant. We see her, in her various posts as 'general domestic', as a sexual, social and economic victim. An important episode here is when Esther goes to an employment agency in the hope of finding work. It illustrates the way in which servants are seen, and come to see themselves, not as people, but as commodities. Esther and her fellow workers are judged in the same way that horse-flesh is judged – how old, strong or weak, how fashionable in appearance? The woman who runs the agency tells Esther:

'it will be difficult to find you the situation you want before people begin to return to town. Now if you were only an inch or two taller I could get you a dozen places as housemaid; tall servants are all the fashion, and you are the right age – about five-and-twenty.'[5]

A few pages later, when Esther is attending an interview for a job, she meets an older woman who is after the same post and who says, when Esther tells her she is hoping for sixteen pounds a year:

'Sixteen! I used to get that once; I'd be glad enough to get twelve now. You can't think of sixteen once you've turned forty, and I've lost my teeth, and they means a couple of pound off.' (p. 191)

Here the suggestion of assessing the value of horse-flesh is unmistakeable – a horse's age is always reckoned by the state of its teeth. But perhaps the greatest humiliation Esther has to undergo is when she hires herself out as a wet-nurse – a job which combines very clearly her double exploitation as woman and as servant. This time the implied comparison is not with a horse, but with a carefully tended cow. Yet even Esther is comparatively lucky when we see her in relation to her mother. Continually pregnant, battered regularly by a drunken husband, desperately poor, Mrs Waters finally dies in a difficult childbirth.[6]

Nineteenth-century feminism was an essentially middle-class movement, so *Esther Waters*, even though it concentrates on the degradation and hardships of working women's lives, has only an indirect connection with feminism as Moore would have understood it. In *A Drama In Muslin* however, Moore took up some of the issues which were very closely related to middle-class feminism – the imbalance in numbers between single women and single men, and the frustrating, humiliating life imposed on spinsters. With this novel he presented his contemporaries with an account of the marriage-market, and showed what it meant in psychological terms when a woman failed to 'catch' a husband and was reduced to competitive, pathetic man-hunting. The sordid in-fighting among women rapidly approaching spinsterhood is one of the most effective, if depressing, things in the novel. But a more original and more important observation made by Moore in the book is the way women regulate and evaluate the way they spend their time according to whether or not a man is present. For in this novel women simply do not feel they exist unless they are in some way relating to men. This is something which was uncritically accepted as normal by most of Moore's contemporaries and predecessors, and is still, I believe, built into the portrayal of women in most fiction today. Describing an evening spent in the sitting-room of the Shelbourne Hotel during the Dublin 'season', Moore tells us how the conversation 'languished':

eyes were raised from wool-work and novel in gentle consideration, and said, as plainly as eyes could, 'there's no use in wasting our time talking here; no more men will come in tonight'. (p. 154)

Or again, a few pages later, they:

... longed that a man might come in – not with hope that he would interest them – but because they were accustomed to think of all time as wasted that was not spent in talking to a man. (p. 189)

But not all the women in the novel are completely immersed in the futilities of man-hunting or match-making. Alice is well aware of how humiliating these are and decides to find an alternative career. She asserts the right of a woman to meaningful and satisfying work, echoing Florence Nightingale when she says:

Give me a duty, give me a mission to perform, and I will live! ... But oh! save me from this grey dream of idleness! (p. 93)

Alice, fortunately for her, has some literary talent and escapes into writing novels, and although she finally does marry, she at least demonstrates one alternative to marriage other than a stultifying spinsterhood. Yet the book is weakened by Moore's failure to think of anything for Alice to do other than writing novels, and by his indifference to the problems a woman would have to confront in actually finding work. It is all arranged too easily.

Another contradiction is the conventional happy ending when Alice finally marries a discerning country doctor. Our belief in this marriage, really nothing more than an unconvincing piece of good luck arranged by Moore so that Alice never has to support herself after all, is subverted both by all the evidence in the novel and by women's experiences in nineteenth-century society. It indicates how difficult it was to break away in fiction from the set pattern of courtship followed by marriage. But, more interestingly, the marriage is also part of Moore's really very original argument that women have a right to sexual fulfilment. And he does not mean by this simply the domesticated idea of sex as the prelude to bringing up a family. Alice is curious about her own sexuality and she consciously dreads the life of celibacy which seems to await her. Moore did not find a way of writing successfully about Alice's sexual anxieties, and he lapses into a melodramatic style quite at odds with the rest of the book when he touches on them. But melodramatic or not, he was still readmitting a whole area of experience which had been lost to the novel since Defoe:

In an hour one truth had become terribly distinct, and in the nightmare terrors of her mind, strange thoughts, thoughts of which she was ashamed, passed and mockingly taunted her, and it required all the strength of her intelligence to regain her mental balance. Was she impure? she did not wish to be, but she trembled to think of her life pure from end to end ... (p. 100)

Alice's feelings of guilt and shame are not what we find in *Moll Flanders*, it is true, but the important point is that Moore believes Alice is right to acknowledge her sexuality. So that the marriage, through which Alice's sexual feelings are, we presume, satisfied, plays a novel and positive role, even though it remains implausible.

Alice's eroticism then, is depicted as normal, not pathological. But the way this is presented is curious. It is done through contrasting Alice with her friend Celia, who is mentally unbalanced, a semi-cripple and, it is strongly hinted, lesbian. Celia's 'abnormality' is used to justify Alice, who remains calm and rational about men and marriage, but it also points to a degree of hostility on Moore's part towards certain expressions of feminism. For with Celia, Moore adopts a new stereotype – the maladjusted man-hater whose feminism is a response to her own homosexuality. The sheer crudity of this portrait seriously damages the novel, which is otherwise a shrewdly characterized work. But Celia is not an isolated aberration. The same kind of hostility to 'advanced' women, who were advanced, in Moore's opinion, in the wrong direction, appears in 'Mildred Lawson', a short story from the collection *Celibates* which was published in 1895. Mildred's feminism is pure egotism, a self-indulgent craving for sensation. And like Sue Bridehead she is a sexual opportunist, benefiting from manipulating men but always stopping short of sexual relations with them. She keeps them in tantalizing, exhausting suspense. One man even dies from this treatment – presumably from frustration and despair. (It will be recalled that Sue Bridehead also 'kills' a young student in the same mysterious way.) It is possible that Moore's unpleasant interpretation of feminism in 'Mildred' was a reaction to a sexual snub – at about this time he had asked the lady novelist John Oliver Hobbes to marry him, but she refused. It has been suggested that Mildred was a nasty way of getting back at 'John Oliver'.[7] But whatever the personal motives and anxieties lying behind Mildred, she still represents a spiteful and deliberately perverse view of the emancipated woman of the 'nineties. He was not alone in using this kind of anti-feminist stereotype (see below in Part Three), but we have only to place Celia or Mildred beside James's Olive Chancellor in *The Bostonians* to see Moore's vulgarity and ill-disguised animosity.

GEORGE MEREDITH

Moore's writing, then, is a puzzling but revealing mixture of penetrating insights into the reality of women's lives, and of barely suppressed anxieties about where feminism might lead, especially in terms of sexuality and sexual relations. In this he really has more in common with Gissing than with Meredith, who shares none of Moore's unevenness of tone or guarded hostility towards emancipated women. Artistically too, these two writers are poles apart, Moore starting out as a disciple of Zola, and Meredith adopting a sophisticated, elliptical, and sometimes almost inpenetrable style of narrative.[8] However, they are linked by the failure of each to resolve the narrative problem of what to do at the end of a novel with a woman character who has struggled throughout it for independence or freedom. We have seen how Moore fell back on an unlikely marriage in *A Drama in Muslin*, the novel in which he explicitly addresses himself to the problem of women's economic status. Meredith finally does just the same thing in *Diana of the Crossways* (1885), another work about a woman trying to live independently of men, and in his most explicitly feminist enterprise, *The Egoist* (1879). In both these novels the conflict between idea and narrative direction remains unresolved.

The *Egoist* is a remarkable and early analysis of male sexual vanity, a theme later taken up in the novel by Gissing in *The Odd Women* and by Forster in *A Room With A View*. Its central character, Sir Willoughby Patterne, is an archetypal if genteel exploiter of women, adeptly making psychological use of every female with whom he comes into contact. (His name, based on the idea of a 'pattern', indicates that Meredith wants us to take him as in some way typical.) Willoughby is surrounded by women – friends, fiancée and doting maiden aunts – and likes to see himself as the focal point in their lives. They are female satellites, revolving around him, the male sun. Yet, though he does not realize it himself, Meredith makes it plain that it is in fact Willoughby who depends on them. His very sense of existence is really no more than his self-image refracted through their adoring, dependent female eyes. Without them, he cannot exist as an individual identity. It is this that accounts for his urgent need to dominate his fiancée, Clara Middleton. He cannot be comfortable until she renounces her individuality. Her independence of mind is a threat to his self-esteem, so he must conquer her.

But Willoughby is not content with simple domination; he wants to incorporate Clara's whole existence into his own. Even her thoughts are to be appropriated until they become his:

He had made the discovery that their minds differed on one or two points, and a difference of view in his bride was obnoxious to his repose ... He desired to shape her character to the feminine of his own ... he wanted her to be material in his hands for him to mould; he had no other thought.[9]

The novel is chiefly concerned with this attempt to colonize Clara's mind – an attempt which fails because Clara gradually understands and then rejects her position as a woman in a society arranged by Willoughbys for their own satisfaction. But parallel to Clara's battle of wills and wits with Willoughby, and her own father – who is Willoughby's willing accomplice – is a second sexual drama. We learn very early on in the novel that for several years Willoughby has been making an emotional convenience of another woman, Laetitia Dale. He takes up with her only when it suits him, and uses her to maintain his self-image as an irresistibly attractive bachelor – an image which sustains the occasional shock when other girls, Clara included, see through him. He is able to feed his male sexual vanity off Laetitia's pathetically faithful and uncritical love. She is a reserve love-force to be drawn upon when there is no-one else available, the faithful mirror to his narcissism. Meredith captures this idea of Laetitia as mirror in a memor-

able encounter between her and Willoughby which takes place
after the young lord has been absent from England for three
years. (He had gone off because Clara's predecessor had had
the wit to jilt him.) Needless to say, during all this time
Laetitia has been faithfully keeping his image bright:

> She was crossing from field to field with a band of schoolchildren, gathering
> wild flowers for the morrow May-Day. He sprang to the ground and seized
> her hand. 'Laetitia Dale!' he said, he panted. 'Your name is sweet English
> music! And you are well?' The anxious question permitted him to read
> deeply in her eyes. He found the man he sought there, squeezed him
> passionately, and let her go, saying 'I could not have prayed for a lovelier
> home-scene to welcome me than you ...' (Vol. 1, p. 29)

The way Meredith skilfully interlaces the pronouns 'him' and
'her' while Willoughby gazes intently into Laetitia's eyes indicates economically and damningly the real nature of Wil-
loghby's interest in her. He gets from her the flattering devotion of an attractive woman who can be relied upon to bolster
his ego in a way that Clara cannot:

> A clear approach to felicity had long been the portion of Sir Willoughby in
> his relations with Laetitia Dale. She belonged to him; he was quite unshack-
> led by her. She was everything that is good in a parasite, nothing that is bad.
> (Vol. 1, p. 177)

And, comparing Laetitia with Clara, we learn that for Willoughby:

> The exceeding beauty of steadfastness in women clothed Laetitia in graces
> Clara could not match. A tried and steadfast woman is the one jewel of the
> sex; she points to her husband like the sunflower; her love illuminates him;
> she lives in him, for him; she testifies to his worth; she drags the world to his
> feet; she leads the chorus of his praises; she justifies him in his own esteem;
> surely there is not on earth such a beauty? (Vol. II, p. 148)

But guided by Clara, Laetitia comes to a mature understanding of Willoughby's character, of the way he makes a convenience of her and of everyone else around him. So that although
she finally does marry him, she does so from a position of
strength and dignity, and there is finally no doubt that she will
be more than his 'match'.

Willoughby's relations with these two women are at the core of the novel, and through them Meredith probes the psychology of what we now call sexism. He is particularly interested in the reasons why men insist that women should be, above all else, sexually pure. Willoughby is extremely anxious that the woman he chooses for his bride should be 'uncontaminated', 'unsullied' by the trading that goes on in the marriage-market:

Miss Middleton had been snatched from a crowd, without a breath of the crowd having offended his niceness. He did it through sarcasm at your modern young women, who run about the world nibbling and nibbled at, until they know one sex as well as the other, and are not a whit less cognizant of the market than men: Pure, possibly; it is not so easy to say innocent; decidedly not our feminine ideal. (Vol. 1, p. 51)

The fine sarcasm of 'our feminine ideal' by which Meredith dissociates himself from Willoughby's opinions, points here to the fact that Willoughby is concerned not with the effect of the 'market' on women, but with its affront to his fastidious pride, his 'niceness'. Later on in the novel, when Meredith extends this analysis, he concludes that the desire to secure an untouched virgin for a wife is fundamentally a more directly sexual impulse;

The capaciously strong in soul among women will ultimately detect an infinite grossness in the demand for purity infinite, spotless bloom. Earlier or later they see they have been victims of the singular Egotist, have worn a mask of ignorance to be named innocent, have turned themselves into market produce for his delight ... But the devouring male Egotist prefers them as inanimate, overwrought polished pure-metal vessels, fresh from the hands of the artificer, for him to walk away with hugging, call his own, drink of, and fill and drink of, and forget he stole them. (Vol. II, p. 148)

Meredith is suggesting here that the demand for purity at all costs is unnatural because it makes women artificial; but the passage also contains unmistakeable sexual overtones which suggest an unacceptable degree of use and control of the woman's sexuality – 'hugging', 'call his own', 'delight', 'devouring'. The image of women as passive, inanimate 'vessels' or containers which men 'drink of', 'fill' and 'drink again', all obliquely hint that Meredith is talking specifically about sexual possession and power.

Another surprisingly progressive part of Meredith's analysis of Clara's situation is the way he manages to show what it feels like for a woman to be treated in this way. Willoughby assumes that once engaged to Clara, he has certain physical claims on her. Given that this was in the mid 1870s, these do not go much beyond the odd kiss, but Clara resents being expected to reciprocate his clumsy sexual advances. She begins to separate what she comes to see as her 'real' self from the self the man appropriates:

With a frigidity that astonished her, she marvelled at the act of kissing, and at the obligation it forced upon an inanimate person to be an accomplice. Why was she not free? By what strange right was it that she was treated as a possession? (vol. II, p. 78)

It is as though she herself, the real Clara, is simply just not there. Her own body has become a separate object which she watches from a safe distance.

Although Clara finally escapes marriage to Willoughby, I think we should still see their relationship as Meredith's paradigm of conventional marriage relations. Willoughby always behaves according to 'pattern', and the pattern of marriage and courtship he follows is one which systematically drains the woman of her individuality. Like Ibsen's Helmer in *A Doll's House* (written, incidentally in the same year as *The Egoist*), he continually patronizes Clara and belittles her abilities:

Whenever the little brain is in doubt, perplexed, undecided which course to adopt, she will come to me will she not? I shall always listen ... (Vol. 1, p. 121)

And Clara's personality, if Willoughby and her father have their way, will be squeezed out of her until she becomes pure Willoughby. Clara is strong enough to resist this warping process:

She would not burn the world for him; she would not, though purer poetry is little imaginable, reduce her self to ashes, or incense, or essence in honour of him, and so by love's transmutation, literally be the man she was to marry. She preferred to be herself. (Vol. 1, p. 61)

Marriage to Willoughby would be like wearing 'a cap of iron' and all she feels she can offer him is 'unwillingness, discordance, dull compliance; the bondwoman's due instead of the bride's consent'. At first she thinks her feelings are simply a reaction to Willoughby's peculiarly oppressive idea of marriage. But she gradually comes to see that what is wrong is not just Willoughby, but the whole socio-sexual system. She realizes that she is an object to be passed, without her consent, from one man to another. She learns that 'women are in the position of inferiors. They are hardly out of the nursery when a lassoo is round their necks.' (vol. 1, p. 213) Meredith sees marriage as a structure which ensured that women stayed in the position of inferiors by preventing them from developing any sense of themselves as individuals.

Clara discovers exactly the same thing about marriage as Nora Helmer. But the novel rests on a major contradiction which Ibsen carefully avoided. Having brought Clara to a lucid understanding of her position, Meredith still ends the story by having her marry. No alternative is presented to her or to us. Ibsen was more consistent – he ended his play by having Nora leave her husband and family in order to discover herself *on her own*. Kate Millett's comment on this unsatisfactory marriage at the end of *The Egoist* sums up what is in fact a serious flaw in the structure of the novel;

Comedies are always concluded in marriages, but there is something poignant in the realization that Clara's marriage is rather like a death. Throughout the novel she was a person in the process of *becoming*, but by the last page she has not succeeded in becoming anyone but Mrs. Vernon Whitford, which is to say, no one at all.[10]

Like George Moore in *A Drama in Muslin*, Meredith's problem was partly a structural one, in as much as the novel was not fully adapted to exploring the ways women might live outside marriage and their emotions. But this finally means that for all its psychological subtlety, *The Egoist* evades the vital question of what the alternatives to married dependence could be. The whole movement of the work is a sustained argument against marriage, and although literature does not and cannot be expected to provide solutions to social and political problems, we can at least expect it to be emotionally and artistically consistent. *The Egoist*, for all its strengths, is not.

6. The Short Story

Developed in France and Russia in the middle of the century, the short story became popular with writers in England during the 'eighties and 'nineties. One reason for this was that a more subtle and flexible narrative form had become necessary if fiction was going to cope at all adequately with the new themes literature was turning to at this time. The short story met this demand. Its characteristic inconclusiveness, its open-ended or deliberately evasive resolutions were particularly helpful in overcoming the narrative problems of traditional realism which we have looked at in Hardy, Moore and Meredith. This is because a story which deliberately examines only a single brief episode or encounter avoids the tendency of the conventional full-length novel to come to definite conclusions, to dispose adequately of all the characters and to unravel what could be a dazzlingly complicated plot. In short, its greater narrative flexibility was instrumental in emancipating fiction from some of the constraints of the realist tradition.

It also incorporated the moral and social commitment of writers like Hardy and Moore into the innovations in style and form which were the particular concern of the so-called 'decadents'. It is significant, for instance, that practically all the leading short story writers of the 'nineties were associated at one time or another with John Lane or with his *Yellow Book*. As well as enjoying a reputation for immorality, the latter was also a forum for discussion of aesthetic and literary issues. Its contributors were as important for their formal experiments as they were for their moral views, and periodicals like *The Yellow Book* and *The Savoy* played an important part in bringing the short story before a public which had been brought up on, and was accustomed to, the more substantial fare of mid-nineteenth-century fiction.

The short story then, extended the 'nineties' rejection of

Victorianism from content to aesthetics, and was far removed indeed from the old three-volume novel which it helped to eclipse. The moral and stylistic characteristics of that literary dinosaur, lovingly mocked by Kipling in his comic poem, belonged to an age which was passing:

> Fair held our breeze behind us – 'Twas warm with lovers' prayers,
> We'd stolen wills for ballast and a crew of missing heirs;
> They shipped as Able Bastards till the Wicked Nurse confessed,
> And they worked the old three-decker to the Islands of the Blest.
> No moral doubts assailed us, so when the port we neared,
> The villain got his flogging at the gangway, and we cheered,
> 'Twas fiddles on the foc'sall – 'twas garlands on the mast,
> For everyone got married, and I went ashore at last.
> I left 'em all in couples a-kissing on the decks,
> I left the lovers loving and the parents signing cheques,
> In endless English comfort by country-folk caressed,
> I left the old three-decker at the Islands of the Blest ...[1]

There were plenty of 'moral doubts' in the short story. And by relying on image and suggestion, rather than on plot and moral prodding, the new form dispensed altogether with the often clumsy aesthetics of the traditional nineteenth-century novel.

But is was not just a simple question of novelty or variety. The inherent brevity, the compression and clarity of the short story, were peculiarly well suited to new and different types of subject matter. As Derek Stanford has pointed out, it was ideal for depicting clashes between the old and new sexual moralities and the problems greater sexual freedom was producing, especially for women:

This new democracy of the touch, this egalitarianism of the erotic senses is clearly to be felt as a presence informing the fiction of the period. In one sense, the short story here was a more suitable medium than the novel. It could offer the reader the bare essentials of the encounter, the dilemma, the choice: a victory for love or a victory for class. In the same way the short story could highlight, with no inartistic augmentation, the debate on the claims of erotic attraction and the demands of a sexual morality geared to marriage and solely marital intercourse.

The short story took for its domain,

Seduction, prostitution, animal magnetism, the sudden change of a personality under the impact or revelation of sex, the state of concubinage, the social status of the divorcée, and even alcoholism in marriage.[2]

Women and sexual relations then, were at the heart of the 'nineties short story. They are explored perhaps most honestly by Ella D'Arcy. Her first book of stories, *Monochromes*, appeared in John Lane's 'Keynotes' series in 1895, and she became literary editor of *The Yellow Book* in the same year. Ella D'Arcy writes almost exclusively about women, but she has no illusions about her own sex. Her aims are similar to Gissing's – she exposes the selfishness, egotism and duplicity of many women – but she is quite unlike him in that she remains detached and analytical where Gissing is all too often partisan and vindictive. With only two important exceptions ('The Elegie' and 'The Engagement'), she depicts men as victims and dupes, women as their cold-hearted, destructive exploiters. It is as though all her stories were a variation on the Rosamond/Lydgate relationship in *Middlemarch*. Her favourite theme is the failed marriage and she invariably sends her couples to the altar as if 'their blood was to be shed'.[3] She even writes a story about a 'nymphomaniac' ('The Pleasure Pilgrim'). In short, Ella D'Arcy is never sentimental about women; she never allows herself to be anything but a critical realist. This is due partly to her style, which is sparse, cryptic, ironic, and partly to the shrewd and rigorous way she registers every mental ploy of her selfish characters.

To illustrate the strength of her work I have chosen what is perhaps her most chilling story, 'A Marriage' from her second collection, *Modern Instances* (1898). The story also appeared in *The Yellow Book*. It is a study of the change which takes place in the central character, Minnie, after she marries the man who has been keeping her for some years as his mistress. From being quiet, submissive, and docile – the ideal mistress and housekeeper in fact – she is transformed, once she becomes 'respectable', into a monster of pettiness and cruelty. Her coldness and indifference, her inhuman attitude towards her servants, her steady wearing away of her husband's youth and happiness – all these gradually weaken the husband, erode his will to live, and finally kill him. There is a macabre suggestion that Minnie is in some strange psychological way 'living-off' her ailing husband, for as he sinks into ill-health and depression, she flourishes and blooms:

She was prettier than she used to be, more strikingly pretty at first sight. She had learned perhaps to bring out her better points ... Five years of married life had in no way dimmed the transparency of her skin. Not a line recorded an emotion whether of pleasure or of pain. If she had lived through any psychic experiences, they had not left the faintest trace behind.[4]

In contrast to this uncanny 'immobility of countenance' is the now ravaged face and physique of the husband:

He found him huddled up over the drawing-room fire, spreading out his thin hands to the blaze. Half lost in the depths of the armchair sitting with rounded shoulders and sunken head, he seemed rather some little shrunken sexagenarian than a man still under thirty. (p. 67)

The husband has been crushed over the years by the accumulated effect of small domestic tyrannies and humiliations:

'She has made my life miserable, miserable ... and that's enough for me. And if I were to try and explain how she does it, I daresay you would only laugh at me for there's nothing tragic in the process. It's the thousand pin-pricks of daily life, the little oppositions, the little perversities, the faint sneers. At first you let them slip off again almost indifferently, but the slightest blow repeated upon the same place a thousand times, draws blood at last.' (p. 75)

This sums up one kind of domestic misery, but, interestingly enough, this idea of the effectiveness of the slightest blow repeated on the same place over and over again, also describes Ella D'Arcy's own technique as a writer. For this is exactly what she does in her work, where the steady accumulation of small and individually insigificant incidents gradually builds up a sharp image of the conflict at the heart of the story. There is the minimum of incident in 'A Marriage', but each small detail develops the overall picture of suffering which lies behind the facade of this apparently successful marriage. The same is true of the many other stories in which Ella D'Arcy explores the boredom, stultification or misery which in her view all too often lie hidden in respectable middle-class suburbia, with its appearance of niceness, gentility and comfort.

Ella D'Arcy concludes this survey of writers whose attempts to depict society, social relationships or ethical problems from a critical, unidealized standpoint led them to a comparatively honest portrayal of women. As we have seen, they were not always successful, they were often constrained by the literary form they inherited and they did not entirely reject conventional assumptions about sex or about women, but their writing on women and their attempts to deal with some of their problems – even if only in the form of airing them – were a considerable advance on the complacency of their immediate predecessors. Yet they came to their views on women through their prior commitment to literary honesty and their refusal to accept the conveniently tidy framework of Victorian morality. Their interest in women was secondary. There were, however, a number of writers whose interest in women was primary. These are the subject of my next chapter.

7. Feminist Fiction and The Rejection of Realism

GEORGE EGERTON

Not many people these days have heard of George Egerton. But when her first volume of short stories appeared in 1893 she caused a sensation. They were very 'nineties and very feminist.

Her real name was Chavelita Dunne. (George Egerton was a convenient pen-name, borrowed from her husband, George Egerton Clairmonte, when she turned her hand to writing.) Her father was a charming but aimless gentleman and her Irish family lived from hand to mouth, the mother coping as best she could while Dunne tried first this thing then that. He was certainly a versatile man, but an extremely unsuccessful one – except at fishing, on which he wrote an authoritative but unprofitable book.[1] When the mother died the family split up and Chavelita left Ireland and junketed about Europe, America and London, until she eloped with an acquaintance of her father's called Higginson, who was already bigamously married. They lived in Norway, where she came into contact with progressive, post-Ibsen writers and ideas, and fell in love with the poet and novelist Knut Hamsun. But she was only in Scandinavia for two years. Higginson died, rather conveniently, as he had turned out to be a violent drunkard. Chavelita then returned to England.[2]

In 1891 she married Clairmonte, a penniless idler whose character seems to have exactly reproduced her father's. He proved quite incapable of supporting her and their child, and so, encouraged by the Dublin editor T.P. Gill, she began writing stories as a way of raising some money. She sent a collection to John Lane, who was impressed, and who brought them out under the title 'Keynotes'. The collection was so successful that Lane used the title again, this time for his new modern fiction series.

George Egerton's 'shocking' past provided her with the

kind of material which gave her immediate notoriety. It also made her an important figure in the struggle to force sexuality back into fiction and redefine the literary image of women. Her stories concentrate on women – their relationships with men, their sexuality, the conflicts between their emotional lives and their determination to be free and independent. The question of what it feels like to be a woman is at the centre of nearly every one of her stories. And even if she falls too easily into the accepted notion that women live chiefly through their emotional relationships, at least she tackles the complicated, contradictory and hitherto taboo area of women's sexuality.

Keynotes celebrates the 'new woman'. Egerton sees her as strong, sensitive, varied and fascinating. She is clear-sighted and intelligent but still passionate and powerfully attractive – a real challenge to the anti-feminist stereotype of the new woman as a neurotic, repressed frump, who turns to feminism in desperation because she has failed to 'get' her man. (This frowzy man-hunter was a favourite with *Punch* cartoonists.)[3] Sex and sexual conflict are usually the core of Egerton's stories, which show women coolly analyzing their men, their ménage or their marriage. They calmly weigh up the relative advantages and disadvantages of marriage, sex without marriage, children without a husband, a career instead of children, or both together. But the stories are far from being feebly characterized discussions, dry arguments about women and the treatment meted out to them by men. Instead they are filled with a warm sensuousness which makes the women very much alive. Intelligent, wasted wives, mistresses who are dominating and free or used and exploited, resigned, contented or rebellious mothers, prostitutes, young schoolgirls, writers – all these and more are there in Egerton's stories. And even where she does collapse into the occasional diatribe against men or marriage – for instance in 'Virgin Soil' – she is always worth reading for the passion and articulacy of her denunciations.

No wonder she was attacked. Her name and her stories became synonymous with the literary filth which was supposed to be corrupting the morals of an increasingly degenerate nation. 'Foulness and hysteria', 'erotomania', 'neurotic fiction', 'crude vulgar indecency', 'things too low to be spoken of' – she provoked all these choice remarks.[4] And even the sympathetic T.P. Gill, the first to recognize and encourage her, was most unhappy about the more explicitly sexual passages in *Keynotes*. He advised her to tone down a section in 'The Cross Line' which describes a mildly erotic episode between a husband and wife:

Catching her wrists, he parts his knees and drops her on to the rug. Then perhaps the subtle magnetism that is in her affects him, for he stoops and snatches her up and carries her up and down, and then over to the window and lets the fading light with its glimmer of moonshine play on her odd face with its tantalising changes. His eyes dilate and his colour deepens as he crushes her soft little body to him and carries her off to her room.[5]

Strong stuff for the Victorians. Poor Gill, who entered into a correspondence with 'George Egerton' about the passage, was most embarrassed to find that he was discussing these 'appeals to the sexual senses' with a woman. The outcome was that he advised her to go back, safely, to the 'old reticences'.[6]

Perhaps Egerton's most important characteristic as a writer is that she generally avoids a realist mode altogether. She is a utopian. Here Egerton is in complete contrast to Ella D'Arcy, who was concerned not with what women might become, but with what society had made them – selfish, egoistical, shallow. D'Arcy, writing with remarkable clarity about what she saw around her, was a realist. Egerton, looking to the future and to the potential she saw in women, was a romantic. She could always sympathize with and understand what women had often been reduced to, and she was able to see an ideal future in which sexual discrimination no longer existed, where women were free. So she almost inevitably idealized; sometimes she escaped into fantasy.

'The Regeneration of Two' (from her second volume, *Discords*), gives an unashamedly idealized version of the new woman. Here a woman who at the beginning of the story is a bored and jaded society hostess, sets up a self-sufficient rural community of women. She herself becomes a quasi-feudal lady-of-the-manor figure – she has duties and responsibilities, is the lynch-pin of the whole system. She loves a man, but remains free. More important, she sees her relationship with him as only a part of her life:

She has found fresh interests, new duties, an ambition, and if he judge her rightly no love will ever satisfy her wholly; it will never be more than one note ...[7]

But it is significant that before the woman arrives at this position, she has had to create the kind of co-operative community which makes it possible – something which is extremely difficult in our society and was quite impossible for women at the time Egerton was writing. However, she seems to recognize this herself by setting the story in a strangely wild, isolated rural landscape. In short, 'The Regeneration of Two' is really a social-science-fiction – a useful vehicle for expressing ideals or objectives, but not a realistic assessment of what was actually possible.

Egerton's rejection of realism is I think significant. It has certain fundamental limitations, but is bound up with the imaginative leap she was able to make into the future. It is this vision – of new possibilities, of different ways of living – which makes her work important. It provided alternative models on which women could focus and which could act as a measure of both their achievements and their potential.

OLIVE SCHREINER

Egerton incorporated feminism into fiction more successfully than any other 'nineties woman writer. but she was not the first to have attempted a fusion of feminist commitment with literature. Olive Schreiner, a young English-South African had published her remarkable novel, *The Story of An African Farm*, in 1883 – over ten years before Egerton's work began to appear. Schreiner was both committed and outspoken. She showed in her novel the cost of the discrimination, burdens and injustice forced onto women, and she passionately asserted their rights to a decent education, to economic independence and to sexual liberty.

The Story of An African Farm traces the lives of three children – Waldo, Lyndall and Em – who are brought up on an isolated farmstead by an ignorant, unimaginative Boer woman, Tant Sannie, and Bonaparte Blenkins, a sadistic parasite. Em and

Lyndall are cousins, Waldo is the orphan son of the previous farm foreman, a gentle, humanitarian man who was turned away from the farm for no good reason. But it is Lyndall who is the central figure. She is extremely intelligent and is full of abilities which she is determined to develop and use. But because of her isolation on the farm and because she is a woman, she can do nothing. She is quite different from the submissive Em, who philosophically accepts what seems to her to be her fate – the unending, numbing routine of farm life. Em is the 'little woman' who stays at home while Lyndall, who has money from her English relatives, goes off to broaden her education at a town boarding-school. She is away four years and comes back an ardent feminist, her eyes wide open to what the 'finishing' school, on behalf of society, aimed to do for her:

'They finish everything but imbecility and weakness, and that they cultivate. They are nicely adapted machines for experimenting on the question, 'Into how little space can a human soul be crushed?'[8]

Since she was really more a paying guest than a pupil, Lyndall was able to reject the school and its ethos, using her time more profitably in learning about 'life' from her friends and contacts in the city. In a long conversation with Waldo, really a mono-logue, Lyndall gives us the benefit of her experiences, speaking what is really Olive Schreiner's mind on women. She attacks their humiliating position as marriageable dependents and its degrading effect on their characters: 'a little weeping, a little wheedling, a little self-degradation, a little careful use of our advantages,' she says, 'and then some man will say – "Come, be my wife!" ' (p. 190) She speaks out against the way class distorts love and the way sex is manipulated in the scramble for wealth; she demands education, work and the chance for self-respect for all women. And in the decisions she makes in her own life she deliberately defies the double standard – rejecting marriage and the sexual domination it meant for a woman, she chooses to live with her lover, rather than marry him.

The second part of the novel, with Lyndall's declamatory speeches and her death in childbirth, in no way measures up to the earlier chapters. The story gets cut off from the harsh, sun-dried African landscape and looses its sense of time and place. It becomes thinner and more strident as Lyndall's defiant protest against woman's lot moves away from her experiences on the farm, away from Schreiner's brilliant evocation of the parched no-man's-land of the Karoo, and retreats inside her own head. Although what Lyndall says so passionately and so clearly about women is true, and sounds true, we never see her learning or experiencing these truths. The feminism is not worked satisfactorily into the texture of the novel.

But for all its imperfections, *The Story of An African Farm* is a deeply felt statement of women's rights and an uncompromising outcry against their wrongs. It was an instant success when Chapman and Hall published it in 1883, two years after Olive's arrival in London, and it fired many women into support for feminist struggles. Edith Lees (Havelock Ellis's wife) called it 'a voice from the depths' which could arouse even the most apathetic of women. And she bracketed it together with Ibsen's *A Doll's House* as one of the two works which 'drove most thinking women further together towards their emancipation'.[9] Recently re-published in paperback by Penguin, the *Story* is read by feminists today, and not just as a historical curiosity, for its message simply has not dated. It means as much as it ever did, possibly because women's lives have changed so little since Olive Schreiner was writing.

Where her novel inspired feminists in the 'eighties and 'nineties, her later works, *Dreams* (1891) and *Woman And Labour* (1911), spoke to the next, more militant generation. Lady Constance Lytton, a suffragette whose health was broken by her treatment in prison, called the story 'Three Dreams in A Desert', 'a guide to our journey' which gave the imprisoned women strength to endure.[10] And Vera Brittain refers to *Woman And Labour* in the same enthusiastic way:

To Olive Schreiner's *Woman And Labour* – that Bible of the Women's Movement which sounded to the world of 1911 as insistent and inspiring as a trumpet call summoning the faithful to a vital crusade – was due my final acceptance of feminism.[11]

These quotations point to a characteristic and important feature of Schreiner's work – its prophetic, quasi-religious quality. Her books inspired, revealed and explained the women's movement to itself; grasping in her imagination the spirit and aims of the struggle, she welded them into an impassioned and eloquent whole. The breadth and firmness of her understanding of women's oppression, her vision of the future woman and the new kind of sexual relationships possible in a transformed and better society, give her work a near visionary dimension. Fervour and commitment burn through everything she writes.

Like George Egerton, Schreiner's favourite and most successful vehicle is not realist fiction at all. She works best in parables, allegories and dream visions, in fact in all the narrative methods of religious teaching. Her style, her turn of phrase, are often close to the rhythm and cadence of the King James Bible, and she seems to draw on Bunyan – in her use of symbol and allegory, and in the texture and sound of her prose. The Bunyanesque rhythms are at their clearest in the dreams and allegories, but they are always an important part of her narrative technique and give her writing its hypnotic power. Here for example, from the *African Farm*, is her description of the Karoo during a prolonged drought which seems to symbolize the arid, emotionally deprived lives of Lyndall and Waldo:

From end to end of the land the earth cried out for water. Man and beast turned their eyes to the pitiless sky, that like the roof of some brazen oven arched overhead. On the farm day after day, month after month, the water in the dams fell lower and lower; the sheep died in the fields; the cattle, scarcely able to crawl, tottered as they moved from spot to spot in search of food. Week by week, month after month, the sun looked down from the cloudless sky, till the karoo-bushes were leafless sticks, broken into the earth, and the earth itself was naked and bare; and only the milk-bushes, like old hags, pointed their shrivelled fingers heavenwards, praying for the rain that never came. (p. 44)

The parched earth of the desert or bush is never just the well-remembered landscape of Olive Schreiner's youth. It is always in her work an expression of spiritual desolation and longing, a central image for her feminism. In the 'Three Dreams', for example, the desert which the narrator/dreamer sees between her visions represents the world as a waste-land. It will be like this for as long as women are not free:

And all to the East and to the West stretched the barren earth, with the dry bushes on it. The ants ran up and down in the red sand, and the heat beat fiercely.[12]

And in another 'dream' the same image appears, this time as the painful no-man's-land which the woman must cross if she is to give up her comfortable, cushioned life for the hard feminist struggle. Beckoned by the figure of Duty she leaves the (Ruskin-like) Garden of Flowers and wanders away, 'and the grey sand whirled about her'.[13]

One further example, this time from *Woman And Labour*, will show how Olive Schreiner's poetic use of language and image forged an imaginative whole out of the various facets of feminism. Here she is comparing the movement to the slow and painful construction of a gothic cathedral. Although, she says, it may seem to those who stand in the present, admiring the achievements of past ages, that the cathedral stemmed from the clear, unified conception of one mind, it was really the product of generations of countless workers and craftsmen. They could spend a lifetime working on the cathedral, yet never grasp the meaning of the whole or understand its final harmony:

Ages elapsed from the time the first rough stone was laid as a foundation till the last spire and pinnacle were shaped, and the hand which laid the foundation stone was never the same as that which set the last stone upon the coping. Generations often succeeded one another, labouring at gargoyle, rose-window, and shaft, and died, leaving the work to others; the master-builder who drew up the first rough outline passed away, and was succeeded by others, and the details of the work as completed bore sometimes but faint resemblance to the work as he devised it; no man fully understood all that others had done or were doing, but each laboured in his place and the work as completed had unity; it expressed not the desire of one mind, but of the human spirit of that age.[14]

She goes on to compare the cathedral workers with the isolated efforts of individual, often lonely women who were making their contribution to women's freedom. Frequently not understanding the outline or broader implications of the movement, often attempting the wrong things, usually without recognition or reward, these women have a harder time than the visionaries. 'Nevertheless', she says, 'it was through the conscientious labours of such alone, through their heaps of chipped and spoiled stones, which may have lain thick about them, that at last the pile was reared in its strength and beauty.'

But Olive Schreiner's passionate commitment to women led her into the same artistic difficulties as it later did George Egerton. The fiction of both women is flawed by lapses into rhetoric, long passages of angry denunciation or personal bitterness. Both failed to develop as artists. Although Olive Schreiner worked for years on another novel, *From Man to Man*, she could never complete it and it was finally published posthumously and unfinished. George Egerton produced two collections of stories after *Keynotes*, but they were really a repetition of her earlier observations and feelings. T.P. Gill noticed the similarity between the two women when he wrote to George Egerton after the initial success of *Keynotes*:

Olive Schreiner has never written a book worth reading since her *African Farm*. She put all her heart, her experience into that. The rest is bosh. Most people have *one* story to tell. The creative artist does not merely utter his own heart cry.[15]

He wonders whether Egerton can write as well out of her imagination as she had done out of her experience. Even if we can argue against his opinion that everything Olive Schreiner wrote after 1883 was 'bosh' (*Women And Labour* was an important and influential book), it does seem to be true that neither woman was able to build on her original insights. Art was grafted uneasily onto their feminism. Olive Schreiner turned increasingly towards more orthodox politics and became involved in the campaign against the British in South Africa. George Egerton disappeared into obscurity.

GRANT ALLEN AND SARAH GRAND

Obscurity is where we must go to find most of the topical but transient feminist novels of the 'nineties. There were novels on wives, spinsters and virgins, on marriage, sex and motherhood, on career girls and suffragettes (or 'Women's Righters' as they then were). But most of them were treatises first, novels second. Many were confused and sentimental, or bald statements of problems rather than attempts to come to grips with them. But two books deserve special attention, if only because of their notoriety at the time – Grant Allen's *The Woman Who Did* and Sarah Grand's *The Heavenly Twins*. Along with *Jude* and *Keynotes*, these two novels were chief targets of a public outcry about 'moral corruption' and literary 'filth'.

Reading these books now it is difficult to see what all the fuss was about. Anyone going through *The Woman Who Did* would probably be left wondering: 'Did what?' What she 'did' was to have sex and stay single, although it is all much more genteel and respectable than that simple summary suggests. As a priggish and self-styled martyr, Herminia Barton gladly endures the social odium and ostracism which follow her decision. But her image as heroic anti-marriage champion collapses when her lover inconveniently dies and she is left to bring up her child on her own. Unfortunately the daughter does not share the mother's feminist principles. All she wants is to be allowed to live a 'normal' life – dress in pretty clothes, be admired by gentlemen, and marry. So she rejects feminism, and her mother with it, as wicked and immoral. Herminia is shattered by her daughter's defection and commits suicide.

In as much as Herminia is suitably punished for her breach of the 'rules', the story is morally impeccable. And as the above outline of the plot shows, Grant Allen was no feminist. But its critics did not see it like that. They missed the novel's fundamental conformism and saw only the attack on conventional marriage, described in the novel as a 'system of slavery'. Not only that, but Herminia, who has been to Girton and is an animated compendium of every feminist idea in circulation, openly advocates going beyond the token freedom of the vote and into more crucial areas of oppression – sex and morals. No wonder Mrs Fawcett and other orthodox feminists condemned the novel and its author as 'not a friend but an enemy' of the movement.[16] As usual, they were afraid that public discussion of sexual questions would get the suffrage campaign a bad name. *The Woman Who Did* certainly had a bad name, and poor though the novel is, it was still important as an attempt to shift the terms of the feminist argument away from the 'safe' issues of work and the vote and into the more explosive areas of sex, marriage and maternity.

Sarah Grand's *The Heavenly Twins* is a better novel than *The Woman Who Did*; it is less diagrammatic and the figures in it are more, though little more, than Allen's one-dimensional spokespeople for or against emancipation. It also deals with a much more taboo issue than marriage – venereal disease. The heroine, Evadne, marries in ignorance of her husband's promiscuous past, but discovers it in time to refuse intercourse with him. She and the husband come to an agreement to live together in the same house, keeping up the appearance of normal relations. The husband eventually dies and Evadne, by this time a nervous wreck, remarries. In one of the innumerable sub-plots a second woman, Edith, marries another man who is evidently riddled with some kind of disease, though Grand never actually says this. Edith contracts the disease, goes mad, and dies, though not before giving birth to a repulsively sickly child.

The very daring plot is clearly inspired by the Contagious Diseases Acts and the campaign for their repeal (the infected husbands are military men), and Grand believes that it is primarily men, not women, who spread venereal disease. But, more important, she involved nice upper-class girls in the discussion. Only prostitutes were supposed to get infected, but one of her heroines, a high Anglican from an upper-class family, actually dies of an unnamed 'contagious disease'. Brought up in spectacular ignorance about sex, Edith and Evadne are married off by parents whose ideas of a 'good match' are strictly economic. Needless to say, even when a suitor has an extremely unsavoury reputation, no-one is interested in whether or not he has picked up any infections. But Evadne, a clever girl, with the sense to look things up in medical reference books, *is* interested. Edith, dangerously protected by her intensely religious background, remains in a blissful state of ignorance and unwittingly allows herself to be handed over to a slow, painful death.

The Heavenly Twins looks forward to Christabel Pankhurst's pamphlet *The Great Scourge and How to End It*, published in 1913. By then sections of the women's movement had grown out of some of their earlier shyness about sex, and in a blaze of publicity Christabel triumphantly claimed that 'from seventy-five to eighty percent of men' had gonorrhoea and a 'considerable percentage' syphilis.[17] But under the WSPU (Women's Social and Political Union) the campaign against male promiscuity which began when women first organized against the CD Acts, hardened into a platform demanding purity for all. 'Votes for Women and Purity for Men' became a successful slogan. *The Heavenly Twins* was part of this tendency, which in effect demanded equality of sexual austerity rather than greater, equivalent freedom for women.

The Woman Who Did and *The Heavenly Twins* are literary curiosities. They have little intrinsic value, but they are interesting and important historically as they show how far the novel had moved in challenging the moral and sexual *status-quo*. Both Grand and Allen are reticent or coy when they have to deal with sexual encounters and are more fundamentally conservative than either Hardy or Moore. In so far as they understood feminism, they were feminists; yet we only have to place their work beside Olive Schreiner's *African Farm* and it immediately pales into mechanical gestures of support or enthusiasm for a cause which she not only felt passionately, but which she also understood and which inspired in her a remarkable novel.

The feminist novelists arrived at fiction mainly because their interest in the women's emancipation movement coincided with a need to earn money, and writing was still one of the few possibilities open to a middle-class woman who had to work. Olive Schreiner and George Egerton were exceptional in that they were gifted as well as hard up. Most of the feminist writers – women like Emma Brooke (*A Superfluous Woman*), Edith Johnstone (*A Sunless Heart*) and, as we have seen above, Sarah Grand – just were not good enough *as* writers to turn their material into an important challenge to the literary tradition. This meant that at the very moment when literature was beginning to break free from the moral stranglehold of Victorian sexual ideology, the novel was dominated for the first time and quite accidentally by male writers. Had there been a Brontë or an Eliot writing during this period of transition, women might have emerged from it very differently. As it was, Virginia Woolf was the only major female talent writing at the time, and she was both too late and, as I shall argue in my

Conclusion, ultimately too ambivalent to redefine women within fiction. And so the nexus of conservative assumptions about women and about sexuality which we have noted in male writers such as Hardy, Moore and Grant Allen went largely unquestioned.

8. A Postscript

We have seen to what extent a number of important writers and a group of lesser known writers understood and responded to feminism at the end of the last century. We have also examined some of the formal and narrative problems they had to contend with in order to write differently and more convincingly about women. What remains at this point is to outline the important areas they left untouched and the assumptions they left unquestioned.

Marriage was certainly attacked as an institution by many of these novelists. Monogamy and chastity were not. Hardy, Moore, Meredith and, as we shall see below, Gissing, all had important specific objections to make to the marriage contract as it then was, but they failed to question the moral assumptions which underpinned it and the other social structures they criticized. New tensions, problems and conflicts are acknowledged in their work, but with very few exceptions, the old emotional patterns and moral imperatives are still at work. Only Sue Bridehead is trying to work through to new kinds of relationships and feelings.

Grant Allen's Herminia, for instance, rejects marriage as an institution, mainly because it takes away women's freedom. But she thinks about relationships and sexual morality in much the same way as any orthodox heroine. She is pure, chaste and utterly sexless. And when it comes to her wedding night, we see that she is no different from the virgin bride of convention:

She was dressed from head to foot in a simple white gown, as fair and sweet as the soul it covered. A white rose nestled in her glossy hair; three sprays of white lily decked a vase on the mantle-piece. Some dim survival of ancestral ideas made Herminia Barton so array herself in the white garb of affiance for her bridal evening. Her cheek was aglow with virginal shrinking. (*The Woman Who Did*, p. 77)

Sarah Grand, too, accepts without question the damaging ideology of women's superior moral nature, and spends a large part of her creative energies in complaining that men do not feel obliged to adopt the same exacting and oppressive standards. Like Herminia, her heroine, Evadne, is essentially anti-sexual. There is nothing warm or sensuous about her. It is as though these writers felt that to get their ideas across at all, their heroines had to be above reproach. And being above reproach meant, above all, being sexually respectable.

Motherhood too is barely questioned. (Hardy's Sue is again the exception.) For most writers it is still the only real fulfilment for women. And even Olive Schreiner supports emancipation on the grounds that it would make women better mothers.[1] Sex and reproduction are still inseparable – only one woman (in Egerton's 'Virgin Snow') has heard of contraception and, like Anna Karenina, is prepared to use it. 'Negligent' mothers are severely rebuked – in particular by Gissing, whose novels are generously peopled with careless, unloving, indifferent mothers.[2] Grant Allen's Herminia comes to live exclusively for her child; so does Moore's Esther. And many of even Egerton's women yearn for children, a feeling which is seen as innate and instinctive, not culturally conditioned.

Anxious to demonstrate just how 'safe' feminism was, Grant Allen claimed that:

it is good for every woman among us that she and every other woman should be as physically developed and as finely equipped for her place as mother as it is possible.[3]

He also claimed that the 'loveliest thing on earth' is 'a beautiful marriageable woman'. Motherhood for him, and he believes for all supporters of emancipation, is a woman's true vocation. And so in an article which is supposedly about feminism and the progressive novel, he digresses into a lengthy passage on child-rearing:

The parent birds with nestlings, the males which feed their sitting hens, the ewe with her lambs, the cow that moans for her first calf, strike the key-note of something higher than mere aesthetic sentiment. Tenderness and pathos come in ... with the parental and marital relation. The love of the mate, the love of the young, have this common origin. Think of the widowed wren that laments her lost partner; think of the love-bird that cannot consent to live when deprived of its companion; think of the very monkeys that refuse all food and die broken-hearted when the bodies of their dead wives are taken from them.

There is also the more general question of the whole context within which women exist in the novels. Wanda Neff has rightly pointed out that most fiction in the 'eighties and 'nineties, and into the twentieth century, is still dominated by the love interest; women are seen as the centre of the private emotional world and are defined almost exclusively through their personal relationships.[4] In the world in which women had to live and work this was no longer, and indeed for the majority of women, never really had been the case. Working-class women had always worked, and increasing numbers of unsupported middle-class women had been forced to go out of the home as teachers and governesses ever since the financial instability of the 'forties. And towards the end of the century new and different types of work were opening up for women – nursing, typing, GPO work and eventually, for the middle-class woman, the professions. But a woman who worked was very rarely the centre of interest in a novel. And even where the heroine did work the emphasis was still on her emotional life.

This approach to women has always flourished in fiction, as it corresponds to the novel's central concern with private life, its function of translating historical processes into personal terms. But as even middle-class women were forced out into work, this exclusive emphasis on the private area of women's existence became more and more anomalous. The dominant image of women as having the time and leisure to engage in complicated and demanding emotional entanglements had always been a contradiction of most women's lives, but as work gradually became more the norm, this dislocation between image and reality became even greater. Women were and are affected by the material conditions of their lives. Yet in fiction they exist in a material vacuum, an emotional hot-house of love, sentiment and romance.

Thus in the late nineteenth century we find that most of Hardy's women are largely characterized through their emotional lives, even when, like Bathsheba Everdene, they have other and possibly better things to do. Tamsin Yeobright and Grace Melbury are solely defined by their emotional relationships – both are wronged women, little more; they see life refracted through their experiences with men. Marty South is an independent hard-working woman, but this is peripheral to Hardy's vision of her as a steadfast lover. So that although Hardy seems to be aware of the dangers of women depending on emotion and sentiment (in Eustacia and Felice), he himself never moves away from an exclusively emotional-sexual framework for them. In Gissing, even a book like *The Odd Women*, which is ostensibly about a feminist determined to make an independent life for herself and others, a disproportionate amount of time and space is given over to Rhoda Nunn's entanglement with Barfoot. Even the struggle for independence is seen in narrow emotional terms, and Rhoda is still primarily interesting because of her love affair. This remains true of women in the novel throughout the period. Though they may sometimes desire another kind of life (*A Drama in Muslin*), or have to cope with one (*Esther Waters*), they are never freed from their prison of emotion and private experience, and the novelists always guide them firmly back into the enclosed world of personal relations.

The narrative structure of the novels, too, remains tied in many cases to marriage as the only possible resolution of a woman's problems. Even where novelists are critical of existing marriage relations they still tend to marry off the heroine in the last chapter. Meredith falls into just this inconsistency in *The Egoist*. Moore does it in *A Drama In Muslin*. This suggests that many novelists hesitated to give their heroines the independence they allow them to struggle for, if it was at the cost of a life-time of lonely, hard work. Independence clearly had its drawbacks. Ibsen's Norah, Olive Schreiner's Lyndall, Grant Allen's Herminia, George Egerton's women – they all have to go it alone. They opt for independence, but in doing so they also opt for isolation. Rejecting marriage then, was a leap into the dark which most novelists were reluctant to take. George Egerton occasionally attempts to get round this problem by projecting her women into an ideal future where all the problems of freedom have been solved. Grant Allen does the same thing in his utopian novel *The British Barbarians* (1895).

But generally speaking the really independent women are social outcasts, either through choice (Norah Helmer and Lyndall) or necessity (most of Egerton's women, Sue in her anomalous relationship with Jude). And if the independent women have to be self-supporting it is interesting that they are often involved in some kind of literary work; writing is done in isolation and these women choose it partly because they are isolated already.

But the emphasis on isolation as a condition of freedom, and the inability to see a collective solution to women's problems is only to be expected in an age of individualism. Nineteenth-century feminist thinking was rooted in liberalism; its whole emphasis was on the problem of individual self-development and fulfilment, and it focussed on the question of individual rights. If politically minded feminists saw women's problems in this light, then it is hardly surprising that novelists followed suit, and continued to assume that a woman could only 'find' herself through a solitary progress towards self-knowledge, which could go on only outside normal social relations. The problems were seen as collective, shared; but at this stage the solution could only be individual.

Criticisms of the novelists' sexual conservatism, which derive anyway from our contemporary standpoint, must also be seen in relation to the positions taken up by political feminists. In almost every case the writers are well in advance of the feminists, who were opposed to any discussion of sexuality. Extremely careful not to be associated with what they regarded as 'loose morals', they clung to the ideological apparatus of chastity, marriage and motherhood and upheld the doctrine of woman's natural moral superiority. They worked to improve the situation of the unsupported middle-class woman, but only because single women had the misfortune to be excluded from the norms of marriage and motherhood and had to make a different kind of life out of necessity. Consequently the movement was entirely civic in its aims and organization. It was concerned firstly with the issues of education and job opportunities, and then with the franchise. Orthodox feminists were first unable to perceive, then reluctant to acknowledge, that women were exploited sexually as well as economically. Even the Contagious Diseases Campaign was fought primarily on individualistic lines, concentrating on the infringement of personal liberty involved in detaining and examining prostitutes. And as we have seen, the 'Great Crusade' which developed from the C.D. Campaign and openly attacked the double standard, pushed not for a sexually more tolerant society, but for equality of sexual oppression. Even so, it still caused a split in the suffrage campaign, as many feminists were alarmed at the connection with even this impeccable position on sexual morality.

The disappearance of Mary Wollstonecraft as an important feminist figure in the nineteenth century is another indication of the sexual and political conservatism of the women's movement. She was conveniently forgotten from about 1820 onwards. She was an embarrassment. Not only had she preached sexual equality, but she had tried to practise it too. In Victorian terms, her life was a scandal. But it was not even just a case of an illegitimate child and an undignified passion for its father. She was also a revolutionary. Her conception of free and equal sexual relations was bound up with her belief in a free and equal society. For her, oppression and women's oppression were part of the same social and political system, so that freeing women had to go hand in hand with fundamental changes in society. Such a far-reaching interpretation of their movement was anathema to nineteenth-century feminists. Their aim was to integrate women into society as it existed; women were to share the same privileges and rights as a small number of men. No wonder Mary was dropped. But even when she had been partially rehabilitated in the more adventurous climate of the 'nineties, Mrs Fawcett could still write, with evident disapproval, of the 'irregular relations' of her circle and 'the errors' of her life.[5] She would have benefited, we are told, from 'self government'.

On marriage and motherhood the feminists held strictly orthodox views. Frances Power Cobbe for instance believed that the:

great and paramount duties of a mother and wife once adopted, every other interest sinks, by the beneficent laws of nature, into a subordinate place in normally constituted minds.[6]

Clearly, emancipation was strictly for spinsters. Mary Wollstonecraft's 'great redeeming merit' meanwhile was that she did not sanction any depreciation of the immense importance of the domestic duties of women. (Fawcett, Introduction to *A Vindication*)

Corresponding to the elevation of motherhood was an indifference to birth control. The feminists were hostile to contraception and they failed to see any connection between emancipation and control over fertility. Their fierce sexual conservation led them to oppose all birth control propaganda. In 1877 Mrs Fawcett and her husband refused to appear for the defence in the Bradlaugh-Besant trial saying that 'if we were called as witnesses, we could effectively damage your case'.[7] Elizabeth Blackwell, the first woman doctor, called contraception 'a national danger',[8] and Frances Power Cobbe referred darkly to:

women who call themselves emancipated ... who are leading lives if not absolutely vicious, yet loose, unseemly, trespassing always on the borders of vice; women who treat lightly and as of small account, the heinous and abominable sins of unchastity and adultery ...[9]

sins they could indulge in freely only with the aid of contraception.

The hostility to birth control reveals an extraordinary short-sightedness. At the very least, it was a crucial question for all married women, and could make all the difference to the kind of lives working-class women in particular could lead. Its importance had long been recognized by radicals in England. But the feminists were not radical. They were keen to show their political reliability at all costs; to do anything else would jeopardize their chances of getting the vote. Their conception of sexuality was as orthodox as their conception of politics – they were unaware of the limitations of the vote and they were unaware of the part played by the family and its ideology in perpetuating women's oppression. Among contemporaries only the anarchist Emma Goldman attacked the feminists on these grounds. With a clear political analysis of the family, the role of chastity and the function of marriage, she saw sexuality as the crucial area of struggle. Her life and work are a speaking criticism of the narrow conservatism of orthodox feminists and suffragettes.

Sexually then, English feminism was backward-looking and unadventurous. This points to the real break with literary and social conventions which the novelists were attempting. For all their disregard of certain important issues, Hardy, Moore and others were still a threat to various illusions and pretences about sex and women which had successfully permeated public consciousness for nearly a hundred years. We can see this from the near hysterical reaction they provoked. This reaction is the subject of the next section.

PART THREE

RESPONSES

9. The Counterattack

INTRODUCTION

The aims of the women's movement, modest though they
were, taken together with the commitment of a number of
important writers to a degree of sexual honesty in the novel,
were greeted with alarm and dismay by a fundamentally conservative public. The counterattack, when it came in the
'nineties, was ferocious. But its venom cannot be explained
solely in terms of the resistance to change felt naturally by a
society which had systematically ignored sex and had confined
women to a purely domestic existence for the best part of a
century. The character of the response – irrational, hysterical
and dogmatic – can only be explained by the special nature of
the challenge.

We have already seen that as far as most feminists were
concerned their movement was about the political rights of a
fairly small number of propertied women, about education
and about jobs. But feminism *potentially* went far beyond these
limited demands. In its furthest implications it was likely to
question the very basis of social organization – the family – and
it contained the potential for a direct confrontation with the
dominant sexual ideology, which affected everyone, not just
women. Not surprisingly then, it was seen by its opponents as
a dangerous challenge to the stability of bourgeois society.
The feminists themselves were the first to deny this. But if
they were blind to the revolutionary possibilities of their
movement, their opponents were not. They quickly rallied
round in support of the sacred cows of family, marriage and
motherhood, claiming them for God, the Church and the
State. A typical comment claimed, for instance, that divorce
would be 'most detrimental to the very foundation of society,
and for this reason: it would injure materially *family* life,
which, after all, is the bedrock of all well organized states'.[1] It
was quite clear to the positivist Frederick Harrison that votes

for women would pull society 'down from its very roots' and would 'uproot the very first ideas of social order'. And in defence of the family he invokes 'the State, the Nation, Industry, Social Organization, Law'.[2] (The capitals are his.) Mrs Fawcett, replying in the next issue of *The Nineteenth Century* hastened to reassure him and dismissed his attack on feminism as scaremongering. But it was Harrison, not Mrs Fawcett, who was basically correct in his understanding of the function of the family in society. He grasped its role of underpinning existing political and economic structures and saw how it reproduced and re-enforced bourgeois values.

Well aware of the fundamental critique of the entire social order which lay hidden in feminism, anti-feminists attacked the movement in the widest political terms. Feminism, free love and votes for women became firmly connected in the Tory mind with Revolution. One article, 'Tommyrotics' by Hugh Stutfield, attacked modern fiction and feminism on just this basis, linking Hardy, Egerton, the 'new woman' and 'nineties 'decadence' with Anarchy and Rebellion:

Along with its diseased imagining – its passion for the abnormal, the morbid and the unnatural – the anarchical spirit broods over all literature of the decadent and 'revolting' type. It is revolution all along the line. Everybody is to be a law unto himself ...

The connection between revolutionary principles in ethics and politics is obvious. The sensualist and the communist are, in a sense, nearly related. Both have a common hatred of and contempt for whatever is established or held sacred by the majority, and both have a common parentage in exaggerated emotionalism. Everybody knows that among the Jacobins of the French Revolution filthiness of life, ferocity, and maudlin compassion went hand in hand. In these days the unbridled licentiousness of your literary decadent has its counterpart in the violence of the political anarchist. Each is the alter-ego maniac of the other. The one works with the quill, the other with the bomb.[3]

Making a connection between sexual liberty, feminism and revolution is not peculiar to 'nineties reactionaries. Nor is it without historical foundation. For the periods when freedom of sexual relations and equality for women have emerged as real possibilities have always been those of revolution or near revolution. 'It is a curious fact', remarked Engels, 'that with every great revolutionary movement the question of 'free love' comes into the foreground.'[4] During the seventeenth century many Puritan sects, in particular the Ranters, were committed to equality for women. For them it was an integral part of the 'priesthood of all believers'.[5] Free love, too, was practised for a short time by several sects, although this was stamped out by the 'gloomy Puritanism' which set in after 1660. But during the early days of the English Revolution it really looked as though equality for women and free sexual relations might be incorporated into a new vision of society.[6] The question of women's rights was repeatedly raised by women in France after 1789. They argued that 'the rights of man' must include equal rights for women and pointed out to the Assembly that:

You have destroyed all the prejudices of the past, but you allow the oldest and the most pervasive to remain, which excludes from office, position and honour, and above all from the right of sitting amongst you, half the inhabitants of the kingdom.[7]

It was no accident that Mary Wollstonecraft's *Vindication of the Rights of Woman* appeared in 1792 when she and other English radicals were fired by the ideals of the French Revolution.

In 1848 and again during the Paris Commune the issue of women's rights re-emerged, and women once more played an important part in major political struggles.[8] In the early years of the Russian Revolution abortion was legalized, divorce was by mutual consent and collective child-rearing schemes were introduced. And now in China, women's lives are being transformed beyond anything anyone could have imagined before 1947. Revolution and the real possibility of women's liberation have always gone hand in hand.

In 1848 the crop of would-be revolutions in Europe coincided with the remnants of Chartist agitation at home, and triggered off in the English ruling class a milder version of the panic which greeted 1789. *Jane Eyre* was received in this climate of political paranoia and reviewers made the same connection between Charlotte Brontë's feminism and revolution that Stutfield and others made again in the 'nineties. Responses to *Jane Eyre* were political in exactly the way that responses to Hardy and Egerton were political. For example, in her now notorious review for *The Quarterly Review* Lady Eastlake said:

We do not hesitate to say that the tone of mind and thought which has overthrown authority and violated every code human and divine abroad, and fostered Chartism and rebellion at home, is the same which has also written *Jane Eyre*.[9]

It certainly was not any specific political allegiance of the feminists which sparked off these fears. Charlotte Brontë was a staunch Tory, and in 1914 the WSPU calmly swopped feminism for anti-German propaganda. Only Sylvia Pankhurst's East London Federation was working-class and socialist. What disturbed their opponents was the emphasis in feminism on the rights of women as individuals when these rights openly clashed with the needs and demands of the family. In the case of women, liberal individualism was clearly at variance with traditional patterns of authority and social organization. So when feminists refused to 'know their place' and would not stay in it when it was pointed out to them, this individualism was neatly turned on its head. For a man to assert his rights was perfectly acceptable and legitimate. When a woman tried it she was accused of selfishness or self-indulgence.

Mrs Humphry Ward's novels are a useful guide to this kind of conservative reaction. The plots of *Marcella* (1894) and *Delia Blanchflower* (1916) are designed to prove that feminism is dangerous and that women's demands for freedom are pure selfishness. She does this by opposing, in a crude and obvious way, what she sees as the destructiveness of feminist individualism and the values of conservative paternalism. She believes that reform and progress are the responsibility of progressive members of the upper class – to be more specific, model Tory landowners – and in the novels we see these rare creatures looking after the interests of their tenants and their womenfolk. These respond with a suitable degree of deference and respect. The feminist heroines on the other hand, cause friction and unhappiness in personal relationships, to say nothing of 'murmurings' among the local agricultural labourers. But they are eventually converted back to Reason by the handsome Tory landowners, and are finally convinced that the situation of both women and the poor can only be improved through paternalism and charity.

It is significant that Mrs Humphry Ward's novels are always

set in an implausible, idealized rural England where the cosy conservative image of a golden past of semi-feudal relations could flourish. She makes no attempt to adapt her vision of reform by a benevolent aristocracy to modern urban society. But implausible or not, the heroines learn to accept this conception of social relations. Delia for example, once her dangerous feminist ideas have been quelled, miraculously realizes the virtues of 'traditional' English rural life:

how beautiful this common human life seemed that evening – after all the fierce imaginings in which she had lived so long! In the great towns beyond the hills women were still starved and sweated – still enslaved and degraded. Man no doubt was still the stupid and vicious tyrant, the Man-Beast ...

But, we learn, none of this matters any more, not now that she loves Winnington (the local squire) and has undergone a conversion:

Here in this large English village, how the old primal relations stood out! Sorrow-laden and sin stained often, yet how touching, how worthy, in the main, of reverence and tenderness! As they went in and out of the cottages of her father's estate, the cottages where Winnington was at home, and she a stranger, all that 'other side' of any great argument began to speak to her – without words. The world of politics and its machinery, how far away! – instead the world of human need, and love, and suffering unveiled itself this winter evening to Delia's soul, and spoke to her in a new language ...[10]

She gives up the suffrage struggle and accepts in its place Winnington's idea of women as dispensers of charity, 'doing the little things – which make just all the difference'. (p. 265)

The attack on individualism is even clearer in Eliza Lynn Linton. We have already met her denouncing feminism as early as the 'sixties and again in the 'nineties, so it is hardly surprising to find that anti-feminism is the mainspring of several of her novels. In *The New Woman in Haste and in Leisure* (1895) she makes her central character, Phoebe Barrington, into a monster of egoism and vanity. Phoebe's arguments for independence are made a transparent cover for self-indulgence, and it emerges that all she really wants is freedom from all duties and social obligations. She is a malicious parody of feminism, intended to discredit the movement she supposedly represents. She wants to be

... what all these ladies were – absolutely free from any kind of disciplinary control, whether of duty or sex, domestic authority or social law – what a splendid existence! To be the unquestioned mistress of her own time, of her own actions, of her morals, her habits, her self; to own no obedience, no consideration to husband or mother – no self-restraint because of her child; to throw all her energy into that unchecked will which, with her and those wrong headed moralists went by the name of self-development, and to make this the sole object of her life ...[11]

Phoebe's political allies are sinister anarchists – 'whatever made for lawlessness and disorder they upheld; whatever conduced to law and order they condemned' – (p. 108); and her attempts to preach the feminist gospel in yet another version of the ideal English rural community are a disaster – like Delia Blanchflower she triggers off disrespect among the poor and disrupts family relationships.

Individualism then, when applied to and by women, was politically dangerous. But another important strand in the counter-attack against feminism stemmed from a more specific anxiety – about moral decadence. It was widely believed at this time that moral and martial valour were closely linked, so when the whole character of English culture seemed in the 'eighties and 'nineties to be moving rapidly into a more permissive era (Ibsen, Wagner, Wilde, feminism, socialism), widespread anxieties about the supposedly declining 'moral fibre' of the nation combined with fears about Britain's ability to defend the Empire. These essentially imperialist alarms gained momentum with the humiliations of the Boer War and culminated in the invasion scares of the years immediately before 1914.[12]

As an imperialist power under the twin pressures of economic competition and the possibility of nationalist risings in the colonies, Britain depended for its sense of security on a large and effective standing army. But it was widely supposed that the British working class was in such poor physical shape that the army and the Empire could collapse if it came to a large-scale war. There was undoubtedly some basis for this particular worry as *laissez-faire* capitalism still had not progressed much beyond public drainage, and substantial sections of the working class still lived in appalling housing conditions and worked long hours in unsafe, unhealthy jobs for pathetically low wages. Given these conditions, it is hardly surprising to find that large numbers of recruits were found unfit for military service. The government was so disturbed at this that it set up a special commission of enquiry – The Interdepartmental Committee on Physical Deterioration – which reported in 1904. (Incidentally, it is in this context that we should see the grudging efforts of the 1906 Liberal government to provide a degree of state assistance to working-class mothers.)

But the problem was not seen simply as one of manpower and physical fitness. It was also a common assumption that certain sections of the ruling class were becoming morally unfit to govern. The special flavour of 'nineties culture was blamed for this moral and psychological decline. A really remarkable book, Max Nordau's *Degeneration* (1895) is a fascinating guide to this corrupting world of late nineteenth-century art and literature. Wagner, Ibsen, the pre-Raphaelites, Symbolism, Tolstoy, Nietzche and Zola – they are all there and they are all dangerous subversives, burrowing away at the foundations of the British Empire. The book was a best-seller.

These are the ideas surrounding Stutfield's 'tommyrotics' article. His attack on 'nineties fiction is apparently on moral grounds, but his anxieties are really nationalist and racial; for him the 'foulness and hysteria' of modern literature are dangerous because they undermine traditional British virtues:

Hysteria, whether in politics or Art, has the same inevitable effect of sapping manliness and making people flabby. To the aesthete and the decadent, who worship inaction, all strenuousness is naturally repugnant.[13]

Another popular book, this time attacking birth control, was based on the same kind of politics. R. Ussher's bogey in *Neo-Malthusianism* (1898) is underpopulation and the possibility of 'racial decline'. Pointing to the awful example of France where, according to him, contraception had cut the population to a dangerously low level, he asserts that the practice of birth control in England will destroy all that is best in British life. 'Signs are showing that France is nearing a precipice,' he says, 'and if English women don't do their duty, England may well follow her over it.'[14] And if,

Neo-Malthusianism, which is destroying the French people, should extend to the other races which now form the front rank of civilization, they will run the risk some day of being supplanted by the less civilized peoples ... [and] these nations will pour in multitudes upon the effete and dwindling races of the West.[15]

He goes on to criticize novelists who dared to suggest that women should have a right to choose whether or not to have children. He wants to counteract 'the flippant, vulgar and unnatural Englishwomen writers of the day' who 'describe as a "propagating drudge"' women fulfilling what he chooses to call 'the scared tie of motherhood'. In the name of 'the Nation' he calls for 'healthy homes in all senses of the word, healthy sons and daughters'. 'Despise these,' he says, 'and a cataclysm will come.'[16]

These then are the forms in which the opposition to feminism and sexual freedom appeared. Imperial anxieties about race, the manliness of the nation and the declining birth rate became more, not less, pronounced in the early years of the twentieth century. They tended to influence writers away from feminism and towards a mystique of motherhood which subordinated women's real needs and rights to eugenicist concepts of breeding and childrearing. In terms of institutionalized moves against pro-feminist or sexually suspect literature, the 'nineties and the pre-war years saw an intensification of state censorship and an increase in the number of private prosecutions mounted against individuals. Vizetelly was tried and imprisoned in 1889; Oscar Wilde in 1895. Havelock Ellis's work was suppressed in 1897 and a whole series of novels was banned in the opening years of the new century: Eleanor Glyn's *Three Weeks* in 1807, Hubert Wales's *The Yoke* in 1908, and the English translation of Hermann Sudermann's *Song of Songs* in 1910. *The Rainbow* was suppressed in 1915.[17] An energetic campaign was mounted against H.G. Wells when *Ann Veronica* came out in 1909 (see p. 23), and in the same year the Lord Chamberlain's office produced a string of ludicrous decisions against various plays.[18] Shaw's *Mrs. Warren's Profession*, for instance, though written in 1894, could not get a licence for public performance until 1925. There was also an attempt, instigated by the National Purity League – an offshoot of the ever vigilant NVA

– to introduce censorship procedures into the new public library system. In fact the literary challenge to sexual and moral norms, so far from being gradually accepted at the beginning of the new century, met with increasing hostility. For, in the words of a historian,

> There was obviously a good deal more at stake in these questions than simply the right attitude towards sex; the answers, one way or the other, implied ideas about the relation between the public and their rulers, about the place of women in society, about the morality of monogamous marriage, about the role of education in society. A revolution in the public attitude towards sex seemed to the conservative mind to threaten larger and even more sinister revolutions, and they consequently set about a counter-revolution.[19]

THE NOVELISTS

Attacks on feminism, and expressions of outrage at the appearance of sex in literature, were not confined to the daily and periodical press. A number of novelists shared popular fears about free women and freer sex and attempted to counter both feminism and sexual permissiveness. The fictional backlash produced distortions and caricatures of feminism and tried to boost the old images of virgin, wife and mother. This reaction is crude and easily identifiable in popular middle-class writers like Mrs Humphry Ward, but it is there in more important writers as well. Gissing and James both share it, and it permeates their work.

Mrs Oliphant, who was convinced that Hardy was intriguing with what she called an 'anti-marriage league' when he wrote *Jude*, provides us with a useful guide to what she and others like her found objectionable about 'nineties fiction. Her chief complaint is that Hardy, Grant Allen and the rest, insist on describing 'what is now fully discussed as the physical part of the question'.[20] This, she says, is 'immoral and contrary to good manners', as it 'fixes the thoughts upon one subject, and on that subject which has been proved to be the most damaging in the world as a subject for thought and for the exercise of the imagination'.[21] (She means sex, though she manages to avoid actually saying so.) Stutfield has precisely the same objection:

The physiological excursions of our writers of neuropathic fiction are usually confined to one field – that of sex. Their chief delight seems to be in making their characters discuss matters which would not have been tolerated in the novels of a decade ago. Emancipated woman in particular loves to show her independence by dealing freely with the relations of the sexes. Hence all the prating of passion, animalism, 'the natural workings of sex', and so forth, with which we are nauseated. Most of the characters in these books seem to be erotomaniacs.

And as for the 'new woman', she is,

a victim of the univeral passion for learning and 'culture', which when ill-digested, are apt to cause intellectual dyspepsia. With her head full of all the 'ologies and 'isms, with sex problems and heredity, and other gleanings from the surgery and the lecture-room, there is no space left for humour, and her novels are for the most part, merely pamphlets, sermons, or treatises in disguise.[22]

This then is the frame of reference within which the reactionary novelists wrote, and by and large they depict the would-be emancipated women as a compendium of all the moral and intellectual vices Stutfield enumerates with such relish. Mrs Lynn Linton for instance, although she was herself independent and self-supporting, still sees the emancipated woman in just this light. In her eyes she is 'aggressive, disturbing, efficious, unquiet, rebellious to authority and tyrannous ... the most unlovely specimen the sex has yet produced'.[23] She and other novelists caricature her as harsh, sexless and aggressive; in their work she is an ugly or unattractive female who is badly dressed, neurotic, or lesbian. Her desire for freedom is an 'unnatural' rejection of her 'true womanly nature' which is really, underneath it all, submissive, self-effacing, self-sacrificing. 'A woman's own fame is barren', says Mrs Lynn Linton. 'It begins and ends with herself. Reflected from her husband or her son, it has in it the glory of immortality.'[24] In the anti-feminist novels, any departure from this formula is to all intents and purposes little short of a sexual perversion.

Gertrude Marvell, the suffragette demon who leads the heroine astray in *Delia Blanchflower*, Phoebe Barrington, Moore's Celia in *A Drama in Muslin* and Wells's spiteful portrait of Miss Miniver in *Ann Veronica* all share one or more of the standard failings or vices feminists were supposed to have.

And where the heroines in these novels deviate from the paths of true womanhood we learn that they are 'misguided', 'led astray' or influenced against their 'real natures' in spite of their 'better judgment'. Another favourite device is to 'explain' the otherwise irrational and incomprehensible behaviour of the feminist or suffragette by a matrimonial 'disappointment'. Two of Mrs Humphry Ward's termagents are victims of this particular rationalization. One of them has been 'greatly embittered' by a 'disappointment' and for the other, 'the processions and the crowded London meetings, and the window-breaking riots into which she had been led while staying with a friend, had been the solace and relief of a personal rancour and misery she might else have found intolerable'.[25]

The modest wife and the pure young virgin also figure prominently in this reactionary fiction. They are foils to the feminist viragos and through them we are continually being reminded that 'sweet and lovely women who honour their womanhood and fulfil its noblest ideals' still exist.[26] Carefully constructed as models of female virtue, they are exhibited for our admiration and emulation.

GEORGE GISSING

Gissing is one of the leading advocates of this 'sweet and lovely' ideal. But his novels are considerably more complex than any casual association of his work with the oversimplified arguments of Mrs Humphry Ward or Eliza Lynn Linton might suggest. One of the new school of realists he was determined to write honestly about the world as he saw it, and he never shied away from things which shocked or distressed the squeamish. But at the same time he was also a highly subjective writer, seldom able to distance himself from his largely autobiographical material and so achieve the control or clarity of the major realists. Partially digested fragments of his life and experience distort or at least determine the shape and content of his work. In particular he used his novels to examine and re-examine his own relationships with women.

The biographies disagree about the reasons for it, but one thing about Gissing is abundantly clear – he made two disasterous marriages with women whose class and education made them totally unsuited to him. In both cases their domestic incompetence and their intellectual and emotional incompatibility with his own personality drove him to leave them. So it is hardly surprising that we should find in his novels thinly disguised self-portraits of the author either as a struggling young writer dragged down by a selfish and unsympathetic wife (Reardon in *New Grub Street* (1891)), or as a long-suffering husband tied for life to an incompetent shrew (*The Whirlpool* (1897), *In the Year of Jubilee* (1894)).

The men in the novels are essentially weak; they are too gentle and yielding to fight back at their tormentors. Gissing is rather like Hardy is this respect – the men being pallid, often poorly characterized figures, while the women are highly individualized, full of energy and utterly convincing. (Quite the reverse of the orthodox stereotype in fact.) But the defeated men and the shrewish women are too repetitive. They are more a symptom of Gissing's own experience than a balanced attempt to explore sexual relationships. In fact, whether he is attacking women or idealizing them, we have to recognize that Gissing emerges from a reading of the novels as a misogynist. For this reason it is often difficult to distinguish between some of the more thoughtful and valid criticisms he makes about the way women are conditioned by social pressures into behaving as they do, and his own personal bitterness, which pushed him all the time towards dismissing all women as hopelessly trivial and destructive. Yet if we look chronologically at Gissing's novels, a pattern does emerge. It is in the earlier works that he is more likely to support the idea of education and emancipation for women, in the later ones that he firmly adopts the traditional ideal of women solely as wife and mother, the centre of home and family. The most convenient way to treat the problem of the conflicting ideas of women in the novels is, however, to discuss them separately rather than chronologically. For though his essentially reactionary ideal of womanhood appears in some form in most of the novels, it is important to see this in the perspective of his insights into the situation of women in society as a whole. This must come first.

Gissing's most useful contribution to a different and more

truthful portrayal of women is probably his treatment of marriage, which is not dissimilar from Hardy's in *Jude*. During the 'nineties there was a flood of 'marriage problem' novels.[27] Gissing was only one of many here, but his relentless anti-romantic approach places him at the forefront of the decade's attacks on marriage as an institution. The only happy marriages in Gissing are absurdly idealized and unconvincing – they never serve as a point of interest in themselves, but are there solely to provide a contrast to the intolerable wedded unhappiness of the central figures. In the novels, happiness in marriage comes to 'one in a thousand',[28] and the unhappiness is usually caused by the women. Arthur Peachey, one of Gissing's galaxy of long-suffering husbands, thinks for example that in 'his rank of life',

> Married happiness was a rare thing, and the fault could generally be traced to wives who had no sense of responsibility, no understanding of household duties, no love of simple pleasures, no religion.[29]

Like Gissing before him, Arthur finally walks out, taking his child with him. But the wives do not always succeed in driving the husbands away from home. Through their unreasonable financial demands, selfishness or stupidity, they and their daughters quite often wear away all resistance in the wretched husband, and turn him into a human work-horse. He toils away at the business of making money while the women, far from providing that retreat from the sordid cares of the world, swallow up his earnings, and more, in a thoughtless round of extravagance. Gissing's outstanding workhorses are 'the money-making machine known as Mr. Leach' in *The Whirlpool*, Denyer in *The Emancipated* (1890) and Morgan in *The Year of Jubilee*. We get closest to Morgan who has, in desperation, sunk to the humiliations of debt collecting:

> The occupation revolted him, but at present he saw no other way of supporting the genteel appearances – he knew not why – which were indispensable to his life. He subsisted like a bird of prey; he was ever on the look out for carrion which the law permitted him to seize ... Sometimes a whole day of inconceivably sordid toil resulted in the poaching of a few pence; sometimes his reward was a substantial sum ... The genteel family knew nothing of these expedients. (*Jubilee*, p. 220)

Mr Leach finds he cannot afford to commute to London daily so chooses instead the cheaper and more peaceful expedient of spending the week in a disused room in the building where he works. But at least he goes home at weekends. Denyer is never at home. He spends his time travelling round the world looking out for likely business opportunities. From time to time he drops in on his genteel family, who lodge in comfort in Italy, to warn them of impending financial doom and of the necessity of retrenching. Gissing describes him on one of these fleeting visits, comparing his appearance with the sleek, well-groomed turn-out of his women:

He looked at his boots, which had just been blackened, but were shabby, and then glanced at the elegant skirts of his wife and daughters; he looked at his shirt-cuffs which were clean but frayed, and then gathered courage to lift his eyes as far as the dainty hands folded upon laps in a show of patience.[30]

It hardly needs pointing out that in all these passages Gissing's sympathies are unambiguously with the husband.

Far from idealizing women in their domestic role then, Gissing exposed what he had experienced as their irresponsible neglect of husband and children, their frequent inability to perform even the slightest of household tasks (the married women in the novels can seldom 'manage' the servants), and their absorption in mindless pastimes. These are usually an addiction to third-rate fiction or a trivial concern with dress and fashion. Ada Peachey's reading habits, for example, correspond exactly to the taste of the 'quarter-educated' sneered at by Gissing in *New Grub Street*:

On tables and chairs lay scattered a multitude of papers: illustrated weeklies, journals of society, cheap miscellanies, penny novelettes, and the like. At the end of the week, when new numbers came in, Ada Peachey passed many hours upon her sofa, reading instalments of a dozen serial stories, paragraphs relating to fashion, sport, theatre, answers to correspondents (wherein she especially delighted), columns of facetiae, and gossip about notorious people. (*Jubilee*, p. 5)

Miserable marriages in the novels are usually caused by the ignorance and folly of women like Ada. But not always. Gissing often blames bourgeois society itself for what happens to his marriage partners. Many of his young couples are either prevented from marrying at all because the man has too small an income to support an 'establishment' or, having married, they are so hard pressed for money that what might have been a workable relationship collapses under the strain.[31] This is the root of Reardon's problems in *New Grub Street*. Gissing's characters, caught up in the middle-class idea of marriage as a contract based on achieved wealth and status, are continually faced with a choice between unwelcome celibacy, a long, wearing engagement or marriage with poverty. One of his wretched bachelors sums up this typical dilemma:

'We're neither of us young any longer; we've lost the best part of our lives. And all for what? Because we hadn't money enough to take a house three times bigger than we needed! Two lives wasted because we couldn't feed fifty other people for whom we didn't care a damn! Doesn't it come to that' (*Whirlpool*, p. 219)

This is a situation Gissing understood only too well. It recurrs in many of his novels and again stems from his own experiences. Too poor to marry 'well', Gissing married where he could.

Gissing is appalled by the delays and unhappiness which accompanied the financial restrictions on respectable middle-class marriage. But he is equally emphatic about the absurdities of romantic love and the 'runaway' match, so that marriages based on a sudden romantic passion end as miserably as those plagued by incompetent wives or hard-up husbands. For example, he is heavily ironic about Cecily's dewy-eyed optimism in *The Emancipated*. After making a runaway marriage with a plausible scoundrel, she is confident that love is all and that love will last. In the diary she keeps at the time of her marriage she writes that 'my husband loves me, and I believe his love incapable of receiving a soil' (p. 200) and, a few pages earlier on, that 'it may not be true for everyone, but for me to love and be loved, infinitely, with the love that conquers everything, is the end of life'. (p. 217) When her husband's love rapidly collapses into boredom and adultery Cecily has no choice; she has to go on living with a man who is repeatedly unfaithful to her. She has no chance of divorcing him because, as we have seen, the law did not allow a wife to divorce her husband for 'simple adultery'. Unfortunately, Gissing neatly kills the husband in the last chapter of the novel, and in thus freeing Cecily to try again effectively weakens his comments on romantic love and the divorce laws. But in spite of this conventionalized ending, his general position remains clear enough.

A more interesting and more unusual cause of marital unhappiness appears in *The Odd Women* (1893). This is the overbearing and domineering attitude of the husband. The book is devoted almost entirely to examining women's problems of marriage and spinsterhood, financial dependence and lack of employment opportunities – all the major concerns of the emancipation movement in fact. Monica Madden marries the old and singularly unattractive Widdowson simply because he can offer her a way out of what looks like becoming a life-time of stultifying, low-paid work as a draper's assistant. Given that her spinster sisters are always before her, a terrible reminder of what she herself could become, and that Monica herself is very immature when she meets Widdowson, her decision to go ahead and marry him is a realistic if unattractive resolution of her problems. The marriage collapses because of Widdowson's ferocious jealousy, which makes him keep Monica mewed up in claustrophobic seclusion where he can always keep close watch over her. His possessive, over-protective paternalism is suffocating:

His devotion to her proved itself in a thousand ways: week after week he grew, if anything, more kind, more tender; yet in his view of their relations he was unconsciously the most complete despot, a monument of male autocracy. Never had it occurred to Widdowson that a wife remains an individual, with rights and obligations independent of her wifely condition.[32]

He even recommends that Monica read what Ruskin had to say about women. He hopes in this way to instill in her a proper understanding of his idea of wifely duty and submission:

'Women's sphere is in the home Monica. Unfortunately girls are often obliged to go out and earn their living, but this is unnatural, a necessity which advanced civilization will altogether abolish. You shall read John Ruskin; every word he says about women is good and precious. If a woman can neither have a home of her own, nor find occupation in any one else's she is deeply to be pitied; her life is bound to be unhappy. I sincerely believe that an educated woman had better become a domestic servant than try to imitate the life of man.' (p. 153)[33]

Monica, quite rightly, cannot take all this; she runs away, but finally dies as an indirect result of her husband's tyranny.

The emphasis on male chauvinism in *The Odd Women* is unusual in Gissing's work. He generally concentrates on castigating female vanities and ignorance. In a letter to his sister, Ellen, dated 1882, he states that the 'pigheadedness, ignorance and incapacity of women' is the cause of great misery, but, more important, that this is the result of their trivial education. He looks forward, therefore, to the improvements 'all these new opportunities for mental and moral training' will bring about, and he is confident that women can become 'better'.[34] He stresses the importance of improved education and opportunities for women in *Born in Exile*:

The defect of the female mind? It is my belief that this is nothing more nor less than the defect of the uneducated human mind. I believe most men among the brutally ignorant exhibit the very faults which are cried out upon as exclusively feminine. A woman has hitherto been an ignorant human being; that explains everything.[35]

But for all his expressed belief in the educability of women, Gissing devotes the greater part of his fiction and his creative energy to exposing and attacking 'the defects of the female mind'. This produced a frightening number of selfish, egotistical, pretentious or ignorant women who are poles apart from the conventional ideal. Ada Peachey and her sisters are typical examples. Wholly destructive and utterly selfish, Gissing paints them as black as he can. At one point in the novel (*In the Year of Jubilee*) two of the sisters actually fight together and Gissing describes them with all the contempt he can muster:

Now indeed the last trace of veneer was gone, the last rag of pseudo civilization was rent off these young women; in physical conflict, vilifying each other like the female spawn of Whitechapel they revealed themselves as born – raw material which the mill of education is supposed to convert into middle-class young ladyhood. (p. 253)

Even if Gissing goes further here than usual, we can find

passages very like this one in almost any of his novels. I find them very ambiguous, in the same way that Gissing's overall attitude to women is ambiguous. There is no doubt about what he thinks of the Peachey sisters – he regards them almost as another species from himself; they are sub-human, 'spawn' who will always be inferior to his own class. The ambiguity does not lie here. The problem is rather how this new yet very unfair way of writing about women relates to the old fictional ideal. Gissing attacks the mystique which had surrounded women and marriage in the novel, but he does so by elaborating a new but misogynist stereotype.

The same process is at work in *The Emancipated*, where we find another trio of sisters, the Denyer girls. They are another anti-feminist type which we find creeping into the novel in the 'nineties as a corrective to the 'new woman'. The Denyer sisters regard themselves as emancipated intellectuals, when they are in fact merely ignorant and pretentious. Here for instance is Madelaine's academic armoury:

French she had read passably; German she had talked so much of studying that it was her belief she had acquired it; Greek and Latin were not indeed linguistically known to her – one must pick one's phrases in speaking of Madelaine – but from modern essayists who wrote in the flamboyant style she had gathered so much knowledge of these literatures as to be able to discourse of them with a very fluent inaccuracy. With all schools of painting she was, of course, quite familiar; the great masters – vaguely known – interested her but moderately, and to praise them was to subject yourself in her eyes to a suspicion of phillistinism. From her preceptors in this sphere, she had learnt certain names, old and new, which stood for more exquisite virtues, and the frequent mention of them with a happy vagueness made her conversation very impressive to the generality of people. (p. 75)

Gissing's harsh judgment of the Denyer girls is part of his exploration in the novel of what 'emancipation' really means. The conclusion he comes to here, in *In The Year of the Jubilee*, and in *The Whirlpool* is that there can be no real independence for women without responsibility, self-knowledge and self-discipline – the old liberty and licence chestnut in fact. Although he believes in education for women, it must be education of the right kind, and he will have nothing to do with women's individualistic demands for self-fulfilment. As far as he is concerned, this is merely selfishness and will lead to a rupture in the 'natural' relationship between man and wife. Quite contradictorily, given what Gissing usually has to say about marriage, it is this relationship which is made in the novels to incorporate the love and sympathy he himself valued and searched for all his life. Thus it is that alongside the shallow, aggressive women and the down-trodden men in the fiction, we increasingly find as points of comparison, unconvincing, 'ideal' marriages.

But before he hardened into this position in the later novels, Gissing wrote *The Odd Women*. It is his most impersonal and finely controlled work and it clearly sets out the needs and rights of women – the need for economic independence, the right to work and to the self-respect work brings a single woman. I have already discussed the fate of Monica Madden, who married for money, security, and an escape from poverty. She represents in the novel the slim chance, the unrealistic hope of finding a husband – a hope to which the genteel girl of middle-class family, left penniless by an improvident or unfortunate parent, usually clung. Alice and Virginia, her spinster sisters, are much more distressing figures; they have none of Monica's modicum of resourcefulness or common sense; they work in arduous low-paid jobs as teachers or governesses; they are worn out emotionally and physically by the time they reach early middle-age. Virginia finds her life of loneliness and genteel poverty, always having to keep up appearances, so intolerable that she takes to drink. Alice manages to keep on working, but is broken in health and spirits. Both sisters can only survive at all through their pathetic belief that they will one day start a school together in their home town. This they will clearly never do.

In complete contrast to the two tragically pathetic Madden sisters is Rhoda Nunn. She also is single (her surname is deliberate), is in her thirties and apparently has no chance of marriage. But she is energetic, resourceful and determined to win for herself and for other single women self-respect and a useful place in society – emancipation if not liberation. She and a friend run a small business school which trains girls for work in commerce and encourages them to be independent. The school is a hot-bed of feminist ideas and, at this stage, Gissing is not unsympathetic to them. But he does have reservations about Rhoda, who deliberately encourages and then dismisses an attractive and eligible suitor:

> Offer what he might, she could not accept it; but the secret chagrin that was upon her would be removed. Love would no longer be the privilege of other women. To reject a lover in so many respects desirable, whom so many women might envy her, would fortify her self-esteem, and enable her to go forward in the chosen path with a firmer tread. (p. 148)

Gissing cannot accept that a woman might actually be indifferent to the idea of marriage, and so he implants in Rhoda a secret jealousy of those women who have succeeded in attracting a lover. He makes her both arrogant about love and peculiarly vulnerable to it when it comes along. But he is equally censorious of Rhoda's suitor, Barfoot. Barfoot is a skilful and surprisingly honest study of male sexual vanity, similar in conception to Meredith's Sir Willoughby Patterne in *The Egoist*. Barfoot's interest in Rhoda stems from his desire to subdue and humiliate her; he is affronted by her independence and he is determined to prove to her that she cannot exist, as she wants to, without love and a man. Attracted by her independence, he wants to crush it:

> The keener her suffering the sooner her submission. Oh, but the submission should be perfect! ... He had seen her in many moods, but not yet in the anguish of broken pride. She must shed tears before him, declare her spirit worn and subjugated by a torrent of jealousy and fear. Then he would raise her, and seat her in the place of honour, and fall down at her feet, and fill her soul with rapture. (p. 279)

He 'must have the joy of subduing her to his will'. (p. 265)

Both Rhoda and Barfoot then, are criticized because they approach love in a spirit of levity and pride. But where Rhoda comes to love with deep feeling, Barfoot quickly consoles himself after the failure of their relationship by marrying another girl – one who is flattering enough to appreciate him without any reservations. Rhoda is evidently the superior person. But it is interesting that a disproportionate amount of space is given over to Rhoda's love-life – which suggests that Gissing still saw the emotional area of a woman's life as the most important and significant.

Rhoda is not Gissing's final version or ideal of womanhood.

In *In the Year of Jubilee*, published only a year after *The Odd Women*, and in *The Whirlpool* (1897) he went some way towards resolving some of the contradictions about women and feminism which are always present in his work. But he did so through adopting the traditional image of women as the focus of domestic peace and comfort. In these later novels, much greater emphasis is laid on this essentially sentimentalized version of marriage and home life. But the idealized couples or families he makes use of fall far short, in force and interest, of the depressing yet utterly convincing reality of the ill-assorted marriage partners. These continue to dominate the foreground of the novels. For this reason the novels are increasingly disjointed or broken-backed, the fiction suffering as much as its author did in his private life from the failure to reconcile image and reality.

The domestic dream and the idealized wife play a characteristically contradictory role in Gissing's work. They are partly used as vehicles for his criticism of what he saw as the selfish, empty-headed, incompetent women mass-produced by poor education and a society which regarded women as innately trivial or inferior. But, like Dickens before him, Gissing goes further than this. They are also used in an indictment of the would-be emancipated woman who attempts to throw off the oppression of existing social or sexual relations. It is at this point that Gissing joins more explicitly anti-feminist writers such as Eliza Lynn Linton or Mrs Humphry Ward. This is especially true of the later novels where the struggle for freedom has become futile in his eyes. But it has also become dangerous. For example, Alma in *The Whirlpool* destroys herself and her friends through her determination to be independent. At the beginning of the novel her husband is a tolerant man who wants to allow Alma a degree of freedom within their marriage. But he learns that given the 'unchangeable', 'unstable' nature of women, such freedom is impossible. He retreats into a benevolent paternalism, though not in time to prevent his wayward wife from committing suicide. In this novel Gissing even uses conventional female stereotypes as a stick to beat women who have intellectual ambitions, so that the Gissing who supports the idea of women benefiting from a useful education in *The Odd Women* has turned, a year later, into the tough opponent of higher education for women we find in *In The Year of the Jubilee*. Here we discover Jessica Morgan, an unstable, neurotic girl whose determination to pass various examinations ruins her health and, in a mysterious way which is hard to follow, her moral nature. To become a B.A.,

... to have her name in the newspapers, to be regarded as one of the clever, the uncommon women – for this Jessica was willing to labour early and late, regardless of failing health, regardless even of ruined complexion and hair that grew thin between the comb. (p. 17)

Gissing gives Jessica a nervous breakdown from which she never fully recovers.

To find out exactly what kind of creature Gissing's ideal woman was, we can turn to his critical book on Dickens. Here he claims that:

If Dickens were now writing, I believe he would have to add to his representative women the well-dressed shrew who proceeds on the slightest provocation from fury of language to violence of act ... Nowadays these ladies would enjoy a very much larger life, would systematically neglect their children (if they chose to have any), and would soothe their nerves, in moments carefully chosen, by flinging at the remonstrant husband any domestic object to which they attached no special value. (*Charles Dickens*, p. 135)

To put this feminist shrew in her place Gissing proposes a revival of the Dickens heroine – all blushes, innocence and domesticity:

Truth to tell it was no bad ideal. Granted that the world must go on very much in the old way, that children must be born and looked after, that dinners must be cooked, that houses must be kept sweet, it is hard to see how Ruth Pinch can ever be supplanted. Ruth is no imbecile – your thoroughly kind-hearted and home-loving woman never will be; with opportunities, she would learn much, even beyond domestic limits, and still would delight in her dainty little aprons, her pastryboard and roller. Ruth would be an excellent mother; when in the latter days she sat greyhaired and spectacled, surely would her children arise and call her blessed. A very homely little woman, to be sure. She could not be quite comfortable with domestics at her command; a little maid for the little babies – this is her dream. But never, within those walls, a sound of complaining or of strife, never a wry face, acidly discontented with the husband's doing or saying. Upon my word – is it a bad ideal? (p. 161)

The similarity to Dickens and to Ruskin is striking, particularly the longing for a home which is essentially a retreat, a barrier between himself and the stresses of the outside world. As usual women are kept firmly on the domestic side of the fortifications.

The homely wife is used by Gissing in novel after novel, and the formula is always the same. Here she is in *The Whirlpool*:

> Mrs. Morton had the beauty of perfect health, of health mental and physical. To describe her face as homely was to pay it the highest compliment, for its smile was the true light of home that never failed ... She rose early; she slept early; and her day was full of manifold activity. Four children she had borne ... and it seemed to her no merit that in these little ones she saw the end and reason of her being. Into her pure and healthy mind had never entered a thought in conflict with motherhood. Her breasts were the fountain of life; her babies clung to them and grew large of limb. From her they learnt to speak; from her they learnt the names of trees and flowers and all things beautiful around them; learnt too, less by precept than from fair example, the sweetness and sincerity wherewith such mothers, and such alone, can endow their off-spring ... By method and good will she found time for everything, ruling her house and ordering her life so admirably, that to those who saw her only in hours of leisure she seemed to be at leisure always. She would have felt it an impossible thing to abandon her children to the care of servants. (*Whirlpool*, p. 328)

Gissing's domestic saint is worth emphasizing because she is carefully assembled from practically every available component of the dominant stereotype. She is virtuous, industrious, selfless and homely. She is inexhaustibly fecund and is completely fulfilled by her exclusively domestic role. But her contradictory co-existence alongside the numerous selfish, unfeeling and thoroughly unpleasant women who form the central focus of so many of the novels does point to a genuine conflict between ideology and reality. It was a conflict which Gissing could never resolve.

HENRY JAMES

If in Gissing we meet a sharp clash between reality and a desired ideal, in James we meet pure ideology and an anti-feminism so subtle and fused so completely with the form and texture of the novels that it can be overlooked altogether. His hostility operates at such a sophisticated level, and enters so closely into the fabric of his thought that it becomes all pervasive yet invisible. Ultimately his artistic control is so complete that the reader is tricked into accepting the unacceptable.

James's whole approach to experience and the recording of experience intervenes between the reader and his or her assessment of the values and assumptions of the Jamesian world. Dealing always with the highly organized, refined and sensitive consciousness, with the private inner world of the intelligent and the articulate, James appears to be so concerned with the particular individual, with the unique response to experience, that generalizations about his choice and representation of situations seem irrelevant and arbitrary. And the critic who tries to grasp and assess James in terms of social typicality, asking how far the experience and consciousness of the Jamesian world measure up to the way life is actually lived, is likely to feel like a bull in a china shop, trampling on James's sensitive network of relationships and his subtle moral schema. This problem is complicated even further by the way James's characters live in a kind of material vacuum. Not that they or James are unmaterialistic. Rather the leisure, ease and freedom which wealth confers on his creations prevent us from making sound judgments or comparisons from the world of real experience. To put it crudely, his people never have to stop and wonder where the next meal is coming from. None of their actions have serious material consequences. They live on an entirely moral plane. (Even Catherine Sloper's dilemma in *Washington Square* (1881) is not really about money; the cash is only part of the apparatus of the plot, just another way in which Dr Sloper controls his daughter. And in *The Spoils of Poynton* (1897) the wealth and beauty of the 'things' have a primarily moral, not monetary significance.)

All this has an important bearing on James's women characters. It means that their actions and decisions are represented as the product of free choice, a choice which quite simply did not exist for women in the social and political conditions of late nineteenth-century Europe. There is no external material pressure nagging at Isobel Archer, for instance, in *The Portrait of a Lady* (1881). James goes out of his way to bestow on her an unexpected and unearned fortune, specifically to give her the independence which freedom from financial constraints makes possible. Isobel's situation is far removed from the economic pressures most women would have experienced in a similar situation. George Eliot's Gwendolen Harleth, though like Isobel in many ways, is very different from her in this one important respect. Her fatal decision to marry the odious Grandcourt is largely dictated by her own and her family's poverty.

James's commitment to the individual, and his uncompromising rejection of whatever distorts or crushes individual freedom, should have made him a natural ally of feminism. After all, Victorian feminism was essentially an extension of liberal individualism – as J.S. Mill, for one, was well aware. And sure enough, an alert, developing woman is generally the centre of interest in James's novels and the manipulation or exploitation of one person by another is the cardinal sin in his moral world, forming the structural centre of all his works. He is quite clear that distorting an individual's potential is a moral crime. His horror of psychological suffocation is unmistakable in *The Portrait of a Lady* – (see especially Ch. XLII) – and his chilling picture of the cold-blooded way Sloper experiments with his daughter's feelings in *Washington Square* indicates quite clearly how James felt about people who treat those around them as objects to be manipulated for their own entertainment or interest. The distorted or manipulated characters are invariably women. But in spite of this, what I take to be an underlying hostility to feminism controls James's presentation of the 'used' women and sharply limits his sympathy. This anti-feminism surfaces most clearly in *The Bostonians* (1886), but as we shall see, it is also an important element in other novels where he apparently sides with the woman victim.

The first general point to make about James's attitude towards his women is that like the repellent Dr Sloper of *Washington Square*, he sees them and their problems as 'interesting'. They are objects for him to study and observe. All novelists, of course, find their subjects interesting, but not quite in the way James does. For the important difference between James and a writer like Hardy is that he accepts both the external environment and the inner moral compulsions that produce the conflicts so damaging to his heroines. The social setting is taken as given, is never questioned. It is 'there' only as a background against which James can see what his women will 'do', how they will cope. He never protests against the environment or its values because without them the very things he finds 'interesting', the things he assumes are worth writing about, could not exist – that is, the consciousness of leisured and sensitive men and women.

Yet it is the social structures and moral pressures engendered by the world of James's novels that distort and damage his women. This means that women can never really be free in his fiction. They must always remain victims of the oppressively refined scruples and niceties of the cultured bourgeois society which James finds so fascinating. The only way women could break free of the pressures of their society was to break away from the society itself. But if they do this they forfeit James's sympathy and are disqualified as Jamesian heroines. This is exactly why James so dislikes a woman like Henrietta Stackpole. She is a forthright woman with a vulgar insensitive mind which allows her to act without any of the moral dithering James admires so much.

James then, is primarily concerned with individual psychology, and his approach to character excludes a genuinely critical interest in the conflict between the individual and his or her class or environment. Thus when he is analyzing and recording consciousness he is more a scientist than a moralist or social critic. It is curious to note, for instance, that the terms James uses to describe Dr Sloper, the cold manipulator, are very similar to those he uses to describe his own interest in his fictional characters. We are told of the doctor that he was 'never eager, never impatient or nervous; but he made notes of everything and he regularly consulted his notes'. (*Washington Square*, p. 32) Yet this is also an accurate account of the way James builds up his stories in the *Notebooks*. Sloper's interest in Catherine is that of an impartial observer. He is quite uninvolved with her as a person, never mind as his own daughter. All the time he wants to see what she will 'do' in the difficult situation he deliberately creates for her. He hopes she will 'give me a surprise' (p. 13) and he 'waits with suspense – with

positive excitement' for which he is 'really much obliged to
her', adding that 'there will be a great deal to observe'. (p. 102)
Mrs Almond, his confident at this point in the story, comments that Sloper is 'shockingly cold-blooded'. She is quite
right. But James's attitude is much the same. For instance in his
preface to *The Portrait* he wonders how Isobel will cope with
the situation he has planned for her – 'Well, what will she 'do'?'
he asks.[36] Or again, later on in the same preface he says that 'the
key' to the novel lies in the question 'what will she do?' (p. xvi)
The same 'cold-blooded' spirit of observation underlies his
comments on *The Spoils of Poynton*. Here we again find him
wondering how his heroine will respond to the pressures he
builds into her situation.

The scheme James usually adopts in the novels is to place a
woman in an impossible situation and then to pose as a neutral
observer of her actions. But his scientific detachment is as
unpleasant as Sloper's coolly dispassionate analysis of
Catherine. Both of them, James and Sloper, are experimenters
with people. And like most experimenters they are far from
neutral – they set up the experiment and they define its terms.
To put it another way, they make up the rules of the game,
select the hurdles and hoops the players will have to jump over
and through, and then sit back and pretend to be impartial
spectators, alert to register how the competitors will cope.
James is really a scientist, not a moralist. He is interested in the
way his women think and feel, not in the fundamental injustice
of their situation.

The second general point to make about James's treatment
of women, is that in spite of their talents, potential and determination to be 'free', they invariably fail. The movement of
the novels is usually a slow journey towards the defeat of the
heroine. We can see this at its clearest in Isobel Archer and
Fleda Vetch. But there is something almost arbitrary in the
way James chooses defeat for his women, even though it is
right and convincing given their character-structure. It is no
accident that his women are always of the same very special
type – refined, sensitive, morally scrupulous. A finely adjusted
conscience and a determination to do the correct moral thing
are the essence of the Jamesian heroine. But they are also the
essence of her defeat, as her 'inner' freedom, the knowledge

that she has acted rightly, is no real compensation for what she loses – independence and liberty (for Isobel), or love and the chance of happiness (for Fleda). As Cox points out in his *The Free Spirit*, for all James asserts in his preface to *The Spoils* that Fleda triumphs, it certainly doesn't look that way to the reader. 'In what way is Fleda successful?' he asks. 'She loses the man she loves, and even Poynton with all its treasures of art is destroyed. What is the value of the freedom with which she is left?'[37]

Fleda and Isobel both act according to their sense of what is 'right' or 'good'. Their decisions are not imposed on them by James, to illustrate or emphasize any particular point. They stem naturally from their own natures. But we must remember that James chooses their natures for them. And the most important single characteristic that unites Isobel and Fleda is this determination to behave impeccably, even if it means renouncing what is dearest to them. James presents this as 'fineness', and we are expected to approve and admire. But really their behaviour is self-destructive, masochistic. Such 'fineness' is extremely dangerous and should be seen as such, and not, as James would have it, as moral integrity which happens to have unfortunate consequences.

Once he has given his would-be free woman a sensitive conscience of doubtful value, James is well set up to plot her into defeat, placing her in the kind of dilemma in which she can never win. Fleda *cannot* have the 'spoils' because she cannot have Owen without dirtying her hands. She ends up with clean hands and a clear conscience, but little else. With Isobel it is just the same. She recognizes her terrible mistake in marrying Osmond, but she is determined to live it out, not repudiate it. She is true to her conscience and sense of duty, but it means renouncing all desire for freedom.

As I have said, James can usually work out his heroine's defeat in terms of her own peculiarities of temperament. This is certainly true of Isobel *after* she marries Osmond. But what of her decision to marry him in the first place? Gwendolen Harleth has credible economic reasons for her marriage to Grandcourt in *Daniel Deronda*; Isobel has only her own failure of judgment to blame. Yet the reasons for her decision are not explored by James at all. It is very important for him that she should marry Gilbert, so he can go on to see what she will 'do' once she has realized just how mistaken she has been. But the decision itself is left unmotivated – a curious omission for such a careful artist. James is a little uneasy about this himself and rather self-consciously writes in the explanation that Isobel, feeling burdened by her money, wanted to off-load it onto someone who would make good use of it. But this still does not explain Isobel's blindness about Osmond, especially when her closest friends, people whose judgment she respects, all urge her against him (Ralph, Mrs Touchett, Warburton). In effect, for all the convincing psychology of James's study of Isobel in the unhappiness which follows, he fails to justify the most important single event of the novel.

Reviewers spotted this as soon as the book came out. One complained that Isobel's decision was not convincing psychologically: ('Such a character as his could not have had any fascination for her and it remains one of the problems of the story why it ever had such a fascination.')[38] Others commented on the way Isobel's engagement is presented as a *fait accompli*. A year elapses between Osmond's first proposal and Isobel's final acceptance. During this time she is travelling abroad with Mme Merle, but we are given no account of this period. Nor does James openly make anything of the possibility that Mme Merle is 'working' on Isobel;

As to Isobel's change of mind, and the means Osmond takes to bring it about, we are left altogether in the dark ... Surely if the portrait of Isobel is to be a living one, we ought to see something of the mental processes which decide her to take the gravest step of her life?[39]

And again, 'It is asking too much that we should believe that a woman of Isobel's intellectual force could be taken in by so transparent a cheat.'[40] Modern critics, too, have been hard pressed to explain Isobel's weakness for Osmond. Tony Tanner, for example, believes that a morbid psychological affinity draws her to him.[41]

So why *does* Isobel marry Osmond? If the decision is, as many critics suggest, out of character, then it must come directly from James himself. Only he failed to integrate it into the psychological texture of the novel. But this interference from James is more than an unfortunate artistic blemish; it reveals something of his antipathy to women who desire freedom. Isobel's fate, to be 'ground in the very mill of the conventional', is the perfect retribution for her pride, she who 'dreamed of freedom and nobleness'.[42] The marriage and the way Osmond crushes her are a peculiarly cruel fate for a woman who dared to want more than her sex obviously entitled her to. The punishment suits the crime perfectly. So the failure to make Isobel's decision convincing is something of a giveaway. Well 'done' though the book is, it is rooted in suspicion, and its resolution suggests a degree of hostility to the idea of real independence for women.

The third important point about James's heroines is that they are scared of sex. They can never respond to men spontaneously and they tie themselves into knots of inhibition and self-consciousness at anything resembling a sexual encounter. It is difficult to disentangle whether this is a deliberate part of James's characterization, and therefore some kind of criticism of the heroines, or whether it is symptomatic of James's own attitudes – towards sex in general and female sexuality in particular. *The Portrait* and *The Spoils* again act as guides.

Fleda Vetch's sexual incompetence appears to be the price she has to pay for her refined Jamesian conscience. With her rival, 'the awful Mona', it is the other way round. In fact Fleda and Mona are extremely genteel versions of the old split between virgin and whore. As far as James is concerned passion and 'fineness' can never co-exist in the one woman, and so he perpetuates the traditional separation of women into contrasting categories – in his case sexual versus intellectual, vulgar versus refined. Given a choice between the two types, the Jamesian woman instinctively opts for 'fineness'. This is the essence of Fleda's situation. It is also the way James saw it in the *Notebooks* where Fleda's subordination of her feelings for Owen to her sense of the 'right' thing to do, gradually become for him the main point of the book. 'If I want beauty for her – beauty of action and poetry of effect, I can only, I think, find it just there; find it in making her heroic.'[43] And so he has her give up Owen.

But James is even more specific than this. He takes, for him, the most unusual step of presenting Fleda with a chance of clinching both Owen and the spoils by making a sexual 'advance'. When Mrs Gereth sees that Fleda and Owen are attracted to each other she more or less openly suggests that Fleda should seduce her son. She commands her to 'get him away from her' – that is, Mona. But Fleda does not understand:

'Away from Mona? How in the world? ... How can I get him away from her?'
'By letting yourself go.'
'By letting myself go?' She spoke mechanically, still more like an idiot.[44]

Mona, however, understands perfectly well. She knows the advantages of 'letting herself go' at just the right moment. And having done so, she quickly secures Owen at the nearest registry office. The threat of Fleda determined her:

'Determined her to what?'
'To act, to take means.'
'To take means?' Fleda repeated.
'I can't tell you what they were, but they were powerful. She knew how,' said Mrs. Gereth. (p. 172)

Fleda's innocence and bewilderment during these exchanges are comic. But they are also part of her low-keyed sexual desire. Her moral refinement has left her no room for passionate action. As one contemporary put it, her strength is

'... undermined by a terribly active conscience and a sense of refinement which inconveniently goes far beyond the aesthetic region, and pervades her whole being.'[45]

But the most interesting thing about Fleda's sexual personality is that James appears to approve of it. This is certainly the impression which emerges from the *Notebooks* where Fleda is 'distinguished' and the 'fineness of the book' is 'the fineness of Fleda'.[46] As for Mrs Gereth, the woman who suggests the sexual manoeuvre, James definitely disapproves: 'she sets the girl on him – cynically almost, or indecently'.[47] He cannot endorse such direct action.

We find the same sexual inhibitions in Isobel. Her ostensible reason for refusing first Goodwood and then Warburton is that marriage to either of them would threaten her liberty. But concealed behind this sound and rational belief is a more instinctive fear of their masculinity. They threaten her sexually. Cox suggests that James intended this as a careful modification of Isobel's real freedom: 'her sexual coldness demonstrates the ambiguous quality of her independence'.[48] But when at the end of the novel the choice for Isobel is no longer between independence and sexual domination, a relatively clear-cut situation where her decision is fairly easy, but between the living death of the marriage to Osmond and the challenge of freedom offered by Caspar Goodwood, James's position is different. Isobel's sexual hesitancy is no longer seen as a chink in her armour of independence; it is still that, and it is cruelly damaging to her, but it has also, for James, made her heroic. It gives her the strength to reject Goodwood and the ambiguous freedom he offers. It is the passionate kisses in the garden that convince Isobel, or rather scare her into her decision. ('She had not known where to turn; but she knew now. There was a very straight path.' (p.591)) This is the path back to Rome and suffocation with Osmond. This, to her, is preferable to the sexual suffocation threatened by Goodwood. She fights the feeling of abandonment she experiences when he kisses her and she revolts against the loss of individuality it brings:

> She had wanted help, and here was help; it had come in a rushing torrent. I know not whether she believed everything he said; but she believed just then that to let him take her in his arms would be the next best thing to her dying. This belief, for a moment, was a kind of rapture, in which she felt herself sink and sink .. (p. 590)

James then has her recoil specifically from Goodwood's masculinity:

> His kiss was like white lightning, a flash that spread, and spread again, and stayed; and it was extraordinarily as if, while she took it, she felt each thing in his hard manhood that least pleased her, each aggressive fact of his face, his figure, his presence, justified of its intense identity and made one with this act of possession. (p. 591)

For her, sexual activity is entirely one-sided and to reciprocate is a kind of submission, a loss of independence. And James asks us to sympathize with this view. He apparently admires Isobel for the moral integrity which makes her return to Rome, accept the consequences of her original mistake and stand by Pansy. But he is also endorsing her rejection of passion, her denial of her whole sexual nature. To quote Cox once more: 'this was always James's attitude towards sex. He admired reason and self-discipline and deliberately tried to attract sympathy for Isobel's eventual refusal to be dominated.'[49]

George Moore spotted James's preference for reason above instinct. His view is perhaps characteristically crude, reflecting as it does his own moral and aesthetic prejudices, but there is more than an inkling of the truth about James in his remarks in his *Confessions of a Young Man* (1888):

Why does he always avoid direct action? In his stories a woman never leaves the house with her lover, nor does a man ever kill another man or himself. Why is nothing ever accomplished? In real life, murder, adultery, and suicide are of common occurrence; but Mr James's people live in a calm, sad, and very polite twilight of volition. Suicide or adultery has happened before the story begins, suicide or adultery happens some years after the characters have left the stage, but in front of the reader nothing happens ... The interviewer in us would like to ask Henry James why he never married; but it would be vain to ask, so much more does he write like a man to whom all action is repugnant.[50]

But the sexlessness which Moore finds so odd is a handicap which James inflicts only on his women. Basil Ransom, Caspar Goodwood and Owen Gereth are all sexually attractive, indeed sexually overbearing enough to scare off the nervous heroines. The thing we find in James's novels is not so much an indifference to sex, but a refusal to recognize *women's* sexual and emotional nature.

In *The Bostonians* James confronts feminism head-on, and here, at last, he lets slip the mask of neutral observer and, it seems to me, commits himself to an anti-feminist position. He is more engaged in the conflicts he unfolds than is usual with him, and he even goes as far as sneering at the people he wants us to disapprove of – a very uncharacteristic attitude.

The crux of the book is a struggle between a man and a woman over a young girl. Verena Tarrant, the girl, dominated by her feminist friend Olive Chancellor, is determined to prove to the world that 'a woman *could* live persistently, clinging to a great, vivifying, redemptory idea without the help of a man'. Her aim is to 'testify to the end against the whole stale superstition – mother of every misery – that those gentry were indispensable'.[51] *The Bostonians* 'proves' that this is impossible, and that Verena is destined to be the wife, the essentially private possession of an individual male. Verena is accordingly plotted into submission to the ultra-masculine Basil Ransom, and her attempt to live another kind of life, one where she is independent of men and commits herself to the feminist struggle, is presented as a distortion of her nature.

As usual with James, the names he selects for his characters give an indication of the overall pattern of the novel. Olive, who has such a strong grip on Verena, is given the surname 'Chancellor' which suggests custodianship or ownership. Basil, the strong-willed Southerner who lays siege to Verena, is called 'Ransom'. Here the name suggests rescue or redemption, with a strong hint of the Divine Saviour thrown in. But there is more to it than just a name when it comes to James's attitude towards Olive and her influence over Verena. She is an ardent feminist, totally and passionately committed to emancipation, and it is she who grooms and trains Verena for her public career as an inspired speaker on the women's movement. But Olive is a lesbian. So her feminism, her intensely magnetic personality and the power this gives her over Verena are immediately rationalized as the product of 'perversion'.

Once Olive has been established as a morbid lesbian, James is free to depict her relationship with Verena as unnatural. She is extremely possessive and controls or supervises most of Verena's life. Right from the beginning Verena is uneasy about Olive – when the older woman first proposes friendship with her, the girl is vaguely alarmed:

Verena wondered afterwards why she had not been more afraid of her – why, indeed she had not saved herself by darting out of the room.

And she notices Olive's unusual intensity: 'there was a light in Miss Chancellor's magnified face which seemed to say that a sentiment, with her, might consume its object, might consume Miss Chancellor, but would never consume itself'. (p. 72) As their complicated relationship develops and the threat of Ransom draws nearer, Verena slowly comes to fear Olive. Olive is determined to prevent Verena from marrying and she skilfully out-manoeuvres, among others, one extremely eligible young man long before Ransom becomes a serious challenger. She guards Verena from men like a Gorgon: 'she was haunted, in a word, with the fear that Verena would marry, a fate to which she was altogether unprepared to surrender her; and this made her look with suspicion on all male acquaintance'. (p. 102) Again it is Olive's lesbianism which provides the explanation; one character comments that 'Olive stands between them,' (Verena and one of her suitors) because 'she wants to keep her in the single sisterhood; to keep her, above all, for herself'. (p. 203)

Yet Olive is still a strong and dignified personality, and James enters with some feeling into the anguish of her defeat in the long silent tussle with Ransom. All the other feminists in the novel are either shabby, pathetic figures or unpleasant opportunists, and Verena's father, Selah Tarrant, is a shady quack. Verena is used by these people; used in a crude way by her father who 'works her up' for her feminist speeches, used financially by Mrs Farrinder who is quick to realize that Verena, as a crowd-drawer, is a real discovery, a good business investment for the movement, and used as a money-spinning entertainment by that 'gentleman' of the press, Matthias Pardon. To James, Pardon is the essence of indelicacy, vulgarity and materialism:

For this ingenuous son of his age all distinction between the person and the artist had ceased to exist; the writer was personal, the person food for newsboys, and everything and everyone were everyone's business. (p. 107)

Pardon sees himself as Verena's husband–cum–road–manager, and even suggests to Olive that they might 'run Miss Verena together'. (p. 124) But it is no accident that James associates such figures with feminism. This is how he saw feminism. And even Miss Birdseye, the ageing and generous champion of all good causes, is mocked. She is a 'poor little humanitarian hack' who extends to Ransom 'a delicate, dirty, democratic little hand'. (p. 25)

Verena, at the beginning of the book, is shown off by these people, exhibited like some kind of funfair freak. When he sees her 'doing' one of her speeches, Ransom thinks to himself that:

She had the sweetest, most unworldly face, and yet, with it, an air of being on exhibition, of belonging to a troupe, of living in the gaslight, which pervaded even the details of her dress, fashioned evidently with an attempt at the histrionic. If she had produced a pair of castanets or a tambourine, he felt that such accessories would have been quite in keeping. (p. 51)

The exploitation of the naïve Verena, first by the Birdseye circle and then on a more select and genteel basis by Olive, is central to James's argument against feminism. The feminists distort Verena's real self – which when left to develop under different influences turns out to be the very different self of female submission and domesticity. This insistence on the 'real Verena', hiding somewhere underneath the false super-structure of feminism foisted on her by her 'friends', is pre-sented mainly through Ransom. He consistently sees her in this way. The important question of course is whether or not this is also James's interpretation.

The answer to this is that there is perhaps no 'real' Verena at all. She is not a forceful character and only falls so completely under the influence of the feminists and Olive because she is young, a little simple even, and quite unformed intellectually. Her father has made her into what we find at the opening of the novel, and it is only because she is so guileless that she has not been completely vulgarized by him. Olive takes her and makes her into something else. Then along comes Ransom and he tries to make her into something else again – the sweet and charming but helpless wife of a Southern gentleman. He gradually gets to work on her with his reactionary ideas and she is so impressionable that she swallows them, just as she has earlier been swept along by Olive's strong personality:

The change that had taken place in the object of Basil Ransom's merciless devotion ... was, briefly just this change – that the words he had spoken to her ... about her genuine vocation, as distinguished from the hollow and factitious ideal with which her family and her association with Olive Chan-cellor had saddled her – these words, the most effective and penetrating he had uttered, had sunk into her soul and worked and fermented there. She had come at last to believe them, and that was the alteration, the transformation. They had kindled a light in which she saw herself afresh and, strange to say, liked herself better than in the old exaggerated glamour of the lecture-lamps.

She could not tell Olive this yet, for it struck at the root of everything, and the dreadful, delightful sensation filled her with a kind of awe at all that it implied and portended. She was to burn everything she had adored; she was to adore everything she had burned. The extraordinary part of it was that though she felt the situation to be, as I say, tremendously serious, she was not ashamed of the treachery which she – yes, decidedly, by this time she must admit it to herself – she meditated. It was simply that the truth had changed sides; that radiant image began to look at her from Basil Ransom's expressive eyes. (p. 332)

Verena is eminently manipulable and so becomes the centre of a tug-of-war between Olive and Basil.

We have already seen something of James's attitude towards Olive, but what is his attitude towards Ransom in this battle? Basil's exaggerated Southern masculinity, the crude chauvinism which leads him to see women as private playthings purely for home consumption, does not pass without ironic comment. But given what is for Verena a choice between two evils – Olive's lesbianism, her feminism and determination on a gaslight career of public speaking for her protégée, or marriage to Ransom, the archetypal male who will clearly suffocate her – James opts for marriage and dependence. It seems that this is the nearest thing to what suits the nebulous 'real' Verena. On the other hand, it is clear when she is carried off by Ransom at the end of the book (he only needs a suit of armour and a white charger to do it in complete style), that she is not about to live happily ever after; and so the novel ends on a characteristic note of ambiguity. There is only one winner, Ransom. Both the women have lost – Olive has lost Verena for ever and Verena is clearly going to be unhappy for some time to come:

'Ah, now I am glad!' said Verena, when they reached the street. But though she was glad, he presently discovered that, beneath her hood, she was in tears. It is to be feared that with the union, so far from brilliant, into which she was about to enter, these were not the last she was destined to shed. (p. 390)

But even this complication can be seen as an essentially temporary difficulty which Verena will have to cope with in readjusting to a domestic role after such prolonged contact with the feminists and Olive. It is *not* a clear statement that she is basically unsuited to the sheltered dependence she is now committed to.

So the novel ends on a deliberate note of uncertainty. But weighing up all the evidence, even if James has important reservations about Basil Ransom, he certainly has greater ones about feminism. The feminists, Olive and Basil are all manipulators, and Verena is at the centre of their desires. But the feminists come in for much wider and often much cheaper criticism than the chauvinistic Southerner. For instance there is the minor character Dr Prance. She is an emancipated career woman, but the most striking thing about her is that she is totally desexualized. James approves of her and likes her when she functions as a wry, somewhat cynical commentator on the posturing and extravagance of the professional feminists. She has no time for such things. But it is curious that James still casts her in the role of sexless spinster:

Spare, hard, dry, without a curve, an inflection or a grace, she seemed to ask no odds in the battle of life and to be prepared to give none ... She looked like a boy, and not even like a good boy. It was evident that if she had been a boy she would have 'cut' school, to try private experiments in mechanics or to make researches in natural history. It was true that if she had been a boy she would have borne some relation to a girl, whereas Doctor Prance appeared to bear none whatever. (p. 36)

Dr Prance is a likeable enough character, but her masculinity suggests that, for James, real emancipation and the hard work it brought went hand in hand with a kind of withered sexlessness. Hard, cynical and physically unattractive, Dr Prance is at once a curiosity and a warning. Like Olive's homosexuality, she is a stock response to feminism.

I have devoted a fair amount of space to my attempt to disentangle and expose James's anti-feminism for two main reasons. First, he can be taken to represent the kind of ideas about feminism which hostile writers worked up and used in their books at the end of the century. Second, and more important, his undeniable skill and subtlety as a writer can show us that a network of ideological assumptions – about women, about behaviour, about how people live their lives, about what is valuable in life – can be so closely woven into the texture and structure of a work of literature, that we, the readers, find ourselves drawn into the writer's world view without pausing to examine it for ourselves. Art works through being at once compelling, satisfying and true. A writer like James can make us feel that something is true and right when it is not.

PART FOUR

THE NEW CENTURY

10. Introductory

The death of Victoria did not mean the death of Victorianism, and the opening years of the century saw if anything an intensification of the struggles between moralism and sexual liberty, between feminism and anti-feminism. The moral rearmers flourished as never before in their new organization, the National Social Purity Crusade. Sponsored by the National Vigilance Association, in 1908 they mounted a campaign called the 'Forward Movement' which aimed to raise standards of public and private morality.[1] It was based quite openly on the usual imperialist concerns about contraception and the declining birth rate, about so-called decadence and general laxity in sexual behaviour.

There were enough groups thinking along these lines in London alone for a regional conference to be held in 1910. It called itself the Conference of Representatives of London Societies Interested in Public Morality. At least fifteen organizations attended. The following year the National Social Purity Crusade, which had by now changed its name to The National Campaign for Public Morals, had a letter published in *The Times* which revealed the 'vice' societies' basic concern with social and political issues:

We, the undersigned, desire to express our alarm at the low and degrading views of the racial instinct which are becoming widely circulated at the present time, not only because they offend against the highest ideals of morality and religion, but also because they therefore imperil our very life as a nation. Many causes, old and new, are conducing to the evasion of the great obligations of parenthood, and the degradation of the marriage-tie: evidence of this being found, to some extent, in the decline of the birth rate.

Our youth of both sexes is in danger of being corrupted by the circulating of pernicious literature for which no defence can be offered – a circulation which has today reached an extent and developed a subtle suggestiveness without parallel in the past. This is an evil that can be controlled, and, so long as we knowingly permit it to continue, the serious consequences lie at our door.

Certain laws of heredity and development, no less natural or divine than other laws which are universally acknowledged, must also receive due recognition, and govern our national policy. A high proportion of immorality and inebriety is due to neglect of the incurably defective minded, whose progeny, lamentably numerous under present conditions, too frequently resemble their parents, and largely reinforce the ranks of degradation and shame. The cases must receive permanent care apart from the community, that they and posterity may be protected. We believe that only along these lines – by raising the ideals of marriage, by education for parenthood, and by intervention to prevent degeneracy – can we cope with the demoralization which is sapping the foundations of national wellbeing. We earnestly recommend these suggestions, therefore, to all who love the good cause, and desire to maintain through the coming time our national traditions of marriage and the home. (*The Times*, May 31st. 1911)

The letter was signed by representatives of more or less the whole British establishment and shows just how widespread the idea of national decline was at this time.[2] (The same wave of anxiety inspired Baden-Powell to set up the Boy Scouts in 1908 and, with his sister, the Girl Guides in 1910.) Eugenics was a fashionable science and was accepted even by many people who should have known better – the Webbs and Shaw among them. The Fabians welcomed eugenics as another tool in their social engineering equipment, and associated themselves with efforts to improve the physique of the working class, which might be called upon to defend the Empire and was therefore expected to be physically fit. Karl Pearson of the Social Democratic Federation (SDF) was another keen supporter of both eugenics and imperialism.[3] And we shall see below how H.G. Wells's support for feminism was hopelessly tangled up with his ideas about breeding an élite. But there was not any real debate about eugenics in the pre-war years, because no-one saw it for what it was – a cheap way of avoiding the political changes which could alone eliminate rickety children and the 'feeble-minded', who were the subject of a government report in 1904.[4] Ideas like these were very much in the air and formed an important part of the climate of opinion in which women and their emancipation were discussed in the pre-war years. The decidedly 'unfeminine' anger and determination of the WSPU, to say nothing of Christabel

Pankhurst's attack on marriage in 'The Great Scourge', was profoundly disturbing at a time when an insecure ruling class was calling on society to breed more and fitter children.

For if the period preceding the First World War can be characterized at all, it was, certainly for the ruling class, one of doubt and indecision. The certainties of the past had receded beyond recall and the *status-quo* which had begun to dissolve with the recession of the 1870s, was now disintegrating as political and social developments quickly outdistanced the liberalism brought back to power by the 1906 election. Between the death of Victoria and the Great War the establishment came under tremendous pressure from all sides, and in spite of its huge electoral majority the Liberal Government was unable to act effectively to meet or counter any of its opponents' demands. Well supported and well organized strikes temporarily paralyzed the economy in 1911/12 and the government, hampered by its traditional commitment to *laissez-faire* liberalism, was slow to recognize the need for economic reforms. Lloyd George's cajoling of the Cabinet into accepting a degree of state intervention – pensions, unemployment and health insurance – came too late and was too half-hearted to defuse working-class militancy. His measures split apart an already deeply divided party and precipitated a constitutional crisis when they were rejected by the House of Lords. The Government was flouted over Home Rule by the Ulster 'loyalists' when, openly supported by sections of the Tory Party, they went into rebellion in 1914. And from 1905 onwards, right up to the outbreak of the war, the WSPU followed a new policy of militancy. Under the relentless leadership of Emmeline and Christabel Pankhurst, thousands of women were prepared to take the kind of direct action which was alarming to a nation which had seen no mass political movement in action since the Hyde Park railings went down in 1867. Their tactics included attacks on property – arson, window smashing and letter-box burning – monster demonstrations, marches on the House of Commons and assaults on ministers. Their propaganda machine was probably the most imaginative and effective ever seen in England.

After 1910, all these groups (trade unionists, women, the Ulster rebels) were active at the same time as the long-drawn-out constitutional crisis over the power of the House of Lords. The impotence of Parliament and the disintegration of traditional liberal politics was on such a large scale that historians have argued that had it not been for the interruption of the war, England could well have been on the road to more far-reaching political changes than ever before.[5] For the ruling class the war could not have been more convenient; it swallowed up this potentially revolutionary phase so effectively that it never re-emerged. But at the time, the establishment was being pushed onto the defensive: attitudes hardened and progressive writers, along with socialists and feminists, were attacked with greater bitterness than ever before.

11. Mr. Wells's Sexual Utopia

This sense of disintegration produced a particular kind of novel. Pre-war England was highly conscious of its problems, and its fiction, like the industrial novels of the 1840s, focused on the specific social symptoms of a wider economic crisis. It was a fiction with an obtrusive moral conscience, and its most typical novelist was H.G. Wells, a writer who shows on every page that he is primarily concerned with the state of society. But like many of the feminist novelists working in the 'nineties, he never found a way of incorporating his politics successfully into his fiction, though he experimented tirelessly with the novel form in his efforts to do so,[1] producing a flamboyant amalgam of fiction, prophesy, science-fiction and utopian daydreaming.

But because he was only partly committed to literature, the artistic quality of Well's work is probably the most uneven of any major novelist. He worked too *quickly*, he tended to handle his themes crudely, and he all too often concentrated myopically on a particular idea, clarifying his political position at the expense of the complexities of human experience. This is part of Virginia Woolf's objection to the Edwardian novel in her essay 'Mr Bennett and Mrs Brown', and although her criticisms of Bennett's meticulous recreation of everyday reality perversely ignore what he was trying to do, her comments on Wells are both justified and useful. She says that if Wells was called upon to write a novel about 'Mrs Brown', a very ordinary lady sitting in the corner of a railway carriage, he would:

... instantly project upon the window-pane a vision of a better, breezier, jollier, happier, more adventurous and gallant world, where these musty railway carriages and fusty old women do not exist; where miraculous barges bring tropical fruit to Camberwell by eight o'clock in the morning; where there are public nurseries, fountains and libraries, dining-rooms, drawing-rooms, and marriages; where every citizen is generous and candid, manly and magnificent, and rather like Mr Wells himself. But nobody is in the least like Mrs Brown. There are no Mrs Browns in Utopia. Indeed I do not think that Mr Wells, in his passion to make her what she ought to be, would waste a thought upon her as she is ...[2]

Yet, for all his obvious faults, Wells reminds us that Edwardian literature was essentially a literature of ideas – of commitment, argument and dissent. Wells, in the novel, Shaw and Granville-Barker in the theatre, made their audiences acknowledge and confront their own society and its contradictions. Virginia Woolf found this disconcerting:

Yet what odd books they are! Sometimes I wonder if we are right to call them books at all. For they leave one with so strange a feeling of incompleteness and dissatisfaction. In order to complete them it seems necessary to do something [sic!] – to join a society, or, more desperately, to write a cheque ... ('Mr Bennett and Mrs Brown')

Shaw, Wells and even Galsworthy in his earlier novels and plays, refused to divorce art from politics; they tried to show how society was structured and how people actually lived. They made mistakes, but they never retreated from the pressures of life behind an aesthetic smoke-screen like Mrs Woolf.

But approach him how we may, Wells was definitely attempting to make the novel do things it had done only sporadically in the nineteenth century, something which with the advent of 'Bloomsbury' it again ceased to do – confront inequality and the social structures which produced inequality. He was determined to write about 'everything'; nothing was to be taboo:

We are going to write about it all. We are going to write about business and finance and politics and precedence and pretentiousness and decorum and indecorum, until a thousand pretences and ten thousand impostures shrivel into the cold clear draught of our elucidations. We are going to write of wasted opportunities and latent beauties until a thousand new ways of living open to men and women. We are going to appeal to the young and the hopeful and the curious, against the established and the dignified and defensive. Before we have done we will have all life within the scope of the novel.[3]

For Wells the novel was a vehicle which would express his

generation's rejection of Victorianism. In particular it was to be the antithesis of the sentimental evasions and proprieties which were all too common during the nineteenth century, so that in one of his utopian works, *In the Days of The Comet* (1906) he writes of a glorious public bonfire on which people joyfully burn:

> ... a whole dustcart full of cheap ill-printed editions of the minor English classics ... and about a truckload of thumbed and dog-eared penny fiction, watery base stuff, the dropsy of our nation's mind ... warped and crippled ideas and contagious base suggestions, the mean and defensive ingenuities of sluggish habits of thinking and timid and indolent evasions.[4]

This was always Wells's attitude towards the moral niceties of the Victorian past, and he set out to build on the work of the iconoclasts of the 'nineties. In particular, he saw himself as the champion of sexual freedom in the novel. He was determined to deal openly and truthfully with sex,[5] so he necessarily had quite a lot to say about women, marriage and the social control of sexuality. Much of what he said was penetrating and valuable and makes him the most important writer on sexual liberty between Carpenter and Lawrence. But much of what he said was also confused and contradictory. He allowed his personal experiences and his own sexual needs to dictate the direction of his ideas, so that he is frequently misleading, misinformed and opportunistic when he writes about women. However, before moving on to examine these less attractive aspects of Wells's work, it is only fair to outline the contribution he made to the fictional emancipation of women.

First, Wells developed the late nineteenth-century attacks on marriage and the ideology of sexuality on which it rested. In the autobiographical novel *The New Machiavelli* (1911)[6] he carefully analyzes the reasons behind the failed marriage of the central character, Remington. Pondering on the Remington marriage he notes the unintentional but fatal dishonesty which has kept the relationship going for a while, but finally destroys it:

> Coupled people never look at one another. They look a little away to preconceived ideas. And each from the first days of love-making hides from the other, is afraid of disappointing, afraid of offending, afraid of discoveries

... They build not solidly upon the rock of truth, but upon arches and pillars and queer provisional supports that are needed to make a common foundation, and below in the imprisoned darkness, below the fine fabric they sustain together begins for each of them a cavernous hidden life.[7]

But the main problem in Wells-Remington's marriage is not this self-deception so much as the marriage's basis in the ideology that desexualizes 'ladies'. Remington tells us that he married Margaret because she seemed to offer an escape from the sensuality which was undermining his career. To him she was:

A shining slender figure, a radiant reconciliation coming into my darkling disorders of lust and impulse ... I could contemplate praying to her and putting all the intricate troubles of my life at her feet. (p. 177)

But Margaret, a well-finished product of conditioning, is frigid, so that Wells-Remington is left longing for a woman who is both sexually responsive and high-principled. He finds her in Isabel, a Wellsian version of the 'emancipated' woman. (More of Isabel later.)

The break-down of the marriage is seen exclusively from the man's point of view. This is characteristic. It is merely inconvenient for Remington that Margaret is unresponsive, imprisoned by a damaging ideology; he is not interested in how she sees her own situation, or his use of her, so that Margaret herself remains a shadowy figure, always on the periphery of the novel which is dominated by Remington and his needs. But even if it is hopelessly one-sided, *The New Machiavelli* is still a useful analysis of what, from the outside, looks like a successful bourgeois marriage.

In a number of novels and essays Wells quite openly supported the idea of free love. He had suffered himself from the suffocating atmosphere of monogamous marriage and saw all around him how it produced frustrated men and women living in a claustrophobic world of suspicion and jealousy. For Wells a favourite way of attacking conventional marriage was to look back in incredulity from the vantage point of the utopian novels at the 'old world' theory that,

... there was only one love ... The whole nature of man was supposed to go out to the one girl or woman who possessed him, her whole nature go out to him. Nothing was left over – it was a discreditable thing to have any overplus at all. They formed a secret secluded system of two, two and such children as she bore him. All other women he was held bound to find no beauty in, no sweetness, no interest; and she likewise, in no other man. The old-time men and women went apart in couples, into defensive little houses, like beasts into little pits, and in these 'homes' they sat down proposing to love, but really coming very soon to jealous watching of this extravagant mutual proprietorship.[8] (*In the Days of the Comet*, p. 313)

Wells's views on free love got him into trouble. But when he was attacked for them he backed down, saying that that was not what he meant at all. Some years later, when he looked back on the controversy surrounding *A Modern Utopia* (1905), *In the Days of the Comet* (1906) and the Fabian essay 'Socialism and the Family', he regretted his apostasy. 'Instead of explaining I spluttered', he says in the *Experiment in Autobiography* (1934). But his spluttering was inevitable. He arrived at a position supporting freer sexual relations not primarily because he was intellectually committed to it, but out of personal necessity. It was largely a rationalization of his own sexual behaviour. So when he was attacked he could produce no well-argued defence and could only withdraw, afraid for his already shaky reputation.

Wells's most important break-through in terms of women and fiction was in presenting female sexuality not just as powerful, but as natural and welcome. This was quite new. Hardy had explored female sexuality but saw it as a threat, something alarming and dangerous. Egerton had also written about women's sexual problems and needs, but, with her, women were sentimentalized. Wells in *Ann Veronica* (1909) openly asserted for the first time in fiction not just that sexual desire existed in women, but that this was quite normal and acceptable. Ann Veronica, a capable and intelligent girl, rejects what Wells calls the 'wrappered' life she leads at home with her old-fashioned, unreasonably strict father. She finds the 'nice' bourgeois suburb she lives in utterly boring – all it has to offer are polite tea parties and dull, stupid young men for suitors. She leaves home, goes to London and immediately gets entangled with an ageing philanderer whom we have already met as a respectable neighbour at home in suburbia. After this

quick side-swipe at middle-class sexual hypocrisy, Wells
moves Ann Veronica on, via the aid of a loan from the philanderer, to the science college in Kensington where she wants to
study for a degree. Here she falls in love with her teacher,
Capes, who is divorced and therefore disreputable. She flirts
briefly with the WSPU and even takes part in the raid on the
House of Commons which actually took place in 1908. However, after a spell cooling off in Holloway she decides it is not
political rights she is after, but Capes. She promptly proceeds
to tell him so. ('What do you want?' Capes asks her bluntly.
'You!' says Ann Veronica.) She then persuades him to run off
with her. The novel ends with an implausible reconciliation
between the run-away pair (now respectably married) and
Ann Veronica's father. But although unconvincing, the point
about ending the novel in this way is that Ann Veronica is not
punished. She has claimed the right to love how and where she
wants, and Wells allows her to do this without bringing down
an awful retribution on her guilty head.

   In the *Experiment in Autobiography* Wells makes his own
comments on *Ann Veronica* and its significance:

Ann Veronica was a virgin who fell in love and showed it instead of waiting
as all popular heroines had hitherto done, for someone to make love to her. It
was held to be an unspeakable offence that an adolescent female should be
sex-conscious ... But Ann Veronica wanted a particular man who excited her
and she pursued him and got him. With gusto ...
   After Ann Veronica, things were never quite the same again in the world
of popular English fiction; young heroines with a temperamental zest for
illicit love-making and no sense of an inevitable Nemisis, increased and
multiplied not only in novels but in real life.[9]

Needless to say the book caused a scandal. It was banned from
the libraries and Wells's usual publisher, Macmillan, refused to
handle it. Frederick Macmillan wanted nothing to do with it
because 'the plot develops along lines that would be exceed-
ingly distasteful to the public which buys our books'.[10] The
novel was widely attacked by the press, *The Spectator* being
particularly abusive. It ran a sustained campaign against Wells
and the novel which it chose to call 'this poisonous book'. (See
p. 23) On this occasion however, Wells and his book benefited from their notoriety, and sales were very good.

Wells had other interesting ideas about women and sex. He believed, for instance, that an analysis of the family and its relation to capitalism should be incorporated into socialist theory. Only then would women's oppression be properly understood. This is now a commonplace of socialist–feminist thinking, but when Wells was saying it, his was an isolated voice. Apart from the idealist Edward Carpenter, this area of theory had been neglected in England since Engels's *The Origin of the Family, Private Property and the State* first appeared in 1884. Hyndman of the Marxist SDF regarded feminism and the attempt to understand the role of sexuality under capitalism as a diversion and called Engels's work 'a colossal piece of impudence'; Blatchford, editor of the socialist *Clarion* thought that Carpenter's *Love's Coming of Age* would get the socialist movement a bad name. He was as afraid as any orthodox *pater familias* for the sanctity of the family.[11] So the discussion of sexuality had been carried on by isolated individuals. It remained outside the mainstream of socialist and Marxist thinking in England.

Wells was a prominent member of the Fabian Society between 1903 and 1908. In 1906 he read a paper to the society called 'Socialism and the Middle Classes' (later published as 'Socialism and the Family'), which inaugurated a struggle with Shaw and the Webbs over the issue of sex and socialism. He wanted the society to make a clear statement on how it regarded women and the family, but his efforts to push it into a more progressive direction failed. After a public clash with the Webbs he resigned in 1908. Petty though it was, the quarrel with the Fabians is revealing. It shows how advanced Wells was when it came to socio-sexual problems. It would not have occurred to the Webbs that sexual relations and the family could have any place in Socialist theory.

Beatrice in particular was most unsympathetic towards anything which would tend to relax the strict taboos governing sexual behaviour. Commenting on Wells's views in *Our Partnership*, she calmly states that freer sexual relations would 'mean a great increase in sexual emotion for its own sake and not for the sake of bearing children. And that way madness lies.' As far as she is concerned *In The Days of the Comet* ends 'with a glowing anticipation of promiscuity in sexual relations'.[12] She is clearly horrified. Of Shaw's play *Misalliance* she says that 'it is amazingly brilliant – but the whole 'motive' is sordid – everyone wishing to have sexual intercourse with everyone else'.[13]

The distance between the Webbs and Wells is most clearly set out in *The New Machiavelli*, where Wells hits out, wittily but rather meanly, at his former allies and ridicules their austere, frigid version of socialism. The attack is unkind, but it demonstrates Wells's alienation from any social theories which failed to include a progressive analysis of sexuality. In the following passage from the novel 'Bailey' is Sidney Webb and 'Altiora' is Beatrice:

I don't know what dreams Altiora may have had in her schoolroom days, I always suspected of her suppressed and forgotten phases, but certainly her general effect now was of an entirely passionless worldliness in these matters. Indeed, so far as I could get at her, she regarded sexual passion as being hardly more legitimate in a civilized person than – let us say – homicidal mania. She must have forgotten – and Bailey too. I suspect she forgot before she married him ...

   I couldn't dismiss the interests and the passion of sex as Altiora did. Work, I agreed, was important; career and success; but deep unanalysable instincts told me this preoccupation was a thing quite as important; dangerous, interfering, destructive indeed, but none the less a dominating interest in life. (pp. 172/3)

Unlike the Fabians' 'gas and water socialism', Wells's political utopias are always moral and sexual utopias as well.

   We now come to the more ambiguous aspects of Wells's feminism. Firstly there is his attitude to the WSPU and the suffragettes. He supported the demand for the vote, but seeing that more than access to parliamentary democracy would be required if women were really to be free, he had no patience with the limited perspectives of Emmeline and Christabel Pankhurst and their movement. In the *Experiment in Autobiography* he summarizes his position on the suffrage question. His tone is complacent and brings to mind Norman Mailer's authorial egotism, but there was clearly some truth in what Wells says:

Helpfully and with the brightest hopes he produced his carefully reasoned diagnosis of their grievances; he spread his ingenious arrangement of

Neo-Malthusianism, Free Love (ton corps est à toi), economic independence, the endowment of motherhood and the systematic suppression of
jealousy and animal vice, and he found his lucid and complete statement
thrust aside, while the riot passed on, after the manner of riots, vehemently,
loudly and vacuously, to a purely symbolic end – the Vote in this case – and
essential frustration and dispersal. (p. 486)

Whenever a suffragette appears in the novels she is made to
look ridiculous. The heroines, women like Ann Veronica and
Lady Harman (in *The Wife of Sir Isaac Harman* (1914)) who are
struggling for a degree of personal and sexual freedom, are
always disappointed by the suffragettes, by their narrowness,
prejudice and sexual orthodoxy. 'The real reason why I'm out
of place [with the WSPU] is because I like men. I can talk with
them. I've never found them hostile. I've got no feminine class
feeling', says Ann Veronica. (p. 248)

Wells's criticisms of the WSPU may have been justified
politically, but it is another matter whether he is justified in
caricaturing the suffragettes as sexless, doctrinaire zealots.
Miss Miniver in *Ann Veronica* is treated mercilessly. She is a
neurotic freak, a convenient if comic contrast to Ann Veronica's healthy sexuality:

'No', cried Miss Miniver almost vehemently. 'You are wrong! I did not
think you thought such things. Bodies! Bodies! Horrible things! We are
souls. Love lives on a higher plane. We are not animals. If ever I did meet a
man I could love, I should love him' – her voice dropped again – 'platoni-
cally'. (p. 176)

This kind of cheap laugh smacks more of sexual hostility to
feminism than a serious criticism of the WSPU's puritanism.
But it is no doubt explained by Wells's commitment to sexual
permissiveness as a principle. In his own life too, he saw
women in an exclusively sexual light; this made him naturally
suspicious of a movement which was militantly anti-sex.[14]

An important part of Wells's thinking about women was a
pet scheme which he called the 'endowment of motherhood'.
This was to be a comprehensive system of state support for
women who wanted to have children but did not want to be
economically dependent on men. The scheme is an important
part of his *A Modern Utopia* and is further developed in *The
New Machiavelli*. The idea seems quite inadequate today when

feminists realize that women need much more than hand-outs from the state. These would leave them marginally better off in terms of financial independence but would do nothing to free them from domesticity. But at least Wells was moving in the right direction and understood something of the economic aspects of women's oppression. He also realized that women needed to have control over pregnancy and childrearing, and so contraception was to go hand in hand with his scheme of state allowances.

This scheme may have been an attractive alternative to dependence on individual men, but it was not primarily motivated by feminism. Wells's commitment to the idea of state support for mothers was rooted in his fascination with eugenics and the possibility of breeding an élite. It is easy to forget that Wells started out as a scientist. He was influenced by Darwin, taught by Huxley and believed that the theory of evolution could lead, where social conditions were bad enough, to the decline of the race as a whole. In this he was simply a child of his age which, as we have seen, was obsessed with the physical quality of the British people and fascinated by the idea of 'breeding out' weaknesses.[15] Social Darwinism was to be a substitute for the political action which could eliminate the real causes of 'racial decline' – poverty and inequality.

Wells's grounding in Darwinian science led to an intolerant élitism, a Nietzschean belief in the emergence of natural leaders – something which he and other Fabians found quite compatible with their version of socialism. Elitism dominates the thinking behind the utopian works, where the new social order will be run by a select group called the 'Samurai' and the rest of the population will be strictly classified according to ability and temperament. Among the lowest strata will be 'the dull' and the 'base'.[16] More important, Wells's interest in eugenics also determined his views about women, so that in *The New Machiavelli* he finds a happy coincidence between the solution to the racial/imperialist problem and the solution to women's sexual problems. Women are to be freed from economic dependence on men and are to be handed over to the state as breeders instead. A reorganization of sexual relations is necessary, but chiefly because it will lead to a more efficient state:

I came to the conclusion that under modern conditions the isolated private family, based on the existing marriage contract, was failing in its work. It wasn't producing enough children, and children good enough and well trained enough for the demands of the developing civilised state ... The old haphazard system of pairing ... no longer secures us a young population numerous enough or good enough for the growing needs and possibilities of our Empire. (p. 306)

Wells is quite prepared to jettison the family, but not for feminist reasons. Women are to be free but only because they must be at liberty to mate with eugenically suitable males. Motherhood is still the Great Good, and even better is motherhood carefully regulated to benefit British imperialism:

Women must become less and less subordinated to individual men, since this works out in a more or less complete limitation, waste and sterilization of their essentially social function; they must become more and more subordinated as individually independent citizens to the collective purpose. (p. 306)

These views are not an isolated aberration. Wells justified *Ann Veronica* on exactly the same grounds. Replying in *The Spectator* to some of his critics, he claimed that women will produce sturdy children only if they are free to choose the mates they desire.[17] And where in *Anticipations* (1902) he argues for effective birth control, he is mainly interested in eliminating undesirables. He wants to breed out:

the spectacle of a mean-spirited, under-sized diseased little man, quite incapable of earning a decent living even for himself, married to some underfed ignorant, ill-shaped, plain and diseased little woman, and guilty of the lives of ten or twelve ugly ailing children. (p. 269)

He is not interested in contraception as a useful piece of technology which could revolutionize women's lives.

In *A Modern Utopia* we again find feminism running a poor second best to eugenics and the needs of the state. It certainly is not much of a utopia for women. They stand no chance of evading the regulation number of births and have to tolerate an interesting new version of the double standard, based this time on Wells's concern with racial purity. All relationships are monogamous and the woman is heavily penalized if she has sexual relations with any but her genetically approved partner. 'Legitimate' offspring are supported by the state, but women who produce genetically suspect children by an unapproved man have their state benefits withdrawn. The man, on the other hand, is not penalized:

A reciprocal restraint on the part of the husband is clearly of no importance whatever, so far as the first end of matrimony goes, the protection of the community from inferior births.[18]

Clearly we need to be extremely cautious about Wells's apparently feminist interest in state provision for mothers.

We can see fairly easily how Wells's thinking about women was shaped by the particular anxieties of pre-war England, but it was also a product of his own personal experiences. When we look closely at his private life, we can see that his interest in free love and the sexual liberation of women was too closely related to his own sexual needs. Wells was notorious for his affairs and liaisons. He was married twice – this is not of course significant in itself, but his first wife Isabel divorced him for adultery and he was repeatedly unfaithful to the second, Catherine Wells. Catherine seems to have been a remarkable woman who was able to adjust to Wells's affairs. These included, among others, Rebecca West, Amber Reeves and one of Hubert Bland's daughters. In 1909 a scandal over the Amber Reeves affair became a serious threat to his career and fixed his public image as a philanderer. (It was this that caused him to back down over the free love issue.) And his involvement with the daughters of two members of the Fabian executive contributed to his breach with the society in 1908. (Beatrice was particularly shocked that the affair with Amber Reeves was 'consummated within the very walls of Newnham College'.)[19]

Wells was the prisoner of his own sexual and emotional needs. He respected Catherine and needed the stability and security she provided, but at the same time he was suffocated by marriage, its ties, duties and responsibilities. He suffered from what he called 'domestic claustrophobia' and was driven to lead a permanent and hectic double life, living now at home with Catherine and his legitimate family, now with his current mistress. This meant that in his personal life he exploited women. He used his wife, and he used his mistresses. He suffered only in reputation, but Catherine and his lovers suffered in their whole lives. Amber, for instance, became pregnant by Wells, and apparently loved him, but realizing that marriage to him was out of the question, she married another man who was prepared to accept the child. Wells meanwhile was boasting to Arnold Bennett that the affair went on after the marriage, which was apparently untrue.[20]

It is very important to see Wells's proselitizing in the cause of freer sexual relations for women in the light of these adventures. At a time when contraception was not widely available and was far from reliable, pleas for 'free love' only too often meant the sexual exploitation of the woman. Wells's relations with Amber and with Rebecca West both resulted in children, children the women brought up.

In spite of his permissive ideas about sex, Wells was always extremely sentimental about women. In all his affairs and flirtations one side of him clung to Catherine and their marriage. She gave him a degree of stability and support which helped him to keep going his turbulent and demanding public life. She was an extraordinarily tough woman. But when this side of Wells's life, the hard-won, precarious but ultimately sustaining marital compromise, goes into the novels, it comes out as conventional domesticity. Even the struggling Ann Veronicas collapse into dutiful wives, as rebellion and independence submit to the apparently inexorable laws of motherhood. Ann Veronica herself is finally plotted into a conventional marriage and Wells expects us to believe that the Ann Veronica of the first half of the novel – rebellious, forthright and independent – will be content with the purely domestic future mapped out for her in the second.

All Wells's spirited modern women are invariably encumbered by this same uneasy combination of freedom and domesticity. Ann Veronica, Isabel in *The New Machiavelli* and Lady Harman (*The Wife of Sir Isaac Harman*) all believe in women's emancipation, but conveniently concede that:

A woman wants a proper alliance with a man, a man who is better stuff than herself. She wants that and needs it more than anything else in the world. It may not be just, it may not be fair, but things are so. It isn't law, nor custom, nor masculine violence settled that. It is just how things happen to be. She wants to be free – she wants to be legally and economically free, so as not to be subject to the wrong man; but only God, who made the world, can alter things to prevent her being slave to the right one. (*Ann Veronica*, p. 248)

Ann Veronica is bad enough, but Isabel is even worse. Wells has her, poor woman, make terrible scenes in which, emancipated and independent though she is, she craves and cries out hysterically for babies and motherhood. 'Children', she says, 'get into a woman's brain,

'... especially when she must never hope for them. Think of the little creatures with soft, tender skin, and little hands and little feet! At times it haunts me. It comes and says, Why wasn't I given life? I can hear it in the night ... The world is full of such little ghosts, dear lover – little things that asked for life and were refused. They clamour to me. It's like a little fist beating at my heart. Love, children, beautiful children. Little cold hands that tear at my heart! Oh, my heart and my lord!' She was holding my arm with both her hands and weeping against it, and now she drew herself to my shoulder and wept and sobbed in my embrace. 'I shall never sit with your child on my knee and you beside me – never, and I am a woman and your lover!' (*New Machiavelli*, p. 343)

Equally worrying is the autobiographical basis of this novel and Wells's tendency to use his fiction to re-interpret his relationships with women. *Ann Veronica*, *The New Machiavelli* and *Love and Mr Lewisham* were all based more or less directly on women he had been involved with. Ann Veronica is a combination of Catherine, as Wells saw her before marriage to her bored him, and of Amber Reeves. Isabel in *Machiavelli* is Amber again, while Catherine has become Margaret, the unsatisfying wife. The portrait of Ethel in *Love and Mr Lewisham* is based on Wells's first wife, another Isabel. (She was also his cousin.) This novel suggests that for Wells wives must always be a burden. The whole of *Lewisham* demonstrates that marriage is a trap, not primarily for the woman, but for the man. Through a misplaced sense of chivalry, Lewisham marries the stupid and ill-educated Ethel. She is a perfect product of ideology – dependent, submissive, 'feminine' in the worst possible way. Lewisham is a budding author of considerable talent. But for him the marriage means the end of what could have been a successful and satisfying career. He is immediately caught up in the usual financial difficulties and gives in to the routine of domesticity and money-making, accepting that 'for this we are made'. All this again comes direct from Wells's first marriage, only, unlike Lewisham, Wells got out. He never dreamed for a moment that he was 'made' for domesticity.

The novel is convincingly 'done', but like *The New Machiavelli*, the whole thing is seen exclusively through the husband's eyes. If Ethel is a burden and a responsibility, then so much the worse for Lewisham. Wells is just not interested in how a woman like Ethel might feel about her ignorance (and she knows she is that), her inability to earn money, her stupidity. All he wants to show is that a woman like that and a marriage like theirs ruin a man's career. He is not concerned with how Ethel came to be as she is, or how she can grapple with her problems. In short, he takes an exclusively male point of view. The woman is secondary; something for the man to cope with, never something of interest in herself.

There are so many limitations to Wells's feminism, so many specious arguments and so much sexual self-interest in his apparently advanced views on women, that one has to ask, was he really a feminist at all? In answer to this all one can say is that he offers a confusing and complicated bundle of ideas about women and sex, and that while some of them were useful, others were dangerous. This contradiction is partly explained by Wells's complete lack of self-criticism in either his life or his work. An acute observer of what he saw around him in political and social life, he was incapable of applying the same critical spirit to his own actions or assumptions. He thought of himself as a leading supporter of feminism, but held other political views which were manifestly incompatible with it. He supported sexual liberty for women, but because his ideas came primarily out of his own personal needs, he still saw women first and foremost as sexual partners. This pushed his fictional women towards even more complicated forms of sexual exploitation than straightforward inhibition or repression. In this he looked forward to the narrow, debilitating view of women endlessly written up by Lawrence. In the nineteenth-century the only acceptable image of women was as pure beings who were both repulsed and mystified by sexuality. By the middle of the twentieth century this had been largely reversed, so that the popular fictional image of women became sexualized to a point where they had little reality beyond a psycho-sexual one. Wells must bear some of the responsibility for this development.

12. *The Sober Realism of Arnold Bennett*

Wells is peculiarly representative of his age in that his novels relate in a direct, unmediated way to the central concerns of his contemporaries. Practically all his work was written with a distinctly public intention. This is particularly true of the later novels, where Wells more or less abandons fiction as an integrated aesthetic structure, and concentrates on offering his own often highly idiosyncratic solutions to the world's problems to an audience which had learned to expect from him a strong diet of popularized political theory served up with fictional trimmings.

Unlike Wells, Bennett seldom allowed undigested chunks of sociology or politics to intrude on his art. He certainly held views on important issues and he worked for many years as a journalist. He was also a Fabian socialist. In short he took a keen interest in contemporary questions. These provide the basis for many of his novels, but when they appear in his best work they are always carefully subsumed into the structure and overall meaning of the text. He avoids the uneasy combination of fiction, political prophesy and narrowly contemporary comment that is the undoing of so much of Wells's work. His novels are technically and artistically more accomplished than anything Wells produced, and at his best Bennett achieves an utterly convincing realism, an impression of ordinary lower-middle-class life at a particular time and in a particular place which has never been surpassed in English fiction. But the painstaking effort not to take 'sides', not to adopt a definite position on the political issues that give rise to the central themes of the novels, produces a curiously grey and enervated result.

As an inheritor of the essentially liberal concerns of the nineteenth-century novel, Bennett is sensitive to problems of individual development and is keenly aware of the economic and social forces which determine or distort the shape of people's lives. He understands in particular some of the special psychological problems women have to contend with as a result of generations of oppression. But he ultimately stops short of the kind of unanswerable, total protest of a tragic writer like Hardy. The movement of his novels is always away from revolt and towards a profoundly depressing acceptance of what comes to be seen as the inevitable. His people always 'shake down' in the end; they learn to live with their own and their society's inadequacies. Struggling against these is useless; what is valuable is the wisdom which comes with experience. This is what Bennett understands by maturity.

He generally focuses on a changing and maturing character, tracing his or her development over a period of years, or even over a generation. This approach is related to his belief that experience makes sense only in relation to the passage of time. Time dominates the Bennett novels. Not historical time, the character of a particular epoch, but everyday time, 'the time that is the ticking of the clock'.[1] It trickles slowly by, giving an urgency and importance to the uneventful daily lives of ordinary men and women. Because of the steady pressure of time passing, the process of ageing and assimilating experience becomes all important. In face of a finite world protest is meaningless and stoicism becomes the only reasonable posture to adopt.

We see this most clearly in Edwin Clayhanger. His growth towards the Bennett idea of maturity is traced in the trilogy known as the Clayhanger novels – *Clayhanger* (1910), *Hilda Lessways* (1911) and *These Twain* (1916). In early manhood Edwin has had humanitarian misgivings about the lot of his employees. (He has a successful printing works which he took over from his father. More ruthless than Edwin, Darius Clayhanger claimed that he had not been able to afford his son's delicate conscience.) But this and other nagging feelings of class guilt fade away as Edwin comes to see 'injustice' as something to be 'faced and accepted'; 'to reconcile oneself to injustice was the master achievement'.[2] This is a political and personal statement of crucial significance, not just for Edwin but for Bennett too, as he shares his hero's philosophy. It is a conception which makes Bennett a fine realist, but deprives him of greatness.

This defeatism plays an important part in Bennett's presentation of women. He understands something of what it means to be a woman living in a patriarchal society, and he builds on the critical insights of the nineteenth-century novel. But, in the end, his sympathy for women remains just that, and we see that for them too the greatest wisdom is in acquiescence.

The Old Wives Tale (1908), the novel which is generally recognized as Bennett's best, is rooted in the idea that protest is futile. The book is permeated by a sense of ageing and time passing; it is also a book about women. In it Sophia Baines breaks away from the dullness of her lower-middle-class family, their dreary drapery business and narrow nonconformism. She is young, imaginative and determined to take an independent course. She wants to become a teacher – hardly a revolutionary demand, but she is still forbidden to do it. So she runs off with Gerald Scales the sales rep. of a big Manchester store who occasionally visits the shop. Coming from such a provincial background and with such a narrow range of experience, Sophia easily mistakes Scales's shallow airs for a real knowledge of the world and his easy sales talk for real intelligence. She quickly learns her mistake but for her there is no going back, and so when Scales deserts her she begins to build a new but solitary life. Her experiences have made her capable and self-reliant, so that she runs a successful guesthouse in Paris which gradually earns her a comfortable income. But she has become a sadder as well as a wiser woman and Bennett wants us to see that her revolt has gained her nothing. When at the end of her life Sophia returns to her home-town in the Potteries, we learn that her existence has really been as narrow and uneventful as her stay-at-home sister's. Her daily round in glamourous Paris was basically no different from Constance's in provincial Burslem. If anything she is worse off; Constance has been married, has a son, and so, in a sense, has got more out of life than the rebellious Sophia, who is now a lonely old woman. Sophia's break with her family has only isolated her, and in terms of the overall balance of the novel it is relatively unimportant; it recedes into the far past as the passage of time brings both sisters other concerns, everyday problems to absorb into their experience of life.

The pattern of initial resistance followed by submission to experience is repeated in most of the novels. Only in one work, the early *Anna of the Five Towns* (1902), does Bennett side with the rebellious impulse. Anna is the daughter of the miser Ephraim Tellwright. She is an heiress, but has no real control over either her person or her property because she is tyrannized by her harsh, mean-spirited father. The connections between capital and power, cash and sexual relations are closely intermeshed in the novel, so that Anna becomes engaged as a matter of course to Heny Mynors, a successful young manufacturer who has an eye on Ephraim's wealth. She is never much more to him than a route to her father's capital. Anna has little feeling for Mynors and slowly recognizes that she is in love with Willie Price, the son of a bankrupt who committed suicide when his creditors foreclosed on him – these included Anna, who was bullied by her father into demanding the money Price senior owed her. Yet although she loves Willie deeply, out of habits of obedience and renunciation Anna still goes ahead with the engagement to Mynors, the socially and economically respectable suitor. She is so thoroughly conditioned into crushing her own wishes that she never even considers marrying the man she loves. In despair and bankrupt himself, Willie, too, commits suicide. Anna never knows this; she and everyone else believes he has emigrated to Australia. Anna herself is left to live out a kind of half life, being economically useful to her husband.

Although Anna is ultimately defeated, her feelings of guilt and compassion over Titus Price's suicide and her unacknowledged love for Willie do lead her to one bold act of defiance. She secretly burns a forged promissory note which is in her father's keeping and which, if it came to light, would incriminate Willie. This initiative leads to a rupture with Ephraim, but her conditioning is too strong for her to break with Mynors as well:

She who had never failed in duty did not fail then. She who had always submitted and bowed the head, submitted and bowed the head then. She had sucked with her mother's milk the profound truth that a woman's life is always a renunciation, greater or less. Hers by chance was greater.[3]

Here the cost of acquiescence is too great for Bennett to be able to present it as commendable stoicism. Anna has no real choice at any time, but her quiet submission emerges quite clearly as a great wrong. It costs Willie's life and Anna's happiness.

Anna is the only book where Bennett allows a real tension to exist between submission to authority and possible defiance. In all the others the consequences of submission to the 'inevitable' are played down (*Clayhanger*), or he neatly slips out of a potentially tragic conflict by dexterously plotting obstacles out of the way (*Leonora*).

Bennett generally managed to duck important issues in this way, but this did not prevent him from presenting women and their problems in an intelligent, sympathetic light. This is particularly true of *The Old Wives Tale*, for even if Sophia's rebellion is lost amid the onrush of new experiences, the original rejection of her oppressive home and the limited future it offered her remains one of the most striking sections of the book. Her father is paralyzed, a permanent invalid. But he still attempts to dominate his womenfolk. He represents a decaying patriarchy – as his body grows weaker, so his authority over the girls declines. Yet he is still strong enough to forbid Sophia to take up the career she wants. She is outraged:

... here was this antique wreck, helpless, useless, powerless – merely pathetic – actually thinking that he had only to mumble in order to make her 'understand'! He knew nothing; he perceived nothing; he was a ferocious egoist, like most bedridden invalids, out of touch with life – and he thought himself justified in making destinies, and capable of making them.[4]

Old Man Baines is a just-living symbol of the authority which dictated the shape and direction of women's lives. In a neat piece of plotting he is significantly, if accidentally, killed by Sophia, the spirit of modernity and women's emancipation. And so Bennett finds an effective way of presenting the conflict between the declining order of the past and the demands for freedom made by a new generation of women. At this point he is also openly on Sophia's 'side'; it is only later in the book that he implies that there are no sides, only life and time.

With *The Old Wives Tale* Bennett also opened up a whole new subject area for the novel. He showed that in the hands of a sensitive imaginative writer the lives of very ordinary women become interesting. There is absolutely nothing remarkable about Constance Baines, except perhaps her very ordinariness. She is not poor or wretched like Esther Waters or Zola's working-class women. She is possibly the most unsensational woman in fiction, but Bennett makes us see the everyday reality of her life, makes her important. Virginia Woolf may have scorned her as a version of 'Mrs Brown' and criticized Bennett's concentration on the mundane details of her life, but she is extraordinarily real. In her, Bennett gives us a picture of average experience, and with her we briefly come into contact for the first time in fiction with the neglected and unrecorded lives of thousands of anonymous women. The genesis of Sophia Baines on the other hand goes back to Emily and Charlotte Brontë, Hardy and Flaubert. Her passionate revolt and somewhat sensational existence through the Paris Commune make her less real, more of a fictional stereotype than Constance. It is Constance, not Sophia, who is an important addition to the range of women's experiences recorded in the novel.

Much the same is true of two further categories of women who feature in Bennett's fiction. These are spinsters and domestic servants. These appear so often in the novels that it is as though Bennett saw himself as a champion of both groups. Certainly his spinsters are never the cruel caricatures of frustrated or embittered old women, the figures of fun who feverishly chase every unmarried man in sight through the pages of so much English fiction. They are once again ordinary women, but women who have had no opportunity to marry. They are always treated with respect. Yet Bennett still looked on spinsters as sad and wasted. Maggie Clayhanger and Janet Orgreave are both attractive young girls at the beginning of the Clayhanger trilogy, but they fade in beauty and charm as the novels develop, passing imperceptibly through the twilight zone between marriageability and being old maids. Bennett assures us that they are very kindly and would have made the best of wives and mothers, but he never suggests that they might have become anything else, or that they might have wanted to do anything else had it not been for the claims of parents and family. These claims are very real and both 'girls' become indispensable as parents and other relatives grow older and need looking after:

She [Janet] sat there rather straight and rather prim between her parents, sticking to them, smoothing creases for them, bearing their weight, living for them. She was the kindliest, the most dignified, the most capable of creatures; but she was now an old maid. You saw it even in the way she poured the tea and dropped pieces of sugar into the cups. Her youth was gone; her complexion was nearly gone. And though in one aspect she seemed indispensable, in another the chief characteristic of her existence seemed to be a tragic futility.[5]

The narrow range of options open to Janet and Maggie is a convincing picture of the restricted opportunities and cramped lives which single, middle-class women still faced as late as 1910. Yet Bennett never goes beyond regretting that they never married. He does not believe that like Hilda Lessways, a 'new' woman from a family with little money, they should have gone out to work. His attitude is one of mingled sympathy and regret, but he has no constructive suggestions to make.

We find the same pattern in his handling of female domestics. They haunt the background, the cellars and attics of these novels of middle–class domestic life, and even if his bourgeois characters can conveniently forget about them, he cannot. They never play an important part in the books, but they are there all the same, one of Bennett's 'causes', written in to jog the consciences of his public. Here for example is Florrie from *Hilda Lessways*:

... today Florrie was a charming young creature, full of slender grace. Soon she would be a dehumanised drudge. And Hilda could not stop it. All over the town, in every street of the town, behind all the nice curtains and blinds, the same hidden shame was being enacted.[6]

Just why Hilda cannot do something to 'stop it' we are not told. As an interim measure she could always try shortening Florrie's hours and raising her wages. It is the same as with the spinsters – Bennett fails to get beyond sympathy. He presents the exploitation, feels bad about it and then passes on to some other issue. Samuel Hynes believes this was typical of pre–war fiction, of what he calls the 'literature of right feeling'. Here a social problem becomes a humanitarian test for author and reader, the novel demanding a sympathetic response to a stated problem, but its resolution being carefully structured to avoid the kind of absolute contractions which would be more profoundly disturbing.[7] Much the same is true of Galsworthy. The feeling that this allows, that injustice is part of the nature of things, is related to the liberal dilemma of the pre-war years. It was a feeling that Bennett increasingly came to share and which produced his stoicism, the value he places on intelligent resignation.

But even if he holds out little hope for Hilda's Florrie, in Hilda herself Bennett shows that he was very much alive to the way some middle-class women were refusing to accept the traditional role which we see crushing Maggie Clayhanger and Janet Orgreave. She is Bennett's version of a liberated woman, one of the many who began entering white-collar jobs in large numbers during the pre-war years. The war accelerated this development, but the trend towards employing women in administrative and clerical work had already emerged well before 1914,[8] as industry and administrative expansion increasingly needed large numbers of workers for office jobs of all kinds. The invention of the typewriter had mechanized and downgraded clerical work and meant that women could now be safely employed in what became a rapidly expanding area of low paid work. Hilda is the first woman in Bennett's 'Five Towns' to learn typing and shorthand and she becomes secretarial assistant to a local newspaper-man. She is independent and determined to succeed as a single woman, but she is still drawn towards the idea of marriage. The tension between the value she places on her self-sufficiency and her 'instinctive' need for marriage is the crux of *Hilda Lessways*. But it is a problem which Bennett cannot solve because at this point marriage was, for a woman, still quite incompatible with anything but token gestures in the direction of independence – as we see only too clearly in *These Twain*, the novel which concentrates on Hilda's and Edwin's married life. The only possible solution – sexual relationships outside marriage – was not available to women in 1911.

When he began work on *Hilda Lessways* Bennett's intention was to put across the 'point of view' of 'the whole sex', 'against a mere background of masculinity'.[9] He frequently thought he was doing this, but all he generally managed to achieve, especially with young women, was to foist onto them his own very confused ideas of what 'women' were really like. The fact that he does not individuate, but imagines that all women can be lumped together in the catch-all phrase 'the sex', should prepare us for his failure, both in *Hilda* and elsewhere. No-one, as yet, has considered writing a novel about men as a group in which they all share the same consciousness, simply because male dominated culture habitually sees men as individuals; only women are presumed to hold an entire mentality in common and share identical responses to experience. Women as a class clearly do stand in a particular relation to society, and this is what Bennett was probably getting at, but he made the mistake of assuming that *all* women shared the same 'female' consciousness.[10]

The contradictions in Hilda's personality are perfectly explicable in terms of the psychology of a woman divided between inherited culture and changing social conditions. In this sense she is certainly 'typical'. But her emotionalism and the elusiveness which Edwin finds so fascinating and attractive come straight out of Bennett's preconceptions about women being mysterious, in some way unknowable beings. Part of him recognized that women could be, and often were, tough, independent and efficient, but at the same time he never quite relinquished a romantic image of them as something quite apart from everyday reality.[11] This confusion in Bennett's mind about what women actually were and what he wanted them to be runs through his characterization of Hilda in all three Clayhanger books. It meant that he was sympathetic to her feminism but could never credit her with the strength to act it out – and so he has her welcome the chance of settling down peacefully with Edwin, all doubts about marriage swept aside in spite of a previous failure.

The same kind of confusion marks *These Twain*, the novel which shows us Hilda as a wife. As usual Bennett is receptive to feminist ideas. We see this in the way he handles the problems which Hilda has to work through before she and Edwin can really get on together. He enters into her feelings of frustration and bitterness when she is forced to accept that she can only act through her husband, as Mrs Clayhanger; he understands her resentment of her financial dependence, and he shows how domesticity trivializes her. Yet, at the same time, when the marriage seems to be going seriously wrong, he clearly supports Edwin's irritation at Hilda's 'excesses', forgetting what he has already shown he understands – the narrowing of the wife's range of interests and its impact on her self-respect. The novel ends with an uneasy truce between husband and wife after Edwin has capitulated to one of Hilda's whims. But the truce is only possible because Edwin recognizes that 'giving in' is the wisest thing to do. This ability to give way when he knows he is right is the final proof of Edwin's 'maturity'. It supposedly shows his superiority to Hilda, who remains petulant, unreasonable and demanding. So although Bennett has some idea why Hilda behaves as she does, he finally sees her in the same way as Wells saw Ethel in *Love and Mr Lewisham*. She is an overgrown child whose handling requires patience, tolerance and a placid disposition. The wife is still something to be put up with; it is she who is at fault rather than marriage itself.

In short, there are almost as many qualifications to Bennett's feminism as there are to Wells's. He, too, was never able altogether to abandon the assumptions about women he grew up with, and so there is always a tension in his work between what he knew women *could* be and what he still half consciously expected of them. He supported women's rights to work and economic independence but he never really looked on them as equals, continuing to believe they could only find fulfilment through marriage. In a book of essays called *Our Women* (1920), subtitled *Chapters on the Sex Discord*, he spells out some of his basic ideas. Here he openly upholds the Ruskinian doctrine of separate spheres for men and women, alleging that the two sexes have complementary but essentially different psychologies – aggressive/affectionate, rational/irrational, outgoing/domestic. 'Jack leans towards reason', he tells us. 'Jill leans towards sentiment.' 'Jack dominates by intellect. Jill seeks to outflank him by attacking his heart.'[12] He even admits that he believes women are inferior:

In creation, in synthesis, in criticism, in pure intellect women, even the most exceptional and the most favoured, have never approached the accomplishment of men. (p. 104)

And subscribing to the convenient myth that women 'love' to be dominated, he takes it as final proof of 'intellectual inferiority'. (p. 206)

Either Bennett was being unusually candid about his own beliefs or he had an eye on what he thought people wanted to read, especially when it came to work versus marriage. For work in *Our Women* is only an emergency stand-by; it is there to fall back on if Mr Right fails to turn up. As for the 'salary earning girl':

She is not creative; she is not fully capable of self-defence; she does not shine in initiative; she is less complete in herself than a bachelor is in himself; she is very human in that she does not love to work for work's sake; she would like a change; she has dreams, hopes; she is afraid of the reproach, half-pitying, half-disdainful, which society still puts upon the maid who passes a certain age without capturing a man; she longs for the unique feminine dignity of wifehood and motherhood and home-mistresship; she is not averse from ruling a man and a family. (p. 148)

In all, it is hardly surprising to find that Hilda Lessways longs for a husband and home:

She dreamed ... of belonging absolutely to some man. And despite all her pride and independence, she dwelt with pleasure and longing on the vision of being his, of being at his disposal, of being under his might, of being helpless before him. She thought, desolated: 'I am nobody's ...' She scorned herself for being nobody's. To belong utterly to some male seemed to be the one fate for her in the world. And it was a glorious fate, whether it brought good or evil. Any other was ignobly futile, was despicable. (*Hilda Lessways*, p. 282)

The bulk of *Our Women* is given over to outlining women's domestic responsibilities and how best to go about them. Bennett's ideal wife is a graceful hostess in a tea-gown, carefully schooled in cooking, 'the principles of comfort', taste and decor, accounts, the management of servants, first-aid and 'the principles of infant education'. (pp. 56/59) Women are the 'natural creators' of the domestic machine and their primary function is to soothe the troubled male mind:

Jack's got a life job. And so have you. And part of yours is to keep the savage charmed. (p. 91)

The most interesting thing about *Our Women* is its date – 1920. It appeared at a time when women were struggling to keep the jobs they had done during the war, many of them for the first time, but which the Government wanted to hand back to men returning from the Front.[13] In addition, millions of men had been killed in the war and now had to be replaced if British capitalism was to recover its manpower. These two factors helped push women back into the home in the 'twenties and 'thirties and Bennett's book clearly did its bit to encourage them to go quietly. True, it was aimed at bourgeois women, but it was important for middle-class women to be seen to be adopting the ideals of motherhood. As they had only just begun to question these it was relatively easy to persuade them that the home was where they really belonged.

Leonora (1903) is a much earlier book than *Our Women* but it shows that this had perhaps always been Bennett's attitude. It has some strengths. In it he allows a married woman in her early middle-age to love another man without having to pay in guilt and disgrace for the rest of her life. It marks a significant departure from the *Anna Karenina* pattern of tragic remorse. But, this aspect of the plot apart, *Leonora* is a deeply conventional book. Leonora herself is a model of elegant domesticity, and the narrative is based on a very clear division between the factory, where the husband works, and the drawing-room, where Leonora and her daughters wait patiently for the men to return and for life to start again. It is curious to note that the adjective Bennett uses most frequently to describe Leonora is 'supine'. Nor is he being critical. For him it is a word of approval (as long as it is applied to a woman) and is supposed to sum up Leonora's calm relaxed manner, her poise. To me is simply suggests unlimited boredom. And without realizing it, Leonora is bored, for while the men exist in a bustle of work, worries, production and money, the women languish in a world of inactivity, futility, decoration and consumption.

Leonora is in its way bad enough, but a much more alarming novel from the point of view of Bennett's image of women is the little known *Sacred and Profane Love* (1905). It reads like a fictionalized version of some of the worst aspects of *Our Women*. Its heroine (and she really is a heroine, in passionate nineteenth-century style) is Carlotta Peel, Bennett's quite extraordinary idea of a fully emancipated woman. In theory she is intellectually, emotionally and sexually liberated. At the beginning of the novel she has already sloughed off her conventional upbringing and is ready to live according to her new individualistic principles.

The first thing she does, to clinch her liberation, is to sleep with a famous concert pianist who specializes in Chopin (of course) and is giving a recital in her provincial town. She encourages him to seduce her and then drops out of his life as suddenly as she dropped in, giving him the slip in the early hours of the morning. Inevitably she thinks she is pregnant, so she goes off to London to 'avoid discovery'. On arrival she conveniently finds that she is not pregnant after all, but she stays on anyway becoming (overnight and with no difficulty whatsoever) a famous and successful novelist. She then has an affair with her (married) publisher. His wife commits suicide; so does he. Filled with remorse Carlotta disappears again, living this time in romantic seclusion on the Continent. After some time as an intriguing recluse she again comes across Diaz, the pianist. He is in a terrible state, has taken to drink and is ruined as a performer for ever. Needless to say, the reason behind his moral and artistic collapse is Carlotta's desertion after the one-night-stand. (*Cherchez la femme.*) Predictably, she decides that she can save Diaz and his career and so carries him off to convalesce in a handy French château. She now abandons her own career as a novelist, puts her talents at his disposal and writes him a libretto for the opera with which he is to make an astounding comeback as a composer. He makes the comeback alright, but she, unfortunately, dies of appendicitis at the first night. But this does not really matter, as she dies happy in the knowledge that she has saved a great man.

It is difficult to avoid the conclusion that the novel is some kind of male sexual fantasy. What could be more pleasing than for a 'liberated' woman to voluntarily subordinate herself to a man's unspoken needs? Carlotta shows that a career and independence are really nothing to her. What she wants, we are to understand, is the opportunity to obliterate herself in an orgy of self-abnegation:

Wondrous the joy I found in playing the decorative, acquiescent, self-effacing woman to him, the pretty pouting plaything! I liked him to dismiss me, as the soldier dismisses his charmer at the sound of his bugle. I liked to think upon his obvious conviction that the libretto was less than nothing compared to the music. I liked him to regard the whole artistic productivity of my life as the engaging foible of a pretty woman ...[14]

Carlotta, we must remember, is an artist. This makes the form of her renunciation (giving up her career) particularly interesting. Bennett clearly enjoyed entertaining the idea of a liberated lady novelist admitting male artistic superiority. Looked at this way, the whole plot becomes an elaborate exercise in self-flattery by its author.

A yet more startling element of fantasy in *Sacred and Profane Love* is the seduction at the beginning of the novel. The whole scene is artificial and 'stagey' – music, soft lights, velvet furnishings – but more unreal still is Carlotta's cool decision to go with Diaz to his hotel and calmly offer herself to him. No hesitations, no anxieties, no traumas at all. Yet Diaz is a complete stranger and she is sexually inexperienced. Hardly a convincing scenario for 1905. The whole thing is quite fantastic, a sexual daydream in which the author becomes the romantic artist, lonely and misunderstood but sexually magnetic, and Carlotta functions as a cross between a turn of the century groupie and the faithful redeeming woman of mythology.

One critic has called *Sacred and Profane Love* 'almost the most tasteless book ever written by a major novelist', and he is right.[15] The whole conception of the novel is vulgar and sensational, closer to Ouida's or Marie Correlli's romances than Bennett's customary sober realism. The story is told in the first person by Carlotta, and Bennett devised a gushing semi-hysterical narrative style especially for her. He went to great trouble over this and presumably thought it suitable for his 'liberated' heroine. And extraordinary though it may seem, Bennett actually believed, certainly at the time of writing, that *Sacred and Profane Love* was a good novel. He called it 'a serious work', 'a third to *Anna* and *Leonora*'.[16]

Such gross misjudgment is quite unlike the unconceited, down-to-earth man Bennett generally appeared, certainly at this stage of his career. He was genuinely unaware of the novel's offensiveness and artificiality. That he could write such a book illustrates his misconception of what women's liberation would be about. It also shows how far he was from being able to recognize his own quite unconscious prejudices. For, like Wells, Bennett really believed he was a feminist; again like Wells this claim is disproved by a close examination of his texts.

13. Mr Forster's Telegrams and Anger

Forster was a consciously intellectual novelist and he understood the dilemmas facing his generation in a way which was beyond the everyday sobriety of Bennett. He is a world away from the slow capitulation which Bennett's novels enact time and time again in the face of the social and economic problems presented by pre-war England. He was anything but complacent about the developments he saw taking place around him. The novels show this quite clearly. But Forster's reaction to the essentially political problem posed by the waning of liberalism as a progressive ideology and then even as a viable parliamentary grouping, was to retreat into a private world of personal relations and good feeling. He could not embrace socialism because for him it was an ideology which would override individual freedom. For although he rejected the competitive economics of liberal individualism, he continued to believe in a liberal hierarchy of values in which the rights of the individual are sacred. He gives up, if you like, the public and economic aspects of liberalism, but clings to its private morality. 'If we are to answer The Challenge of Our Time successfully', he said, 'we must manage to combine the new economy and the old morality. The doctrine of *laissez-faire* will not work in the material world ... On the other hand, the doctrine of *laissez-faire* is the only one that seems to work in the world of the spirit.'[1]

Forster appears to us now as the artist of liberalism in retreat. His novels rehearse over and over again the tired platitudes of a past world – 'tolerance', 'good temper', 'sympathy', 'personal relationships'. These are the corner-stone of his faith, but though, in a general way, they are important, they are supremely irrelevant to the crises of the contemporary world. They were fairly irrelevant to Forster's own. They could do nothing to ease the growing conflict between capital and labour or, in the 'thirties, to withstand the advance of Fascism. But they were all that was available to a man like Forster who continued to believe that 'programmes mean pograms'[2] and that socialism could only be a totalitarian nightmare.

Forster's commitment to the idea of personal relationships as something to cling to 'in a world of violence and cruelty'[3] has an important bearing on his conception of women. It finally slams in their faces the door to the outer world where all that violence and cruelty actually happens, but where other things go on as well. I shall expand this idea later; meanwhile it is important to appreciate the more positive side of Forster's liberalism.

As a liberal Forster was unusually consistent, and he applied to women the idea of individual freedom which the nineteenth-century had carefully labelled 'men only'. Even more important, his idea of individual freedom included the right to sexual fulfilment – for women as well as for men. Here Forster echoes Edward Carpenter, a friend and writer who is acknowledged as an influence in *Two Cheers for Democracy* (1951). Many of the ideas in *A Room With A View* (1908), *Where Angels Fear to Tread* (1905) and *The Longest Journey* (1907) are very close to what Carpenter had said in *Love's Coming Of Age*, and one of the characters in *A Room With a View*, the utopian socialist and free thinker Mr Emerson, could almost be a portrait of Carpenter. Certainly their views are strikingly similar.

Forster asserts, in a milder form than Lawrence, everyone's right to a fully developed sexuality. The damage done by either sexual inhibition or moral hypocrisy is a key theme in all his novels, the most obviously 'Carpenterish' of these being the two 'Italian' works – *A Room With A View* and *Where Angels Fear to Tread* – where he opposes sexual vitality, passion and what he loosely calls 'the holiness of the heart's affections', to the serile conventions of the respectable, repressed English middle classes. In *A Room With A View* he specifically argues in favour of sexual freedom for women. For here Lucy Honeychurch, a girl who has been subjected to the usual 'ladylike' English upbringing, is finally forced to recognize and accept her own sexuality, even though it leads her out of her class and away from her family. Through the sensuous magic of Italy (a country which to Forster always meant emotional and physical liberation), and under the kindly tutelage of Mr Emerson, Lucy at last breaks free from her conditioning, admitting to herself that she is in love with Emerson's son George. She is thus saved from the wasted life of genteel virginity for which she was stubbornly heading. Such a life, Forster tells us, 'sins' against 'passion and truth'.[4]

It is probable that like Carpenter, Forster owed what seems to be an instinctive understanding of women's sexual oppression to his own frustrated homosexuality. Disguised homosexual episodes and relationships appear in most of the novels, and where Forster makes use of images to suggest sexual freedom or energy, they generally have exclusively male associations. For instance, the naked male swimming party in *A Room With A View* is a much more convincing expression of sexual energy than the heterosexual, but curiously abstract, kiss that George unexpectedly gives Lucy among the violets in Italy. The Lucy/George relationship is supposed to stand for sexual and emotional freedom, but it remains oddly unreal. We seldom see them together and we never feel the emotional reality of their relationship. Intellectually, we can see what Forster is getting at, but the whole affair remains calculated and stilted. Lionel Trilling has this to say about it:

Nothing could be more artful, nothing more disembodied than this story about naturalness and the body. Its hero and heroine are as nearly creatures of air or mythology as it is possible for two young people to be in a story about sexuality.[5]

In a general way the relationship manages to *represent* sexual attraction – through symbol and argument. What it does not do is to make us feel the attraction between George and Lucy. This is possibly because for Forster the affair is really an artificial area of interest. He had little knowledge of heterosexual relationships and when he has to write about them he could only draw on his own repressed homosexuality. What Leavis calls 'a spinsterish inadequacy in the immediate presentation of love' is the result.[6]

It is also curious to notice that Forster's women are only

really convincing in their relationships with men when the relationships go badly wrong. Thus Lucy's irritation and only half recognized impatience with her fiancé, Cecil, is much more successful than the rather forced Lucy/George interludes. And Margaret Schlegel's precarious marriage with Henry Wilcox in *Howards End* (1910) is interesting in a way in which her sister's brief intoxication with Leonard Bast definitely is not. It is as though the difficult, uneasy relationship is the norm for Forster. He knows and can write about it.

I think we can fairly say then that Forster's homosexuality gave him a special insight into women's sexual repression, but inhibited him when it came to actually writing about sexual relationships. Less acceptably, it was probably the basis, too, of Agnes Pembroke, Rickie's wife in *The Longest Journey*. Agnes is Forster's chilling version of woman-as-destroyer, the man-trap we have already met closing in on so many of Gissing's hard-pressed husbands. She is heartless, narrow-minded and utterly selfish, so much so that with her Forster verges on Gissing's misogynist hatred. Such women do, no doubt, exist, preying on weak ineffectual men, but Agnes leaves us with an overwhelming impression that Forster was really afraid of women, of what (he believed) they could do to men.

Rickie's friend Ansell is instinctively hostile to Agnes. Motivated by sexual jealousy and without knowing anything at all about her, Ansell denounces her as a predator and predicts disaster if the marriage takes place:

'She is happy because she has conquered ... She wants Rickie partly to replace another man whom she lost two years ago, partly to make something out of him. He is to write. In time she will get sick of this. He won't get famous. She will only see how thin and lame he is. She will long for a jollier husband, and I don't blame her. And having made him thoroughly miserable and degraded, she will bolt – if she can do it like a lady.'[7]

By making Ansell the mouthpiece for his suspicion of Agnes, Forster cleverly displaces his hostility onto an 'outsider'; yet, when Ansell's gloomy forebodings are borne out by the subsequent development of the plot, we see that Forster endorses Ansell's initial suspicion and dislike. Agnes does not 'bolt' – she is much too conventional; but she does much worse in humiliating and destroying her husband.

The feeling that women are always potentially destructive, threats to the moral integrity and dignity of men, is at its clearest in *The Longest Journey*. But it is there in the other novels as well, especially in the later and more ambitious *Howards End*. Among other things this novel is specifically about male/female relationships, but the principal theme is the need to 'connect' and harmonize what Forster saw as conflicting and apparently irreconcileable elements in the English liberal culture of his day. He realized that the personal qualities he valued and respected – generosity, sensitivity, discrimination – do not exist of themselves alone, but grow out of an assured private income, itself based in turn on the distasteful capitalist economics of *laissez-faire* liberalism. So in *Howards End* he hoped to show how what he calls elsewhere the 'private decencies' of 'an aristocracy of the sensitive, the considerate and the plucky' could be 'transmitted to public affairs'.[8]

As usual with Forster, the novel is carefully patterned into opposing groups of characters. It is all clearly signposted. The Schlegel sisters, Margaret and Helen, and their brother Tibby represent the humane liberal culture, based on private morality and the 'inner world' of personal relationships in which Forster himself shares. The Wilcox family represent finance capital and business efficiency. They are involved in the 'outer' material world of 'telegrams and anger'. The Schlegels are all sensitivity, discrimination and refined morality. The Wilcoxes, at their best, are industrious, neat and decisive – in short genuine inheritors of the protestant work ethic. At their worse, and we invariably see them at their worst in the novel, they are hypocritical, obtuse, emotionally dishonest. They are the overgrown public schoolboys whom Carpenter saw as the typical adult middle-class Englishman. But without them, says Forster, the cultured and cushioned lives of the Schlegels could never exist. Margaret recognizes this. She is, she says:

'tired of all these rich people who pretend to be poor, and think it shows a nice mind to ignore the piles of money that keep their feet above the waves. I stand each year upon six hundred pounds a year, and Helen upon the same, and Tibby will stand upon eight, and as fast as our pounds crumble into the sea, they are renewed ... And all our thoughts are the thought of six-hundred pounders, and all our speeches.'[9]

So she marries Henry Wilcox. Forster endorses her decision and the reasoning behind it – the alliance of money and morals is to provide a home for Helen's illegitimate child. The baby's father, Leonard Bast, is Forster's idea of a working-class man struggling to improve himself, and the child itself is a symbol of the future harmony between the best qualities of both classes, between 'liberal idealism and underprivileged effort'.[10] But, as Leavis points out, the marriage remains an unconvincing piece of wish-fulfilment:

We are meant to approve. The novelist's attitude is quite unambiguous: as a result of the marriage, which is Margaret's active choice, Helen ... is saved and the book closes serenely on the promise of a happy future. Nothing in the exhibition of Margaret's or Henry's character makes the marriage credible or acceptable.[11]

The marriage does not lead, as Forster would have us believe, to a final reconciliation between Culture and the sordid business of money-making, between Schlegels and Wilcoxes, the rich and the underprivileged. It leads to the defeat of the Wilcoxes. By the close of the novel Henry is a broken man and his son, Charles, is in prison serving a sentence for manslaughter after accidentally killing Bast in a characteristic fit of Wilcox obtuseness.

So Forster's attempt to convince himself, and us, that there is no contradiction between a tolerant liberal culture and its basis in a system of economic exploitation, fails. But the attempt reveals something very interesting about Forster's idea of women. For Margaret and Helen represent more than the culture and personal values of the bourgeoisie. They also represent 'women'.

Howards End appeared in 1910. The date is important because it was also the height of the WSPU campaign against the Liberal Government. It was a time when the whole question of women's role and position in society was in the forefront of people's minds, a time when middle-class women in particular were acting and mobilizing in a way which hardly corresponded to their official public image. They were still supposed to be helpless but contented dependents. Yet here they were out on the streets, demonstrating, getting themselves arrested and generally behaving in an aggressive, essentially 'unfeminine' way.

There are no suffragettes in *Howards End*, but the book was still very topical in terms of the women's movement because it tried to tackle the whole question of male/female relationships. Margaret and Helen are both, in a limited and rather conventional way, feminists, and the Wilcoxes are ultra-masculine males who disapprove of almost everything the Schlegel sisters do. They are very manly men indeed – almost caricatures of clean-living, hearty Victorians. Forster finds this comic, but for him their masculinity is still part and parcel of their economic efficiency. In *Howards End* the two go together. It is male confidence that makes the Wilcoxes so successful, and they are supremely well-organized chiefly because they are not hampered by 'feminine' sensitivity. 'Once past the rocks of emotion, they knew so well what to do, whom to send for.' (p. 98) They are in complete command of the material world; they run about in those new-fangled motor cars, buy and sell houses, move into them and out of them again, furnish and empty them with no difficulty at all. (Margaret, whose attempts at house-hunting are a complete failure, laments that 'gentlemen seem to be able to mesmerize houses – cow them with an eye, up they come, trembling. Ladies can't. It's the houses that are mesmerizing me. I've no control over the saucy things.') (p. 146) The Wilcoxes are formidable decision makers, dealing neatly and decisively with problems – 'item by item'. But it is just here that their masculinity lets them down; they make the mistake of trying to control the emotional and personal world in the same brisk way as the material world of capital and property. We see this in the way they try to handle Helen Schlegel. When Helen mysteriously refuses to see her sister, the Wilcox tribe automatically presume she is deranged and set about trying to capture her. They succeed, more or less, but only because they cease to treat her as a rational being with rights to be respected. To them she is no longer a person but an animal. 'The pack', we are told, 'was turning on Helen to deny her human rights.' (p. 269) What Forster wants us to see in all this is that manly men may be efficient and powerful, but they are deficient in sensitivity and imagination. This cannot, he believes, be ignored or excused.

Motor cars play an interesting and important part in establishing the Wilcoxes' masculinity. All the Wilcoxes own or drive cars and this in itself is a symbol of their wealth, their grip on the material world. But the association with motors means more than this; it also points out what Forster sees as their typically masculine defects. For the Wilcoxes the cars are useful because they give them greater status, speed, efficiency and mobility. They are only interested in covering distances in them and are quite oblivious of the countryside around them or the people they inconvenience. Margaret, however, dislikes motor cars. For her a journey with the Wilcoxes is unpleasant because she cannot enjoy her surroundings any more. ('She looked at the scenery. It heaved and merged like porridge. Presently it congealed. They had arrived.' (p. 185)) Even worse is Charles Wilcox's insensitivity when he runs over a little girl's dog. He drives on, leaving another man and two servants to deal with the incident. Margaret insists that 'men can't see to it', but Charles will not stop the car and allow her to go back. For a moment she is powerless, but then she jumps out of the car while it is still moving, intending to run and soothe the child with the feminine sympathy the men neither understand nor realize is necessary. 'Charles', says Forster, 'had never been in such a position before. It was a woman in revolt who was hobbling away from him, and the sight was too strange to leave any room for anger.' (p. 199) The next incident of the episode then clinches the sensitive/insensitive opposition Forster has been working to establish. One of the men who has been dealing with the child calls out: 'It's alright ... it wasn't a dog, it was a cat ... I cut as soon as I saw it wasn't a dog.' 'There!' exclaimed Charles triumphantly. 'It's only a rotten cat!'

The Wilcox houses and the Wilcox furniture are also excessively masculine and they too are deliberately connected by Forster with the Wilcox hold on the 'outer' world. When Margaret is looking over their London house she thinks of one room that it 'would never do with her own furniture, but those heavy chairs, that immense sideboard loaded with presentation plate, stood up against its pressure like men. The room suggested men, and Margaret, keen to derive the modern capitalist from the warriors and hunters of the past, saw it as an ancient guest-hall where the lord sat at meat among his thanes.' We learn that 'we fellows smoke' in the entrance hall. And when we are smoking 'we fellows' sit in maroon leather armchairs. Significantly, Margaret thinks that 'it was as if a motor car had spawned'. (p. 153) The drawing-room on the other hand is typically feminine, or at least typical of the Wilcox idea of femininity. 'It was sallow and ineffective. One could visualize the ladies withdrawing to it, while their lords discussed life's realities below, to the accompaniment of a cigar.' (p. 154)

Where the Wilcoxes act out Forster's idea of clumsy masculine insensitivity, the Schlegel sisters represent the sensitivity and moral perceptiveness he identifies with women. The Wilcoxes live in a masculine world of cash and property, the Schlegels in the sheltered but responsive world of personal relationships. The novel attempts to 'connect' these two worlds of masculine and feminine as much as it tries to ease the ethical contradictions of *laissez-faire* liberalism. Margaret believes that there is some good in the 'outer' world of money-getting. It does have something to offer:

'the truth is that there is a great outer life that you and I have never touched – a life in which telegrams and anger count. Personal relations, that we think supreme, are not supreme there. There love means marriage-settlements, death, death duties. So far I'm clear. But here my difficulty. This outer life, though obviously horrid, often seems the real one.' (p. 27)

But the attempt to connect the two opposing realms of masculine and feminine consciousness fails too. What Forster represents as male and female values conflict, mildly in the incident we have already looked at when Charles runs over the cat, and then severely over the moral issues surrounding Helen's pregnancy. Helen is pregnant by a one-night-stand with Leonard Bast; when Henry Wilcox finds out about it he mouths, vociferously and indignantly, all the usual moral platitudes of outraged respectability. Margaret immediately feels that in standing by Helen she is 'fighting for women against men'. (p. 270) More particularly, she is fighting Henry's sexual hypocrisy. For by a rather mechanical piece of plotting, Henry has in the past had an affair with Bast's wife. So he has done no more and no less than Helen herself. But he still condemns Helen, even going as far as invoking against her the dead first Mrs Wilcox – 'canting with her memory', Margaret calls it.

Henry's natural self-deception and moral obtuseness are so great that he simply cannot see his own inconsistencies. He expects Margaret, now his wife, to forgive him for his past affair with Bast's wife, but has no intention of 'forgiving' Helen. This leads to a serious break-down in his relationship with Margaret. They are finally reconciled, but only after Henry has been exhausted by the shock of his son's imprisonment. The conclusion, with Margaret and Henry providing a peaceful home for Helen and the baby at Howards End, is supposed to be optimistic, but, as we have already seen, the rebuilding of the marriage is really very unconvincing. And it is now on quite a different basis. Margaret is in complete control and Henry is a broken man, emotionally and physically dependent on his wife.

His collapse, Charles's imprisonment and Bast's death all point to real anxieties about women on Forster's part. Through a complicated chain of events, Margaret and Helen finally destroy all the men with whom they come into contact, so that in spite of the 'official' happy ending, the fusion of masculine and feminine values remains an unfulfilled dream.

Forster fails in *Howards End* because he accepts the traditionally rigid separation between male and female psychological characteristics. Wilcoxes and Schlegels are the product of highly conventional ideas of masculinity and femininity; the men are defined entirely in terms of the outside world which orthodox opinion still believed was their natural sphere, and the women are restricted to the private 'inner' world of the emotions. This sharp division arises to some extent out of the way Forster uses the Wilcoxes and Schlegels primarily to represent conflicting aspects of contemporary British culture. The ultra-masculinity of the men and the ultra-femininity of the women correspond to the public world of economic competition and the private world of liberal moral values. So the traditional male/female stereotypes are an important part of the political patterning of the whole book. But it is just this that interferes with Forster's obvious intention of exploring exactly what his contemporaries meant by 'male' and 'female'.

It imposes a serious limitation on the way he thinks about women.

The two sisters are fairly emancipated in their everyday lives; they go to lectures and even give them, and (like the Stephen sisters, Virginia and Vanessa, whom Forster knew well) they have their own private establishment and circle of friends. They go on walking holidays in Europe without the customary chaperone. But all this really adds up to is a superficial modernity; fundamentally Forster is still living in Ruskin's ideal world where men are naturally outgoing and aggressive and women inward-looking and affectionate. More important, women still represent for Forster that haven of peace in an intolerable world. The sisters are at the centre of his cult of personal relationships which he looks to to provide 'something to cling to'. This is the image Forster would like to leave us with at the end of the book where we see Margaret, who has now taken over from the first Mrs Wilcox as the spirit of peace and contentment, soothing the scarred and damaged fugitives from the outside world.

Margaret is right when she tells Helen that there is 'a great outer life' that neither of them has ever entered. Yet, although she recognizes its existence by marrying Henry Wilcox, she never really involves herself in it. Neither sister will ever have to dirty her hands – literally through having to work for a living, or metaphorically through adopting Wilcox moral standards. Forster never shows any interest at all in women as workers, and *Howards End* is no exception. Instead he imprisoned them in an ideology which excludes them from the world of work, its concrete experiences and material pressures. Because they are women and because they are upper-class, and so assured of a large private income, this is never a disadvantage for the Schlegel sisters. On the contrary, it is a decided advantage as it saves them from the moral pragmatism of the Wilcox type. But if we turn to Tibby Schlegel, the girls' brother, we can see quite clearly that, for him at least, it *is* damaging to be cut off from work and effort. Tibby is effete, ineffectual, unreliable. Forster makes him an amiable parasite. But the only difference between Tibby and his sisters is his sex and an extra two hundred a year. For Margaret and Helen to cultivate their moral and artistic tastes is apparently alright;

but for Tibby it is not. His life-style, really no different from theirs, is seen as trivial. Theirs is not. This is because they are women, and women, according to Forster, are born to live an exclusively private, emotional life.

This assumption permeates all of Forster's novels, but it is not a result of the complacency we find in Wells and Bennett. It is closer to Ruskin's or Matthew Arnold's reaction to the bewildering contradictions of nineteenth-century liberalism. For, like them, Forster sets women apart from the realities of everyday life, because he needs to reserve for them a special place where peace and affection triumph over the conflicts and anxieties of political and economic life.

Suspicious of political commitment and doubtful of the capacity of human nature to build a just society, Forster placed his faith and his hopes for a better future in the idea of personal relationships, in the vague values of tolerance, sympathy and 'good temper'. His women are central symbols of this idea, but it is an idea which confines them in a prison of private affections, so that they are barred for ever from participating in the material world where political and social struggles take place.

PART FIVE

CONCLUSION

14. Mr Lawrence and Mrs Woolf

One of the clearest developments in the English novel since 1880 has been the disappearance of the virgin heroine and a readiness to recognize and incorporate sexuality into fiction. We can trace this development from Hardy, through Edward Carpenter to Forster and Lawrence. And though H.G. Wells's attempts to fuse politics with literature led him in a quite different artistic direction from that taken by his contemporaries, *Ann Veronica, The New Machiavelli* and the other works in which Wells justifies the full expression of human sexuality place him very firmly within this tradition.

But the recognition of female sexuality does not of itself make a feminist novel. On the contrary, the versions of female sexuality which were evolved by these writers were strictly masculine ones. Hardy, though in many ways a strong feminist, all too often saw women as destructive sensualists; Wells created women who combined intellect and strength of character with sexuality largely for the benefit of his fictional men; Forster was not really competent to write about female sexuality at all. Because at the same time no strong feminist writers emerged to define women differently, it was very easy for these new tendencies to dominate the novel.

There are good reasons why this should have happened. The chief one was the confusion among women themselves about the whole question of sexuality. As we have already seen, political feminists in Britain were militantly anti-sex; this meant that they failed to support even feminist writers if and when their work attempted to break free of the old stereotypes.

Second, women novelists experienced great difficulty in writing about sex. Times had changed since Charlotte Brontë had felt obliged to disguise her sex by adopting a pseudonym, but only a little. George Egerton's pen-name may have been a whim rather than a necessity, but it didn't make it any easier for her to write down her feelings about herself of her sexuality at a time when frigidity in women was still considered quite normal. As many as thirty years later Virginia Woolf found this same problem insurmountable. For her, 'telling the truth about my own experiences as a body' was impossible. 'Outwardly what is simpler than to write books? Outwardly what obstacles are there for a woman rather than for a man? Inwardly, I think, the case is very different: She has still many ghosts to fight, many prejudices to overcome.'[1] As Virginia Woolf recognized, the problem has been one of developing a 'voice', a style in which women can write unselfconsciously about sex. Egerton did not manage it, nor have very many women after her. And although, of her generation, she came nearest to writing convincingly about women's sexual feelings, hers was a single, unsupported voice; alone it was not enough to counter the new versions of female sexuality then being established in the novel.

Yet even if we set aside for a moment the question of the various authors' points of view, it remains true that even though after about 1880 sentiment and discreet evasion in the novel were replaced by an open recognition of sexuality, at a more fundamental level there was no real change either in the framework within which women existed in the novel, or in the general assumptions about them and their lives which have always shaped their literary image. By this I mean the assumptions that women, rather than men, are the central focus of the emotional life, and that they find their greatest satisfaction through their emotional and sexual relationships. These are generally thought of as being in the background of a man's life, but in the foreground of a woman's. The gradual sexualizing of women in the novel has not made any difference at all to this kind of belief. Fictional relationships have become more intense and more physical, but as far as the woman is concerned the relationship is still presented as the most important part of her life, and is usually the only part which is given any prominence at all.

I think these two points – the dominance of male versions of female sexuality, and the novel's continuing indifference to the material, everyday part of women's lives – are still hampering the development of a truthful picture of women in contemporary fiction. They certainly made possible the overwhelming influence which D.H. Lawrence has had in this century, not only on the portrayal of women in fiction, but on the way two generations have thought about sexual relationships.

Kate Millett has already argued the feminist case against Lawrence, so there is no need to go into it again in any great detail here, but leaving aside for the moment the specifically anti-feminist elements in his work, it is worth noting that Lawrence's belief in spontaneous, instinctive living led him to an enormous over-emphasis on sexuality when writing about women. He is simply not interested in their material existence, in what they *do*. After *Sons and Lovers* (1913) and *The Rainbow* (1915), we see nothing of the day-to-day circumstances of their lives; we may learn in passing that they are, or have been, teachers, painters or whatever, but this is supremely irrelevant; their only real function in the novels is as part of an emotional and sexual cult.

Lawrence detested both consciousness of the self and intellectualism, what he called 'knowledge in the head'. These he identified with all that is worst in modern industrial civilization. But they were also an important part of the aggressive feminism which, to use Virginia Woolf's words, turned the English woman into 'a voter, a wage-earner, a responsible citizen'.[2] The militant suffrage campaign, at its strongest at just the time when Lawrence was writing his first novels, was firmly rooted in liberalism, in the ideology which regards the individual and his (now her) rights as sacrosanct. Such a theory could only infuriate Lawrence, who disapproved of this cerebral kind of self-consciousness and believed that individual development – what he called 'personality' – damaged the inner man or woman. Given these views it was both logical and inevitable that he should become an enemy of feminism.

And a very consistent enemy he was. All the women in the novels who have achieved a degree of personal development are presented as misguided individualists who, for their own sanity, must be saved from the twin dangers of equality and independence. Either they learn to repudiate the feminist principle of self-determination, accepting in its place the Lawrencian beliefs in the instincts and the natural superiority of male sexual potency (Ursula in *Women In Love*, Clara Dawes in *Sons and Lovers*, Kate in *The Plumed Serpent*), or, if they fail to conform to this Lawrencian norm, they forfeit the right even to sympathy (Hermione and Gudrun in *Women In Love*, Winifred Inger in *The Rainbow*, Banford in *The Fox*.)

In spite of all this, Lawrence's fiction has had, until recently, a beguiling attraction for women. This is because it stresses the importance of sexual liberation. It has only relatively recently been noticed that Lawrence's idea of sexual liberty entails the obliteration of any real female independence. But there has never been any mistaking the anti-feminism in the essays and journalism, where we find articles like 'Cocksure Women and Hensure Men' in which women who attempt anything out-side their 'natural' sexual sphere, find 'so often that instead of having laid an egg they have laid a vote, or an empty ink-bottle, or some other absolutely unhatchable object which means nothing to them'.[3] We learn both from essays like this one and from the novels, that what women should really be doing is capitulating before the Lawrencian super-male:

Winifred adored her husband, and looked up to him as something wonder-ful. Perhaps she had expected in him another great authority, a male author-ity greater, finer than her father's. For having once known the glow of male power, she would not easily turn to the cold white light of feminine independence. She would hunger, hunger all her life for the warmth and shelter of true male strength.[4]

This is the pattern by which Lawrence always judges women and their sexual relationships. Any deviation is not tolerated. Lesbianism in particular is unpardonable; for example, in *The Rainbow*, Ursula's lesbian friend and school teacher, Winifred Inger, is 'punished' by being married to an industrialist who, like Gerald Crich, handles men and machinery interchange-ably. The marriage supposedly clinches Lawrence's identifica-tion of feminism with 'unnatural' sexuality and a doomed industrial civilization. The chapter which describes Ursula and Winifred's brief affair is, revealingly enough, entitled 'Shame', and another lesbian, 'the' Banford in *The Fox* (1922) is killed off to make way for true male strength when Lawrence arranges a crudely symbolic tree-felling. The tree falls on Banford.

Lawrence then, repudiated what he chose to call the 'cold white light of feminine independence'. As far as he was concerned women should be creatures of instinct, not reason, and his work accordingly defines them almost entirely by their sexuality, so that their emotional lives, their relationships, become the only real area of interest. The only contemporary writer who could perhaps have created an alternative to this vision of women was Virginia Woolf. For if Lawrence presents them in an exclusively sexual light, she, at least in her non-fiction, gives us what had become the traditional feminist view. When she writes about women in her essays and reviews, she concentrates on the everyday reality of their lives, and in *A Room of One's Own* (1929) she argues strongly for a fiction which would record the mundane experience of ordinary women, instead of the passions of the exceptional:

... the majority of women are neither harlots nor courtesans; nor do they sit clasping pug dogs to dusty velvet all through the summer afternoon. But what do they do then? and there came to my mind's eye one of those long streets somewhere south of the river whose infinite rows are innumerably populated. With the eye of the imagination I saw a very ancient lady crossing the street on the arm of a middle-aged woman, her daughter perhaps ... The elder lady is close on eighty; but if one asked her what her life has meant to her, she would say that she remembered the streets lit for the battle of Balaclava, or had heard the guns fire in Hyde Park for the birth of King Edward the Seventh. And if one asked her, longing to pin down the moment with date and season, but what were you doing on the fifth of April, 1868, or the second of November, 1875, she would look vague and say that she could remember nothing. For all the dinners are cooked, the plates and cups washed; the children sent to school and gone out into the world. Nothing remains of it all. No biography or history has a word to say about it. And the novels, without meaning to, inevitably lie ... All these infinitely obscure lives remain to be recorded ... (*A Room of One's Own*, p. 88)

She was also quite well aware of the movement towards the exclusively sexualized idea of women which we have found in Lawrence. Commenting on a novel by an anonymous 'Mr A', she says that 'a shadow, shaped something like the letter 'I' lay across the page:

One began dodging this way and that to catch a glimpse of the landscape behind it. Whether that was indeed a tree or a woman walking I was not quite sure. Back one was always hailed to the letter 'I' ... Is that a tree? No, it is a woman. But ... she has not a bone in her body, I thought, watching Phoebe, for that was her name, coming across the beach. Then Alan got up and the shadow of Alan at once obliterated Phoebe. For Alan had views and Phoebe was quenched in the flood of his views. And then Alan, I thought, had passions; and here I turned page after page very fast, feeling that the crisis was approaching, and so it was. It took place on the beach under the sun. It was done very openly, it was done very vigorously. Nothing could have been more indecent. But ... I am bored ... (*Room of One's Own*, p. 99)

And she is bored because there is 'some obstacle, some imped-iment' in Mr A's mind which is blocking 'the fountain of creative energy'. This obstacle is his deliberately aggressive, self-conscious masculinity – 'He is protesting against the equality of the other sex by asserting his own superiority.'

What Virginia Woolf would like to see in place of this and in place of all the novel's falsifications of women's nature, is women defining their own relationships and defining them in relation to other women:

All these relationships between women, I thought, rapidly recalling the splendid gallery of fictitious women, are too simple. So much has been left out, unattempted. And I tried to remember any case in the course of my reading where two women are represented as friends ... They are now and then mothers and daughters. But almost without exception they are shown in their relations to men. (*Room of One's Own*, p. 82)

Everything else has been 'left out'.

A Room of One's Own shows that Virginia Woolf had a clear-sighted, historically informed view of women and fic-tion – women as writers of fiction and women as they appear in fiction. Yet when it came to her own novels she failed to carry out the transformation of women's image which she knew was necessary and which she herself seemed well-equipped to attempt. This is one of the puzzles of her work.

Most of her novels contain specifically feminist elements. The heroines of the first two books, *The Voyage Out* (1915) and *Night and Day* (1919), vacillate over marriage and sex; there is the brilliant realization of Mr Ramsay's unrelenting male egotism in *To The Lighthouse* (1927); *Orlando* (1928) is a book which explores the nature of sexuality; *The Years* (1937) gives us a number of different women, some married, others spinsters, all of whom have been in some way maimed or cheated by life; the entire narrative consciousness of *Mrs Dalloway* (1922) could be described as an essentially feminine, if not feminist, one. But yet there is no coherent attempt to create new models, new images of women. The feminism is only ever a small part of the novels, is never strong enough to act as a counterweight to Lawrence's mystification of women and their sexuality. Her own frigidity may have had something to do with it, but Virginia Woolf certainly never attempted, either, the exploration of women's sexual feelings which she seems to promise in *A Room of One's Own*. Nor does she bring before us that 'accumulation of unrecorded life' (*A Room of One's Own*, p. 89) which she wanted to see break in on the novel's traditional indifference to women's everyday experience.

This failure to carry her feminism through into her novels seems to stem, at least in part, from her aesthetic theories – in particular from her idea of the relation between fiction as an art and the process of human pe. ception. I think most readers of Virginia Woolf must have felt at one time or another that she was as interested, if not more interested, in experimenting with the formal, aesthetic aspects of the novel as she was in saying something about human experience. She conceived of life as a 'luminous halo, a semi-transparent envelope surrounding us from the beginning of consciousness to the end', and it was as non-stop, if selective, flux of sensory and emotional impressions ('an incessant shower of innumerable atoms') that she set about recreating human experience in her novels.[5] She makes her characters register the external world as 'a myriad impressions – trivial, fantastic, evanescent, or engraved with the sharpness of steel'.[6] But this plethora of impressions, rather than bringing the reader closer to the everyday reality of Virginia Woolf's men and women seems rather to wrap them in a haze of subjective perceptions, to lock them into a private world, which we can relate to any shared material reality only with the greatest of difficulty. In this way her 'characters' (and the most important ones are generally women) become tantalizingly intangible. As their inner consciousness becomes more and more important, their outer lives are increasingly neglected, so that finally, far from presenting us with an 'accumulation of unrecorded life', what Virginia Woolf actually offers us is a version of experience mystified almost beyond recognition.

Her aesthetic and stylistic experiments should not be under-rated – along with her contemporaries Dorothy Richardson and James Joyce she transformed the narrative structure of the English novel – but I think it is true, in spite of what she herself believed, that Virginia Woolf's aesthetic theories actually devitalized her fictional world.

Her primary commitment as a novelist was, quite properly, artistic. Our great misfortune, and possibly hers, is that her artistic theories could not comfortably accommodate her feminism and that she apparently had to choose between them. In *A Room of One's Own* she moves easily between feminist and artistic criteria, but cannot reconcile them. They finally emerge as incompatibles:

It is fatal for anyone who writes to think of their sex ... It is fatal for a woman to lay the least stress on any grievances; to plead even with justice any cause; in any way to speak consciously as a woman ... for anything written with that conscious bias is doomed to death. (p. 102/3)

Her goal is what she calls the 'androgynous mind', which is both masculine and feminine and so free from sexual self-consciousness. When she comes to write, a woman must forget her oppression.

Interestingly, this androgynous creative mind is curiously neutral, inactive. It 'lies' passively receiving impressions from the outside world. This, I think, brings us close to another reason for Virginia Woolf's virtual disregard of feminism in her novels, in as much as this idea of creativity precludes any conflict, any real engagement with external reality:

Not a wheel must grate, not a light glimmer. The curtains must be closed down. The writer ... must lie back and let his mind celebrate its nuptuals in darkness. He must not look or question what is being done ... (*A Room of One's Own*, p. 103)

This concept, with its unmistakeable overtones of sexual passivity, seems to specifically exclude the notion of conflict. It was possibly a way of avoiding the feminist consciousness which Virginia Woolf undoubtedly had, but which seems to have placed almost intolerable pressure on her. It is interesting in this respect that although the creative mind is denoted here as 'he', the 'lying back', the not questioning 'what is being done' (note, too, the use of the passive voice), in fact evoke the traditionally submissive 'she'.

Such a passive attitude towards the writer's mental processes and towards the external world rule out any vigorous (a 'masculine' concept) quarrel with social orthodoxies, whether they affect men or women. This is a habit of mind which Virginia Woolf makes her characters, particularly her women characters, share, and which has the effect of cutting them off from any positive action. Her women are thus cast in a highly traditional mould. Mrs Ramsay and Clarissa Dalloway, like Forster's Schlegel sisters, are all perception and sensitivity. Socially and emotionally creative in a style which links them with an essentially 'female' notion of consciousness, they are far removed from Lawrence's emphasis on instinct and sexuality. Yet they are still confined to a 'female' sphere, distinguished in feeling and perception from Mr Ramsay, Hugh Witbred or the psychiatrist Bradshaw.

Virginia Woolf was a major literary figure in the twenties and thirties; since then there have been a number of important women writers who have set out to do what she deliberately avoided doing – write at a conscious level about what it means to be a woman living in our society. (Ivy Compton Burnett and Jean Rhys in the thirties and forties and, more recently, writers such as Fay Weldon, Doris Lessing, Margaret Drabble, Edna O'Brien and in America, Mary McCarthy.) A common feature of these novelists is that although, with the increased 'permissiveness' of recent decades, many of them have begun to write more freely about women's sexuality, they still have not recognized the importance of incorporating the non-sexual, non-emotional aspects of women's lives into their novels. In their work the tyranny of the intensely personal, of the non-material, is as strong as ever it was, and the privatized world of personal relations which was at its zenith in Lawrence remains the only one in which their women are allowed to exist. This means that there has been no real break with fictional convention. The private world has been sexualized, women have been sexualized, but the assumption that inner experiences are the most significant part of a woman's life remains intact. In Doris Lessing this tendency has become gradually more rather than less pronounced.

Here again the overall historical development of the novel has played its part. One of the major changes which has taken place in fiction during this century has been the movement away from the realist assumption that the novel can, indeed should, explore the contradictory, but ultimately explicable relationship between the individual and his or her society. For the novelist 'reality' used to mean the outcome of countless connections between the individual and the 'outer' world. But in the last sixty years the novel has increasingly adopted the notion that the only true 'reality' is within the consciousness of isolated individuals. The inner voyage, the drama of the alienated consciousness, has become the characteristic theme of twentieth-century literature. This is a truism of contemporary cultural history; but it is worth noting that this development has had an important impact on the way women are portrayed in literature. It has strengthened the dominant assumption about the world of private experience being the only really important part of a woman's life. Simply because the internal consciousness is now seen as the 'true reality' for men as well as for women, it does not make the tyranny of the private world any the less oppressive for those who are actually denied full participation in the 'world outside'.

I think the failure to break away from this subjectivism indicates that one of the problems encountered by explicitly feminist novelists at the end of the last century is being re-encountered by the current generation of women writers. This is a difficulty peculiar to realist fiction – that of how to incorporate into a form whose essential characteristic is the exploration of existing realities, experiences and aspirations which go well beyond the possibilities afforded by that reality. For although women clearly do not live the entirely privatized lives of fictional tradition or of contemporary ideology, it is equally true also that they do not yet live the kind of lives feminists envisage as a real if distant possibility. This explains I think the increasing importance of non-realist narrative forms in contemporary women's writing. I am thinking here of writers such as Monique Wittig, Beryl Bainbridge, Angela

Carter and Patricia Highsmith, all of whom work in fantasy or thriller modes. Like George Egerton and Olive Schreiner, these novelists are deliberately adopting non-realist narrative methods. It is here, and in the equally non-realist and, possibly more important, non-privatized form of drama that a break with the constraints of literary tradition becomes possible. Such a break is, it seems to me, necessary if women are to be freed in literature from the closed world of private experience.

Unless fiction can transcend its own history in this way, it will remain unable to do more than it has always done, albeit done it well – diagnose existing contradictions and existing suffering. Only when novelists, or perhaps we should call them 'fictionists', are able to create women whose experience extends beyond the narrow limits of their own consciousness, beyond the personal world of individual relationships and feelings, will this transformation come about. Thus it may be that what we require is more fiction and less realism. This certainly seems, anyway, to be what we are getting.

Notes

INTRODUCTION

1. See Eli Zaretsky, *Capitalism, The Family and Personal Life* (London, 1976).
2. For an account of the relation between the development of the novel and the growth of individualism in the eighteenth century, see Ian Watt, *The Rise of the Novel* (London, 1963), especially Chap. 6, 'Private Experience and the Novel).
3. Virginia Woolf, 'Women and Fiction', *Collected Essays* Vol. 2 (London, 1966), p. 145.

CHAPTER 1.

1. For a concise account of these changes and their ideological implications see Viola Klein, *The Feminine Character* (London, 1946) and J.A. and Olive Banks, *Feminism and Family Planning in Victorian England* (Liverpool, 1964).
2. Edward Carpenter, *My Days and Dreams* (London, 1916), p. 31.
3. For a chronological account of the progress of the emancipation movement in the mid nineteenth century, see Erna Reiss, *The Rights and Duties of Englishwomen* (Manchester, 1934).
4. The 1851 census showed that women considerably outnumbered men and that it was therefore statistically impossible for every girl to marry – a situation which was aggravated in the middle class by the growing number of men living abroad and administering far-flung posts of the Empire.
5. *The Complete Works of John Ruskin*, ed. Cook and Wedderburn (London, 1905), Vol. 13, p. 122.
6. Mrs Ellis, *The Wives of England*, quoted by Walter Houghton, *The Victorian Frame of Mind* (London, 1957), p. 9.
7. Eliza Lynn Linton, 'The Wild Women as Politicians', *The Nineteenth Century* Vol. 30 (July 1891), p. 81.
8. Frederick Harrison, 'The Emancipation of Women', *The Fortnightly Review* Vol. 50 (October 1891), p. 452.
9. 'An Appeal Against Female Suffrage', *The Nineteenth Century* Vol. 25 (June 1889), p. 781.
10. Harrison, *op. cit.* p. 445.
11. See David Daiches, *Some Late Victorian Attitudes* (London, 1969), p. 33.

12. Humphry House, *All In Due Time* (London, 1955), p. 119.
13. See R.H. Tawney, *Religion and the Rise of Capitalism* (London, 1926), especially Chap. IV 'The Triumph of the Economic Virtues'; C.M. Young, *Victorian England* (London, 1936), p. 2; Herbert Marcuse, *Eros and Civilization* (Boston, 1955).
14. Peter Cominos, 'Late Victorian Sexual Respectability and the Social System', *International Journal of Social History* Vol. 8 (1963). Lawrence Stone's *The Family, Sex and Marriage* was published too late for me to be able to draw on it here, but it provides an extensive survey of sexual behaviour and ideology from 1500 to 1800. This allows us to see nineteenth-century beliefs in relation to earlier ideological formation.
15. William Acton, *The Functions and Diseases of the Reproductive System* (London, 1857), quoted by Stephen Marcus, *The Other Victorians* (London, 1966), p. 31.
16. See R. Hoffman Hays, *The Dangerous Sex* (London, 1966).
17. *Hansard* Vol. 154, p. 134. Quoted by Peter Fryer, *The Birth Controllers* (London, 1965), p. 84.
18. Edward Carpenter, *Love's Coming of Age* (Manchester, 1906), p. 265 in edition used, London n.d.
19. Carpenter, *My Days and Dreams*, p. 94.
20. R. Ussher, *Neo-Malthusianism, An Enquiry into That System with Regard to its Economy and Morality* (London, 1898), p. 84.
21. Quoted by Fryer, *op. cit.* p. 84.
22. Quoted by Duncan Crow, *The Victorian Woman* (London, 1971), p. 246.
23. Quoted by C. Willett Cunnington, *Feminine Attitudes in the Nineteenth Century* (London, 1935), p. 270.
24. Henry James, *The Portrait of a Lady* (London, 1881), p. 58 in Penguin edition, 1964.
25. 'Novelists and Novels', *The Dublin Review* Vol. 16 (1886).
26. *The Spectator*, Vol. 58 (1885), quoted by Kenneth Graham, *English Criticism of the Novel* (London, 1965), p. 79.
27. *The Scots Observer* Vol. 4 (1890), p. 280, quoted by Graham, *ibid.* p. 79.
28. James Ashcroft Noble, 'The Fiction of Sexuality', *The Contemporary Review* Vol. 67 (April, 1895), p. 495.
29. *The Edinburgh Review* Vol. 36 (October 1821), p. 52.
30. M.E. Oliphant, 'The Anti-Marriage League', *Blackwood's Magazine* Vol. 159 (January 1896), p. 139.
31. 'Jude the Obscure', *The Athenaeum* No. 3552 (November 1895), p. 709.
32. E.A. Vizetelly, *Emile Zola, Novelist and Reformer* (London, 1904), p. 278.
33. Quoted by Noel Perrin, *Dr Bowdler's Legacy* (London, 1970), p. 15.
34. *The Saturday Review* and *The Athenaeum* (1872), quoted by Perrin, *ibid.* p. 247.
35. Anthony Trollope, *An Autobiography* (London, 1883), p. 221 in *The Oxford Trollope* Vol. 3 (London, 1950).
36. *Ibid.* p. 225.

37. Oliphant, *op. cit.* p. 138.

38. Thomas Hardy, preface to *Tess of the d'Urbervilles* (London, 1891), p. viii in the 1965 Papermac edition.

39. Quoted by Perrin, *op. cit.* p. 65.

40. Donald Thomas, *A Long Time Burning* (London, 1969), p. 186.

41. *Ibid.* p. 3.

42. For a detailed account of the way fiction was marketed in the middle of the nineteenth century, see Guinevere L. Greist, *Mudie's Circulating Library and the Victorian Novel* (Indianna, 1970).

43. Forrest Reid, 'Minor Fiction of the Eighteen Eighties', *The Eighteen Eighties* ed. De La Mare (London, 1930), p. 111.

44. Hardy did manage to get these two episodes published elsewhere. The seducation appeared under the title 'Saturday night in Arcady' in a Special Literary Supplement of *The National Observer*, Edinburgh, November 1891. The baptism was printed as 'The Midnight Baptism' in *The Fortnightly Review*, May 1891.

45. Hardy, *Tess*, p. 69.

46. M.E. Chase, *Thomas Hardy from Serial to Novel* (Minnesota, 1927), p. 79 in the Russell and Russel reprint, 1964.

47. R.L. Purdy, *Thomas Hardy, A Bibliography* (London, 1954), p. 69.

48. *Ibid.* p. 339.

49. C.E. Mudie, letter to *The Athenaeum* No. 1719 (October 1860), p. 451.

50. George Moore, *Literature At Nurse, or Circulating Morals* (London, 1885), p. 17.

51. George Moore, Preface to English trans. Zola's *Pot Bouille (Piping Hot,* London, 1885).

52. Thomas Hardy, 'Candour in English Fiction', *The New Review* Vol. 2 (January 1890) reprinted in *Thomas Hardy's Personal Writings*, ed. H. Orel (London, 1967), p. 125.

53. Greist, *op. cit.* p. 169.

54. *The Spectator* Vol. 103 (December 1909), p. 934.

55. Quoted by Thomas from the speech made by the Home Secretary when introducing the Bill in the House of Commons, *op. cit.* p. 263.

56. Alec Craig, *The Banned Books of England and Other Countries* (London, 1962), p. 44.

57. E.M. Forster, *Abinger Harvest* (London, 1936), p. 65.

CHAPTER 2.

1. *Household Words* Vol. 14 (December 1865), quoted by Margaret Dalziel, *Popular Fiction One Hundred Years Ago* (London, 1957), p. 84.

2. Quoted by Graham, *op. cit.* p. 33.

3. This was Harriet Martineau's complaint in her review of *Villette*, *The Daily News* 3 February, 1853. And see Françoise Basch, *Relative Creatures* (London, 1974), p. 165.

4. For further comment on Dickens's 'cold' women, see Jenni Calder, *Women and Marriage in Victorian Fiction* (London, 1976) and Basch, *op. cit.*

5. E.F. Benson, *As We Were* (London, 1930), p. 58 in 1938 Penguin edition.

6. Honoré de Balzac, *La Comedie Humaine* (Paris, 1842).

7. See Dalziel, *op. cit.* and Patricia Thomson, *The Victorian Heroine, A Changing Ideal* (London, 1956).

8. Eliza Lynn Linton, 'The Girl of the Period', *The Saturday Review* (August, 1866) and Vineta Colby, *The Singular Anomaly* (London, 1970), p. 17.

9. Lynn Linton, 'The Wild Women as Politicians', *op. cit.* The Wild Women as Social Insurgents', *ibid.* (October 1891).

10. J.S. Mill, *The Subjection of Women* (London, 1869), p. 46.

11. Oliphant, *op. cit.* p. 138.

12. M.E. Oliphant, *Miss Marjoribanks* (London, 1886), p. 595.

13. Oliphant, 'The Anti-Marriage League', p. 136.

14. Quoted by Constance Rover, *Women's Suffrage and Party Politics in Great Britain* (London, 1967), p. 39.

15. Marie Corelli, *Temporal Power* (London, 1902), p. 124.

16. M.E. Braddon, *Aurora Floyd* (London, 1862), p. 151 in stereotyped edition, n.d.

17. For a contemporary view of the sensation novel, see H.L. Mansel, 'Sensation Novels', *The Quarterly Review* Vol. 113 (1863), reprinted in his *Letters, Lectures and Reviews* (London, 1873).

18. Ouida, *Moths* (London, 1880), p. 784 in *Novels of Victorian High Society* ed. Powell (London, 1947).

19. Mrs Humphry Ward, introduction Charlotte Brontë's *Villette* (London, 1899), p. xxviii.

CHAPTER 3.

1. Erna Reiss, *op. cit.*

2. For a detailed account of these conflicts, see Clarence Decker, *The Victorian Conscience* (London, 1952).

3. As far as this discussion is concerned, I do not think it helpful to offer separate definitions of realism and naturalism. I am quoting Zola here to indicate the distance between moral idealism and the general tendency of realism, within which I would include naturalism.

4. Emile Zola, *Les Romanciers Naturalistes* (Paris, 1881), quoted by Decker, *op. cit.* p. 27.

5. George Bernard Shaw, *The Quintessence of Ibsenism* (London, 1913), p. 88.

6. Quoted Thomas, *op. cit.* p. 254.

7. Havelock Ellis, 'The Sexual Impulse in Women', *Studies in the Psychology of Sex* Vol. 3 (Philadelphia, 1920), p. 191.

8. The so-called decadents of the nineties – Beardsley, Wilde, Dowson and

Johnson – were part of the same general trend. The idea of art for art's sake may seem to be poles apart from the realism of Hardy or Gissing, but the realists and the aesthetes had in common this conscious rejection of traditional moral constraints.

CHAPTER 4.

1. Thomas Hardy, 'How Shall We Solve the Divorce Problem?' *Nash's Magazine* Vol. 5 (May 1912).
2. Thomas Hardy, *Jude the Obscure* (London, 1896), p. 64 in Papermac edition, 1966.
3. Thomas Hardy, *The Woodlanders* (London, 1887), p. 298 in Papermac edition, 1964.
4. Hardy, *Tess*, p. 277.
5. For a discussion of Eustacia's relation to Emma Bovary, see Christopher Heywood, 'Miss Braddon and *The Doctor's Wife*, An Intermediary between *Madame Bovary* and *The Return of the Native*', *Revue de Litterature Comparé* Vol. 138 (1964).
6. Thomas Hardy, *The Return of the Native* (London, 1878), p. 191 in Papermac edition, 1968.
7. The similarities with Ibsen's Hedda Gabler are striking.
8. Hardy, *The Woodlanders*, p. 197.
9. Frank Chapman, 'Hardy the Novelist', *Scrutiny* Vol. 3 (1934/5), p. 35.
10. This novel is discussed at greater length below in Chap. 7.
11. Olive Schreiner, *The Story of An African Farm* (London, 1883), p. 238 in Penguin edition, 1971.
12. St Jude in the Roman Catholic pantheon is the patron saint of 'hopeless cases'.

CHAPTER 5.

1. George Moore, *A Mummer's Wife* (London, 1885), p. 125 in 1937 edition.
2. It is interesting that although Moore is 'daring' over Kate's seduction, he still feels sufficiently uneasy about Esther Waters' to provide her with the partial 'excuse' of being drunk when it happened. So Esther, the 'good' woman, and Kate, the 'bad' one, are treated differently and Esther is not completely responsible for her 'fall'. For further discussion of *Esther Waters* see p. 92.
3. George Moore, *A Drama in Muslin* (London, 1884), p. 29 in 1886 edition.
4. See Dalziel, *op. cit.* and Patricia Thompson, *op. cit.*
5. George Moore, *Esther Waters* (London, 1894), p. 86 in 1920 edition.
6. Moore made something of a speciality of childbirth. Kate Ede goes through a difficult and painful delivery; so does Esther. And her confinement in the charity ward of a maternity hospital, complete with

instruments lying at the ready and examination by uncouth and unfeeling medical students, gave Smith's circulating library the excuse they were no doubt looking for, and they banned the novel because of it. See, Moore, *A Communication to My Friends* (London, 1933), p. lii in 1937 edition.

7. See Malcolm Elwin, *Old Gods Falling* (London, 1939), p. 90.
8. Even Henry James called him 'fantastic and mannered'. See F.N. Lees, 'George Meredith Novelist', *The Pelican Guide to English Literature* Vol. 6, p. 366.
9. George Meredith, *The Egoist* (London, 1879), p. 59 in 1897 edition, Vol. 1.
10. Kate Millett, *Sexual Politics* (New York, 1970), p. 134 in 1971 edition.

CHAPTER 6.

1. Rudyard Kipling, 'The Three Decker', *Rudyard Kipling's Verse, Definitive Edition* (London, 1940), p. 330.
2. Derek Stanford, *Short Stories of the Nineties* (London, 1968), p. 39.
3. Osburt Burdett, *The Beardsley Period* (London, 1925), p. 235.
4. Ella D'Arcy, 'A Marriage', *Modern Instances* (London, 1898), p. 16.

CHAPTER 7.

1. For this and other details of George Egerton's life, see Terence de Vere White, *A Leaf from the Yellow Book* (London, 1958).
2. The story of their relationship and Higginson's death is written up in 'Under Northern Sky' in *Keynotes*.
3. See Constance Rover, *Punch's Book of Women's Rights* for the complete gamut of contemporary anti-feminist stereotypes.
4. James Ashcroft Noble, 'The Fiction of Sexuality', *The Contemporary Review* Vol. 67 (April 1895).
5. George Egerton, 'The Cross Line', *Keynotes* (London, 1893).
6. Quoted by de Vere White, *op. cit.* p. 23.
7. George Egerton, 'The Regeneration of Two', *Discords* (London, 1894), p. 246.
8. Schreiner, *op. cit.* p. 185.
9. Quoted by Vineta Colby, *The Singular Anomaly* (London, 1970), p. 71.
10. *Ibid.* p. 93.
11. Vera Brittain, *Testament of Youth* (London, 1933), p. 41.
12. Olive Schreiner, *Dreams* (London, 1895), p. 75 in 1905 edition.
13. Olive Schreiner, 'The Garden of Flowers', *ibid.* p. 95.
14. Olive Schreiner, *Woman and Labour* (London, 1911), p. 140.
15. Quoted by de Vere White, *op. cit.* p. 30.
16. Millicent Garrett Fawcett, 'The Woman Who Did', *The Contemporary Review*, Vol. 67 (May 1895), p. 265.

17. Christabel Pankhurst, *The Great Scourge and How To End It* (London, 1913), p. vi.

CHAPTER 8.

1. Schreiner, *African Farm*, p. 94.
2. For further discussion on Gissing, see Chap. 9.
3. Grant Allen, 'The New Hedonism', *The Fortnightly Review* Vol. 95 (March 1894), p. 381.
4. See Wanda Neff, *Victorian Working Women* (London, 1966).
5. Millicent Garrett Fawcett, introduction to Mary Wollstonecraft, *A Vindication of The Rights of Women*, 1891 edition, p. 27.
6. Frances Power Cobbe, 'What Shall We Do with Our Old Maids?', *Fraser's Magazine* Vol. 66 (November 1862).
7. Quoted by Banks, *op. cit.* p. 92.
8. *Ibid.* p. 93.
9. *Ibid.* p. 103.

CHAPTER 9.

1. 'How Shall We Solve the Divorce Problem?', *Nash's Magazine* Vol. 5 (March 1912), p. 677.
2. Harrison, *op. cit.* p. 448.
3. Hugh Stutfield, 'Tommyrotics', *Blackwood's Magazine* Vol. 157 (June 1895), pp. 837, 841.
4. Frederick Engels, 'The Book of Revelation', *Progress* Vol. II (1883). Quoted by Christopher Hill, *The World Turned Upside Down* (London, 1972), p. 247.
5. Christopher Hill, 'Base Impudent Kisses', *ibid.* Chap. 15.
6. *Ibid.* p. 260.
7. Quoted by Sheila Rowbotham, *Women, Resistence and Revolution* (London, 1972), p. 39.
8. *Ibid.* pp. 104/7.
9. Quoted by Inga Stina Ewbank, *Their Proper Sphere* (London, 1966), p. 32.
10. Mrs Humphry Ward, *Delia Blanchflower* (London, 1916), p. 265.
11. Eliza Lynn Linton, *The New Woman in Haste and in Leisure* (London, 1895), p. 129.
12. See Samuel Hynes, 'The Decline and Fall of Tory England', *The Edwardian Turn of Mind*, Chap. 2 (London, 1968).
13. Stutfield, *op. cit.* p. 842.
14. Ussher, *op. cit.* p. 69.
15. *Ibid.* p. 92.
16. *Ibid.* pp. 77, 69.
17. Alec Craig, *op. cit.* p. 73.

18. Hynes, 'The Theatre and the Lord Chamberlain', *op. cit.* Chap. 7.
19. *Ibid.* p. 162.
20. Oliphant, 'The Anti-Marriage League', p. 137.
21. *Ibid.* p. 145.
22. Stutfield, *op. cit.* p. 836.
23. Lynn Linton, 'The Wild Women as Social Insurgents', *op. cit.* p. 604.
24. Lynn Linton, 'The Wild Women as Politicians, *op. cit.* p. 83.
25. Humphrey Ward, *Delia Blanchflower*, p. 135.
26. Lynn Linton, 'The Wild Women as Social Insurgents', p. 605.
27. William Frierson, *The English Novel in Transition* (New York, 1965), p. 46.
28. George Gissing, *The Whirlpool* (London, 1897), p. 335 in 1948 edition.
29. George Gissing, *In The Year of the Jubilee* (London, 1894), p. 243 in 1947 edition.
30. George Gissing, *The Emancipated* (London, 1890), p. 152 in 1968 edition.
31. An essay by Orwell in *Collected Articles on George Gissing*, ed. Pierre Coustillas (London, 1968) is an interesting discussion of the way Gissing handles marriage and the genteel respectability which so often made it impossible for young couples.
32. George Gissing, *The Odd Women* (London, 1893), p. 152 in 1968 edition.
33. This is an idea which Gissing seriously considers in an interesting short story called 'The Foolish Virgin'. In the story he seems to endorse Widdowson's position, whereas in the novel it is ridiculed.
34. George Gissing, *Letters to Members of his Family*, ed. Algernon and Ellen Gissing (London, 1927), p. 107.
35. Quoted in Stanley Alden, 'George Gissing, Humanist', Coustillas *op. cit.* p. 22.
36. Henry James, preface to *The Portrait of a Lady*, p. xvi.
37. C.B. Cox, *The Free Spirit* (London, 1963), p. 50.
38. *The Spectator* Vol. 54 (November 1881), reprinted in *Henry James, The Critical Heritage* ed. R.G. Cox (London, 1970), p. 94.
39. *The Saturday Review* Vol. 52 (December, 1881), *ibid.* p. 99.
40. *The Dial* Vol. 5 (January 1882), *ibid.* p. 111.
41. Tony Tanner, 'The Fearful Self: Henry James's *The Portrait of A Lady*', *Henry James, Modern Judgments*, ed. Tanner (London, 1968), p. 148.
42. Henry James, *The Notebooks*, ed. F.O. Matthiessen and K.B. Murdock (New York, 1947), p. 90 in 1961 edition.
43. *Ibid.* p. 217.
44. Henry James, *The Spoils of Poynton* (London, 1897), p. 90 in Penguin edition, 1963.
45. *The Bookman* Vol. 12 (May 1897), R.G. Cox, *op. cit.* p. 267.
46. James, *Notebooks*, p. 216.
47. *Ibid.* p. 248.
48. C.B. Cox, *op. cit.* p. 43.
49. *Ibid.* p. 44.

50. R.G. Cox *op. cit.* p. 171.
51. Henry James, *The Bostonians* (London, 1886), p. 39 in Penguin edition, 1966.

CHAPTER 10.

1. Samuel Hynes, *The Edwardian Turn of Mind*.
2. The 68 signatories included two dukes, ten other titles, one archbishop, six bishops, one archdeacon, Ramsay MacDonald, the Deputy Speaker of the House of Commons, Professors of medicine, physics, midwifery and pathology, Mrs Sidney Webb, the editors of *The Lancet* and *Mind*, Rider Haggard, the Master of Downing College and the President of Queen's College, Cambridge, the Moderator of the General Assembly of the Church of Scotland, William Booth, the Moderator of the United Free Church of Scotland, the President of the Primitive Methodist Conference, the President of the Congregational Union of England and Wales, the President of the United Methodist Church, the President of the Baptists' Union and the President of the Wesleyan Conference.
3. For a discussion of how British socialists responded to eugenic theories see Hynes *op. cit.* and Sheila Rowbotham, *Hidden From History* (London, 1973).
4. The report suggested that they should be 'bred out', see Hynes, *op. cit.* Chap. 2.
5. George Dangerfield, *The Strange Death of Liberal England* (New York, 1935).

CHAPTER 11.

1. See Bernard Bergonzi, *The Early H.G. Wells* (London, 1961).
2. Virginia Woolf, 'Mr Bennett and Mrs Brown', *The Captain's Deathbed* (London, 1950).
3. H.G. Wells, 'The Contemporary Novel', *The Complete Works*, Atlantic Edition, Vol. 9 (London, 1925), p. 380.
4. H.G. Wells, *In The Days of the Comet* (1906), *Works* Vol. 10, p. 313.
5. See Wells, 'The Contemporary Novel', *Works*, p. 379.
6. Both the marriage and the 'other woman' in the novel are based on Wells's relationship with his second wife, Catherine, and on his dissatisfaction with monogamy generally.
7. H.G. Wells, *The New Machiavelli* (London, 1911), p. 195 in Penguin edition, 1970.
8. These defensive couples, living out a life of '*egoisme à deux*' look forward to Lawrence's disgust at what he called 'the most repulsive thing on earth ... each couple in its own little house, watching its own little interests, and stewing in its own little privacy'. (*Women in Love*).

9. H.G. Wells, *An Experiment in Autobiography* (London, 1934), p. 470.
10. H. Lovat Dickson, *H.G. Wells, His Turbulent Life And Times* (London, 1969), p. 166.
11. Rowbotham, *Hidden From History*, p. 72.
12. Beatrice Webb, *Our Partnership* (London, 1948), p. 486.
13. *Passfield Papers*, quoted by Hynes, *op. cit.* p. 195.
14. Wells's affairs have been well documented in two recent biographies – Lovat Dickson, *op. cit.* and Norman and Jeanne Mackenzie, *The Time Traveller* (London, 1973). Anthony West's articles about his father (*The Sunday Times*, 11 Jan. and 18 Jan. 1976) support their view of Wells's work as over-dominated by his personal and sexual life.
15. The physical weakness of Leonard Bast in Forster's *Howard's End* is another manifestation of this pre-war anxiety about the health of the British working class.
16. H.G. Wells, *A Modern Utopia* (1905).
17. *The Spectator*, Vol. 103 (December 1909), p. 945.
18. Wells, *A Modern Utopia, Works* Vol. 9, p. 147.
19. Hynes, *op. cit.* p. 119.
20. Lovat Dickson, *op. cit.* p. 83.

CHAPTER 12.

1. Walter Allen, *The English Novel* (London, 1954), p. 32.
2. Arnold Bennett, *These Twain* (London, 1916), p. 505.
3. Arnold Bennett, *Anna of The Five Towns* (London, 1902), p. 235 in Penguin edition, 1969.
4. Arnold Bennett, *The Old Wives Tale* (London, 1908), p. 44 in 1935 edition.
5. Arnold Bennett, *Clayhanger* (London, 1910), p. 525 in 1920 edition.
6. Arnold Bennett, *Hilda Lessways* (London, 1911), p. 38 in 1913 edition.
7. Hynes, *op. cit.* p. 76.
8. Rowbotham, *Hidden From History*, p. 111.
9. Arnold Bennett, *The Journals* ed. Frank Swinnerton (London, 1954), p. 336 in Penguin edition, 1971.
10. His confusion over this problem looked forward to one of the contradictions encountered by the Women's Movement today. One of the most important tasks of the Women's Liberation Movement is to undermine the cultural stereotypes which have refused to acknowledge the strength and variety of women as individuals; yet at the same time the movement seeks to uncover what is in fact a shared experience of oppression and to develop a collective way of combatting it. This means building a collective consciousness among women, but this consciousness must be very different from the old idea of the 'woman's point of view' as Bennett understood it.
11. See Margaret Drabble, *Arnold Bennett* (London, 1974).
12. Arnold Bennett, *Our Women* (London, 1920), p. 107.

13. Rowbotham, *Hidden From History*.
14. Arnold Bennett, *Sacred and Profane Love* (London, 1905), p. 296 in 1917 edition.
15. Georges Lafourcade, *Arnold Bennett, A Study* (London, 1939), p. 92.
16. Bennett, *The Journals*, p. 91.

CHAPTER 13.
1. E.M. Forster, 'The Challenge of Our Time', *Two Cheers for Democracy* (London, 1951), p. 66 in Penguin edition, 1965.
2. E.M. Forster, 'George Orwell', *ibid.* p. 70.
3. E.M. Forster, 'What I Believe', *ibid.* p. 75.
4. E.M. Forster, *A Room With A View* (London, 1908), p. 186 in Penguin edition, 1958.
5. Lionel Trilling, *E.M. Forster* (London, 1944), p. 87.
6. F.R. Leavis, 'E.M. Forster', *The Common Pursuit* (London, 1958), p. 263.
7. E.M. Forster, *The Longest Journey* (London, 1907), p. 86 in Penguin edition, 1960.
8. E.M. Forster, 'What I Believe', p. 82.
9. E.M. Forster, *Howard's End* (London, 1910), p. 59 in Penguin edition.
10. C.B. Cox, *op. cit.* p. 39.
11. Leavis, *op. cit.* p. 262.

CHAPTER 14.
1. Virginia Woolf, 'Professions for Women', *Collected Essays*, Vol. 2 (1966), p. 288.
2. Virginia Woolf 'Women and Fiction', *ibid.* p. 147.
3. D.H. Lawrence, *Assorted Articles* (London, 1930), p. 75.
4. D.H. Lawrence, *England My England* (London, 1922), p. 20 in Penguin edition, 1960.
5. Virginia Woolf, 'Modern Fiction', *Collected Essays*, Vol. 2.
6. *Ibid.*

Bibliography

THE HISTORICAL CONTEXT

Cole, G.D.H. *Socialist Thought – The Second International* (London, 1956).

Crow, Duncan, *The Victorian Woman* (London, 1971).

Dangerfield, George, *The Strange Death of Liberal England* (New York, 1935).

Fulford, Roger, *Votes for Women* (London, 1958).

Hewitt, Margaret, *Wives and Mothers in Victorian Industry* (London, 1958).

Hobsbawm, E.J. *Industry and Empire* (London, 1968).

Houghton, Walter E. *The Victorian Frame of Mind* (London, 1957).

House, Humphry, *All In Due Time* (London, 1955).

Hynes, Samuel, *The Edwardian Turn of Mind* (London, 1968).
   Edwardian Occasions (London, 1972).

Ideas and Beliefs of the Victorians, a BBC symposium (London, 1966).

Kitson Clark, G. *The Making of Victorian England* (London, 1962).

Klein, Viola, *The Feminine Character, History of an Ideology* (London, 1946).

McGregor, O.R. *Divorce in England* (London, 1957).

Neff, Wanda, *Victorian Working Women* (London, 1966).

Pankhurst, E. Sylvia, *The Suffragette Movement*, (London, 1911).

Pinchbeck, Ivy, *Women Workers and the Industrial Revolution* (London, 1930).

Ramelson, Marian, *The Petticoat Rebellion* (London, 1976).

Ratcliffe, R. *Dear Worried Brown Eyes* (London, 1969).

Read, Donald, *Edwardian England* (London, 1972).

Reiss, Erna, *The Rights and Duties of Englishwomen* (Manchester, 1934).

Rosen, Andrew, *Rise up Women!* (London, 1975).

Rover, Constance, *Women's Suffrage and Party Politics in Britain* (London, 1967).
   The Punch book of Women's Rights (London, 1967).

Rowbotham, Sheila, *Women, Resistance and Revolution* (London, 1972).
   Hidden From History (London, 1973).

Stenton, Doris M. *The Englishwoman in History* (London, 1957).

Strachey, Ray, *The Cause* (London, 1928).

Vicinus, Martha, ed. *Suffer and Be Still: Women in the Victorian Age* (Indianna, 1972).

Willett Cunningham, C. *Feminine Attitudes in the Nineteenth Century* (London, 1935).

Young, G.M. *Victorian England* (London, 1936).

SEXUALITY

Banks, J.A. & Olive, *Prosperity and Parenthood* (London, 1954).

'The Bradlaugh-Besant Trial and the Englishnewspapers', *Population Studies* Vol. 8 (1954-1955).

Feminism and Family Planning in Victorian England (Liverpool, 1964).

Carpenter, Edward, *Civilization, Its Cause and Cure* (London, 1889).

Love's Coming of Age (Manchester, 1906).

Cominos, Peter T. 'Late Victorian Sexual Respectability and the Social System', *International Journal of Social History* Vol. 8 (1963).

Crick, Bernard, *Crime, Rape and Gin* (London, 1974).

Ellis, Havelock, *Studies in the Psychology of Sex* (first English ed. London, 1906).

Engels, Frederick, *The Origin of the Family, Private Property and The State* (London, 1884).

Fryer, Peter, *The Birth Controllers* (London, 1965).

Hill, Christopher, *The World Turned Upside Down* (London, 1972).

Puritanism and Revolution (London, 1958).

Marcus, Stephen, *The Other Victorians* (London, 1966).

Marcuse, Herbert, *Eros and Civilization* (Boston, 1955).

Pankhurst, Christabel, *The Great Scourge and How to End It* (London, 1913).

Reich, Wilhelm, *The Sexual Revolution* (1930).

Robinson, Paul, *The Sexual Radicals* (London, 1970).

Rover, Constance, *Love, Morals and the Feminists* (London, 1970).

Rowbotham, Sheila, *A New World for Women* (London, 1977).

Rowbotham, Sheila and Weeks, Jeffrey, *Socialism and the New Life* (London, 1977).

Ruskin, John. 'Of Queen's Gardens' (1865), *The Complete Works*, ed. Cook and Wedderburn (London, 1905).

Stone, Lawrence, *The Family, Sex and Marriage in England, 1500-1800* (London, 1977).

Tawney, R.H. *Religion and the Rise of Capitalism* (London, 1926).

Thomas, Keith, 'The Double Standard', *Journal of the History of Ideas* (1959).

Ussher, R. *Neo-Malthusianism, an Enquiry into that System with Regard to its Economy and Morality* (London, 1898).

Zaretsky, Eli, *Capitalism, the Family and Personal Life* (London, 1976).

FEMINISM

de Beauvoir, Simone, *The Second Sex* (Paris, 1949).

Comer, Lee, *Wedlocked Women* (Leeds, 1975).

Firestone, Shulamith, *The Dialectic of Sex* (New York, 1971).

Friedan, Betty, *The Feminine Mystique* (New York, 1964).

Greer, Germaine, *The Female Eunuch* (London, 1971).

Mill, J.S. *The Subjection of Women* (London, 1869).

Mitchell, Juliet, *Woman's Estate* (London, 1971).

Rowbotham, Sheila, *Woman's Consciousness, Man's World* (London, 1973).

Wollstonecraft, Mary, *A Vindication of the Rights of Women* (London, 1792).

LITERARY HISTORY
Batho, E. and Dobrée, B. *The Victorians and After* (London, 1938).
Cazamian, Louis, *Le Roman Social en Angleterre* (Paris, 1904).
Conn, Edwin H. *The Impact of Madame Bovary on the English Novel* (Columbia, 1952).
Cruse, Amy, *After the Victorians* (London, 1938).
Dalziel, Margaret, *Popular Fiction One Hundred Years Ago* (London, 1957).
Ellis, Havelock, *The New Spirit* (London, 1890).
Elwin, Malcolm, *Old Gods Falling* (London, 1939).
Frierson, William C. *The English Novel in Transition, 1880-1940* (New York, 1965).
James, Louis, *Fiction for the Working Man, 1830-1850* (London, 1963).
Martin, Wallace, *The New Age Under Orage* (Manchester, 1967).
Praz, Mario, *The Hero in Eclipse in Victorian Fiction* (London, 1956).
Reid, Forrest, 'Minor Fiction in the Eighteen Eighties', *The Eighteen Eighties* ed. de la Mare (London, 1930).
Tillotson, Kathleen, *Novels of the Eighteen Forties* (London, 1954).
Watt, Ian, *The Rise of the Novel* (London, 1963).

THE EIGHTEEN NINETIES
Burdett, Osbert, *The Beardsley Period* (London, 1925).
Harris, Wendell V. 'John Lane's 'Keynotes' Series and the Fiction of the Eighteen Nineties, *PMLA* Vol. 83.
Harrison, Fraser, *The Yellow Book, an Anthology* (London, 1974).
Jackson, Holbrook, *The Eighteen Nineties* (London, 1931).
May, J. Lewis, *John Lane and the Nineties* (London, 1936).
Lyon Mix, Katherine, *A Study in Yellow* (London, 1960).
Nelson, James G. *The Early Nineties* (Cambridge, Mass. 1971).
Stanford, Derek, *Short Stories of the Nineties* (London, 1968).
Thornton, R.K. *Poetry of the Nineties* (London, 1970).

FICTION AND ITS READERS
Cockburn, Claude, *Best Seller* (London, 1972).
Cruse, Amy, *The Victorians and Their Books* (London, 1935).
Daiches, David, *Some Late Victorian Attitudes* (London, 1969).
Decker, Clarence, *The Victorian Conscience* (London, 1952).
Graham, Kenneth, *English Criticism of the Novel, 1865-1900* (Oxford, 1965).
Greist, Guinevere L. *Mudie's Circulating Library and the Victorian Novel* (Indianna, 1970).
Leavis, Q.D. *Fiction and the Reading Public* (London, 1932).

CENSORSHIP

Craig, Alec, *The Banned Books of England and Other Countries* (London, 1962).
Fryer, Peter, *Mrs Grundy: Studies in English Prudery* (London, 1963).
Lawrence, D.H. *Sex Literature and Censorship* (London, 1955).
Perrin, Noel, *Dr Bowdler's Legacy* (London, 1970).
Rolph, C.H. *The Trial of Lady Chatterley* (London, 1961).
    Books in the Dock (London, 1969).
Thody, P.M.W. *Four Cases of Literary Censorship* (Leeds, 1968).
Thomas, Donald, *A Long Time Burning* (London, 1969).

WOMEN AND LITERATURE

Basch, Françoise, *Relative Creatures* (London, 1974).
Calder, Jenni, *Women and Marriage in Victorian Fiction* (London, 1976).
Colby, Vineta, *The Singular Anomaly* (London, 1970).
Courtney, W.L. *The Feminine Note in Fiction* (London, 1904).
Ewbank, Inga Stina, *Their Proper Sphere* (London, 1966).
Figes, Eva, *Patriarchal Attitudes* (London, 1970).
Hardwick, Elizabeth, *Seduction and Betrayal* (London, 1974).
Hays, R. Hoffman, *The Dangerous Sex, The Myth of Feminine Evil* (London, 1966).
Johnson, Richard Brimley, *The Women Novelists* (London, 1918).
Killham, John, *Tennyson and the Princess* (London, 1958).
Maison, Margaret M. 'Adulteress in Agony', *The Listener*, 14 Jan. 1961.
Mews, Hazel, *Frail Vessels* (London, 1969).
Miles, Rosalind, *The Fiction of Sex* (London, 1974).
Millett, Kate, *Sexual Politics* (London, 1971).
Moers, Ellen, *Literary Women* (London, 1977).
O'Flinn, Paul, *Them and Us in Literature* (London, 1975).
Rogers, Kathleen, *The Troublesome Helpmeet: A History of Misogyny in Literature* (London, 1966).
Showalter, Elaine, *A Literature of Their Own* (London, 1977).
Thomson, Patricia, *The Victorian Heroine, A Changing Ideal* (London, 1956).
    'The Three Georges', *Nineteenth Century Fiction* Vol. 18 (1963-1964).
Utter, R.P. and Needham, B.B. *Pamela's Daughters* (London, 1937).
Wilson, Angus, 'The Sexual Revolution', *The Listener* Vol. 80 (October, 1968).
Woolf, Virginia, *A Room of One's Own* (London, 1928).
    'Professions for Women', *The Death of the Moth* (London, 1942).
    'Women and Fiction', *Collected Essays* Vol. 2 (London, 1966).

CRITICISM

Allen, Walter, *The English Novel* (London, 1954).
Bellamy, William, *The Novels of Wells, Bennett and Galsworthy* (London, 1971).
Bergonzi, Bernard, *The Early H.G. Wells* (London, 1961).

The Situation of the Novel (London, 1970).

Brunson, Martha L. Carter, 'Towards Fin de Siècle Emancipation: The Development of Independence in Thomas Hardy's Wessex Women', *Dissertation Abstracts* No. 28.

Chapman, Frank, 'Hardy the Novelist', *Scrutiny* Vol. 3 (1934-1935).

Chase, Mary Ellen, *Thomas Hardy from Serial to Novel* (New York, 1964).

Coustillas, Pierre, ed. *Collected Articles on George Gissing* (London, 1968).

Cox, C.B. *The Free Spirit* (London, 1963).

Cox, C.B. *Thomas Hardy, The Critical Heritage* (London, 1970).

Crews, F.C. *E.M. Forster, The Perils of Humanism* (London, 1962).

Delavaney, Emile, *D.H. Lawrence and Edward Carpenter* (London, 1971).

Downs, Brian W. *Ibsen, The Intellectual Background* (London, 1946).

Egan, Michael, *Ibsen, The Critical Heritage* (London, 1972).

Henry James, The Ibsen Years (London, 1972).

Ellman, R. ed. *Edwardians and Late Victorians* (New York, 1960).

Gard, Roger, ed. *Henry James, The Critical Heritage* (London, 1968).

Geismar, Maxwell, *Henry James and his Cult* (London, 1964).

Gransden, K.W. *E.M. Forster* (London, 1962).

Heywood, Christopher, 'Miss Braddon's *The Doctor's Wife,* An Intermediary Between *Madame Bovary* and *The Return of the Native*', *Revue de Littérature Comparé* No. 38 (1964).

Hodgkins, J.R. *A Study of the Periodical Reception of the Novels of Thomas Hardy, George Gissing and George Moore.* (Ph.D. Thesis, Michegan State University, 1960). University Microfilms Inc.

Kettle, Arnold, *An Introduction to the English Novel* (London, 1962).

Korg, Jacob, *George Gissing, A Critical Biography* (Seattle, 1963).

Lafourcade, Georges, *Arnold Bennett, A Study* (London, 1939).

Laredo, Ursula, 'Olive Schreiner', *Journal of Commonwealth Studies* Vol. 8 (December, 1969).

Leavis, F.R. *The Great Tradition* (London, 1948).

The Common Pursuit (London, 1958).

Lucas, John, ed. *Literature and Politics in the Nineteenth Century* (London, 1971).

Arnold Bennett, A Study of his Fiction (London, 1974).

Marder, Herbert, *Feminism and Art: A Study of Virginia Woolf* (Chicago, 1968).

Moore, Harry T. *The Intelligent Heart* (London, 1955).

Parrinder, Patrick, *H.G. Wells, The Critical Heritage* (London, 1972).

Phillips, Walter C. *Dickens, Reade and Collins, Sensational Novelists* (New York, 1919).

Purdy, Richard L. *Thomas Hardy, A Bibliographical Study* (London, 1954).

Raknem, Ingvald, *H.G. Wells and his Critics* (London, 1962).

Simon, J.S. *Arnold Bennett and his Novels* (London, 1936).

Stone, Wilfred, *The Cave and the Mountain, A Study of E.M. Forster* (London, 1966).

Tanner, Tony, ed. *Henry James, Modern Judgments* (London, 1968).

Trilling, Lionel, *E.M. Forster* (London, 1944).
Williams, Iona, *Meredith, The Critical Heritage* (London, 1971).

BIOGRAPHY AND AUTOBIOGRAPHY

Barua, D.K. *The Life and Work of Edward Carpenter*, Ph.D. Thesis, Sheffield University, 1966.
Bell, Quentin, *Virginia Woolf* (London, 1972).
Benson, E.F. *As We Were* (London, 1930).
Brittain, Vera, *Testament of Youth* (London, 1933).
Carpenter, Edward, *My Days and Dreams* (London, 1916).
Chitty, Susan, *The Beast and the Monk* (London, 1974).
Crosby, Earnest, *Edward Carpenter, Poet and Prophet* (Philadelphia, 1901).
Drabble, Margaret, *Arnold Bennett* (London, 1974).
Gissing, Algernon and Ellen, eds. *Letters of George Gissing to Members of His Family* (London, 1927).
Gittings, Robert, *The Young Thomas Hardy* (London, 1975).
The Older Hardy (London, 1978).
Hardy, Florence, *The Early Life of Thomas Hardy* (London, 1928).
Hobman, D.L. *Olive Schreiner, Her Friends and Times* (London, 1955).
Lovat Dickson, H. *H.G. Wells, His Turbulent Life and Times* (London, 1969).
Lynn Linton, Eliza. My Literary Life (London, 1899).
Mackenzie, Norman and Jeanne, *The Time Traveller: A Biography of H.G. Wells* (London, 1973).
Oliphant, Margaret, *Autobiography and Letters*, ed. Mrs Harry Coghill (London, 1899).
Orel, H. ed. *Thomas Hardy's Personal Writings* (London, 1967).
Tindall, Gillian, *The Born Exile, A Biography of George Gissing* (London, 1974).
Tomalin, Claire, *The Life and Death of Mary Wollstonecraft* (London, 1974).
Trollope, Anthony, *An Autobiography* (London, 1883).
Webb, Beatrice, *My Apprenticeship* (London, 1926).
Our Partnership (London, 1948).
Wells, H.G. *Experiment in Autobiography* (London, 1934).
White, Terence de Vere, *A Leaf from The Yellow Book* (London, 1958).
Vizetelly, Ernest A. *Emile Zola, Novelist and Reformer* (London, 1904).

CONTEMPORARY COMMENT

Allen, Grant, 'The New Hedonism', *The Fortnightly Review* Vol. 55 (1894).
Ashcroft Noble, James, 'The Fiction of Sexuality', *The Contemporary Review* (1895).
Beeton, Isabella, *The Book of Household Management* (London, 1880).
Blunt, Rev John Henry, ed. *The Book of Common Prayer* (London, 1898).
Davidson, Mrs H.C. *What Our Daughters Can Do for Themselves* (London, 1894).
'The Family Shakespeare', *The Edinburgh Review* Vol. 36 (October, 1821).

Fawcett, Millicent Garrett, introduction to Mary Wollstonecraft, *A Vindication of The Rights of Women* (London, 1891).
'The Emancipation of Women', *The Fortnightly Review* Vol. 50 (November 1891).
'The Woman Who Did', *The Contemporary Review* Vol. 67 (May 1895).
Goldman, Emma, *The Traffic in Women and Other Essays* (New York, 1917).
Harrison, Frederick, 'The Emancipation of Women', *The Fortnightly Review* Vol. 50 (October, 1891).
'How Shall We Solve the Divorce Problem?' a symposium, *Nash's Magazine* (March, 1912).
Lynn Linton, Eliza, 'The Wild Women as Politicians'; 'The Wild Women as Social Insurgents', *The Nineteenth Century* Vol. 30 (1891).
Mansel, H.L. 'Sensation Novels', *The Quarterly Review* Vol. 113 (1863).
'Mothers and Daughters'; 'The Revolt of the Daughters'; 'A Reply from the Daughters', *The Nineteenth Century* Vol. 35 (1894).
Mudie, C.E. letter to *The Athenaeum* No. 1719 (October 6th 1896).
Nordau, Max, *Degeneration* (London, 1895).
Oliphant, M.E. 'The Anti-Marriage League', *Blackwood's Magazine* Vol. 159 (January 1896).
'A Poisonous Book', *The Spectator* Vol. 103 (November, 1909).
Ratcliffe, R. ed. *Dear Worried Brown Eyes* (London, 1969).
'The Tree of Knowledge', a symposium, *The New Review* Vol. 10 (June 1891), contributions from Hardy, Eliza Lynn Linton, Sarah Grand, Max Nordau and Walter Besant.
Ward, Mrs Humphry and others, 'An Appeal Against Female Suffrage', *The Nineteenth Century* Vol. 25 (June, 1889).
'What Shall We Do with Our Old Maids?', *Fraser's Magazine* Vol. 66 (November 1862).

THE WRITERS

This part of the bibliography includes only works discussed in the test or those which provide further information about their authors' attitudes towards women.

Grant, Allen, *The Woman Who did* (London, 1895).
The British Barbarians (London, 1895).
Arnold Bennett *Anna of the Five Towns* (London, 1902).
Leonora (London, 1903).
Sacred and Profane Love (London, 1905).
The Old Wives Tale (London, 1908).
Clayhanger (London, 1910).
Hilda Lessways (London, 1911).
These Twain (London, 1916).
Books and Persons (London, 1917).
The Pretty Lady (London, 1918).

Our Women, Chapters on the Sex Discord (London, 1920).
   The Journals, ed. Flower (London, 1932).
M.E. Braddon *Aurora Floyd* (London, 1862).
Marie Corelli *Temporal Power* (London, 1902).
Ella D'Arcy *Monochromes* (London, 1895).
   Modern Instances (London, 1898).
George Egerton *Keynotes* (London, 1893).
   Discords (London, 1894).
   Symphonies (London, 1897).
E.M. Forster *Where Angels Fear To Tread* (London, 1905).
   The Longest Journey (London, 1907).
   A Room With A View (London, 1908).
   Howards End (London, 1910).
   Abinger Harvest (London, 1936).
   Two Cheers for Democracy (London, 1951).
George Gissing *The Emancipated* (London, 1890).
   New Grub Street (London, 1891).
   The Odd Women (London, 1893).
   In The Year of the Jubilee (London, 1894).
   The Whirlpool (London, 1897).
   Charles Dickens (London, 1897)
Sarah Grand *The Heavenly Twins* (London, 1893).
Thomas Hardy *The Return of The Native* (London, 1878).
   The Woodlanders (London, 1887).
   Tess of the d'Urbervilles (London, 1891).
   Jude the Obscure (London, 1896).
Henry James *Washington Square* (London, 1881).
   The Portrait of A Lady (London, 1881).
   The Bostonians (London, 1886).
   The Spoils of Poynton (London, 1897).
   What Maisie Knew (London, 1897).
   The Awkward Age (London, 1899).
D.H. Lawrence *Sons and Lovers* (London, 1913).
   The Rainbow (London, 1915).
   Women in Love (London, 1921).
   The Fox (London, 1922).
   England My England (London, 1922).
   Assorted Articles (London, 1930).
   Sex Literature and Censorship (London, 1955).
Eliza Lynn Linton *The New Woman In Haste and In Leisure* (London, 1895).
George Meredith *The Egoist* (London, 1879).
   Diana of the Crossways (London, 1885).
   The Amazing Marriage (London, 1895).
   One of Our Conquerors (London, 1897).
George Moore *A Drama in Muslin* (London, 1884).
   A Mummer's Wife (London, 1885).

Literature at Nurse, or Circulating Morals (London, 1885).

Preface to English trans. Zola's *Pot Bouille* (*Piping Hot*, London, 1885).

Esther Waters (London, 1894).

Celibates (London, 1895).

A Communication To My Friends (London, 1933).

Margaret Oliphant *Miss Marjoribanks* (London, 1866).

Olive Schreiner *The Story of An African Farm* (London, 1883).

Dreams (London, 1891).

Woman and Labour (London, 1911).

Letters, ed. S.C. Cronwright-Schreiner (London, 1924).

From Man to Man (London, 1926).

Ouida *Moths* (London, 1880).

May Sinclair *The Three Sisters* (London, 1914).

Mrs Humphry Ward *Marcella* (London, 1894).

Sir George Tressady (London, 1896).

Eleanor (London, 1900).

Delia Blanchflower (London, 1916).

H.G. Wells *Love and Mr Lewisham* (London, 1900).

Anticipations (London, 1902).

A Modern Utopia (London, 1905).

Socialism and The Family (1906).

In The Days of the Comet (London, 1906).

Ann Veronica (London, 1909).

The New Machiavelli (London, 1911).

The Wife of Sir Isaac Harman (London, 1914).

Virginia Woolf *The Voyage Out* (London, 1915).

Night and Day (London, 1919).

Mrs Dalloway (London, 1922).

To The Lighthouse (London, 1927).

Orlando (London, 1928).

A Room of One's Own (London, 1929).

The Years (London, 1937).

The Three Guineas (London, 1937).

Collected Essays, ed. Leonard Woolf (London, 1966).

Index